Developments in Educational Psychology

What is the relevance of educational psychology in the twenty-first century?

In this collection of essays, leading educational psychologists reflect on the seminal developments which have been made in the field over the past twenty-five years or so and assess how far we have progressed. Given a broad and personal remit to address a range of issues, the contributors review and critique a variety of topics, including:

- intelligence;
- communication;
- family environments;
- individual differences;
- reading;
- peer learning;
- classroom behaviour;
- higher education.

Providing provocative and challenging insights into the state of contemporary educational psychology, the contributors acknowledge throughout the successes and progression in the field, but with a critical edge and a challenge being thrown down to psychologists of education to make study more seriously informed and, as a consequence, reformed.

Now in its second edition, this compelling text for students and researchers is updated and includes four new chapters.

The book's editor, **Kevin Wheldall**, has been Professor of Education at Macquarie University and Director of Macquarie University Special Education Centre (MUSEC) since 1990 and is a Fellow of the prestigious Academy of Social Sciences in Australia.

Developments in Educational Psychology

Second edition

Edited by Kevin Wheldall

Routledge
Taylor & Francis Group

LONDON AND NEW YORK

First edition published 2006
Second edition published 2010
by Routledge
2 Park Square, Milton Park, Abingdon, Oxon OX14 4RN

Simultaneously published in the USA and Canada
by Routledge
270 Madison Avenue, New York, NY 10016

Routledge is an imprint of the Taylor & Francis Group, an informa business

© 2010 Kevin Wheldall for editorial material and selection.
Individual contributors for their contributions.

Typeset in Bembo by Pindar NZ, Auckland, New Zealand
Printed and bound in Great Britain by CPI Antony Rowe, Chippenham, Wiltshire

British Library Cataloguing in Publication Data
A catalogue record for this book is available from the British Library

Library of Congress Cataloging-in-Publication Data
Developments in educational psychology / edited by Kevin Wheldall. — 2nd ed.
    p. cm.
  Previous editon not in LC.
  1. Educational psychology. 2. Learning, Psychology of. 3. Effective
teaching. I. Wheldall, Kevin.
  LB1051.D473 2010
  370.15—dc22   2009004732

ISBN 13: 978-0-415-46998-2 (hbk)
ISBN 13: 978-0-415-46993-7 (pbk)
ISBN 13: 978-0-203-87467-7 (ebk)

ISBN 10: 0-415-46998-8 (hbk)
ISBN 10: 0-415-46993-7 (pbk)
ISBN 10: 0-203-87467-6 (ebk)

Contents

Illustrations

Figures

Tables

About the editor

Kevin Wheldall
BA, PhD, CPsychol, MAPS, FBPsS, FCollP, FIARLD, FASSA

Kevin Wheldall has been Professor of Education and Director of Macquarie University Special Education Centre (MUSEC) in Sydney, Australia since 1990. Prior to this, he was Director of the Centre for Child Study at the University of Birmingham in the UK. A registered psychologist, he is a Fellow of the Academy of Social Sciences in Australia, the British Psychological Society, the College of Preceptors (Teachers) and the International Academy for Research in Learning Disabilities. He has also been awarded the Mona Tobias Award of Learning Difficulties Australia for 2008 'in recognition of an outstanding contribution to the field of learning difficulties in Australia'.

He has researched and written extensively in the area of learning and behaviour difficulties with particular emphasis on classroom behaviour management and helping older low-progress readers. He is the author of more than two hundred books, chapters and journal articles in the field of Educational Psychology and Special Education. He is also the editor of the international journal *Educational Psychology* and joint editor of the *Australian Journal of Learning Difficulties*. He has acted as an adviser to both state and federal government education bodies and ministers on matters relating to Special Education generally and on behaviour and reading in particular.

Notes on contributors

Robyn Beaman is a Research Fellow and Deputy Director of the MULTILIT Research Unit within Macquarie University Special Education Centre which forms part of the Institute for Human Cognition and Brain Science at Macquarie University, Sydney, Australia.

Laraine Bradd was formerly a MULTILIT teacher at Macquarie University Special Education Centre School and is now a Special Education teacher at St. Scholastica's College, Sydney, Australia.

Coral Kemp was formerly a Senior Lecturer and is now an Honorary Associate of Macquarie University Special Education Centre which forms part of the Institute for Human Cognition and Brain Science at Macquarie University, Sydney, Australia.

Alison Madelaine is a Lecturer within Macquarie University Special Education Centre which forms part of the Institute for Human Cognition and Brain Science at Macquarie University, Sydney, Australia.

The late Kevin Marjoribanks was formerly Dean of Education at the University of Adelaide, Australia.

Reg Marsh has been a Professor of Education at the Victoria University of Wellington, New Zealand and at the University of Botswana and has also been Professor of Psychology and Acting Professor of Biostatistics at the University of Malawi and Clinical Associate Professor in Psychiatry at Monash University, Australia and the University of Auckland.

Dennis M. McInerney is Chair Professor of Educational Psychology in the Department of Educational Psychology, Counselling and Learning Needs and Associate Vice President (Research and Development) at the Hong Kong Institute of Education.

Ted Nettelbeck is Professor of Psychology in the School of Psychology at the University of Adelaide, Australia.

John T. E. Richardson is Professor of Student Learning and Assessment at the Open University, UK, where he carries out research into conceptions of learning, approaches to studying and perceptions of academic quality in both campus-based and distance-learning students.

Richard Riding was formerly Reader in Educational Psychology and Director of the Assessment Research Unit in the School of Education at the University of Birmingham, UK.

Jeff Sigafoos is Professor in the School of Educational Psychology and Pedagogy at Victoria University of Wellington, New Zealand. His research focuses on communication intervention for individuals with developmental and physical disabilities.

Keith J. Topping is Associate Dean for Research in the School of Education, Social Work and Community Education at the University of Dundee, UK.

Kevin Wheldall is Professor of Education and Director of the MULTILIT Research Unit within Macquarie University Special Education Centre which forms part of the Institute for Human Cognition and Brain Science at Macquarie University, Sydney, Australia.

Carlene Wilson is Chair of Cancer Prevention (Behavioural Science) at the Flinders University of South Australia.

Gregory C. R. Yates is a Senior Lecturer in the School of Education at the University of South Australia.

Preface

There is a growing realisation by governments and other agencies that education is in crisis, not least as a result of a largely ideological press for change over recent decades for which there was little or no supporting evidence. There is now a growing appreciation, also shared by governments, that there is a need for what has become known as evidence-based practice. Educational psychology is the greatest hope for implementing evidence-based best practice in schools since it is predicated on a scientific approach to education based on quantitative evidence. This is one of the key features of this text.

The origins of this book lie in a special issue I edited to celebrate the twenty-fifth anniversary of the journal *Educational Psychology*. It comprised ten articles by leading figures in the field who serve on the journal's editorial board and who wrote about developments in their specialist topics of interest. The special issue was well received ('about time someone said that,' was a recurrent comment), as was the subsequent hardback book version of this collection of perspectives. In his review in the *British Journal of Educational Technology*, Professor Paul Kirchner of Utrecht University described it as 'a "must read" for all educational psychologists, students of educational psychology, teachers and teacher trainers'.

As a hardback, this edition found its market in libraries rather than among postgraduate students and professionals. Routledge publishers expressed interest in publishing a paperback edition. When my proposal was sent out for review, the feedback was pleasingly positive and suggested that reading and classroom behaviour deserved greater coverage. This was particularly gratifying since these two topics have been my main research interests almost throughout my career. It also provided an opportunity to include some of the work completed by my research students and colleagues reviewing developments in these two key research areas.

What, then, has resulted from this process of revision and expansion? It is clearly not a comprehensive purview of the field as a whole. This collection is more an idiosyncratic overview of recent developments in topics that I consider to be of interest and importance.

The first ten chapters comprise a series of perspectives on general topics within the field of educational psychology and were originally published as the special anniversary issue of *Educational Psychology*, volume 25, and also constituted the first edition of this book (as noted above). With the exception of my opening chapter (Chapter 1), which has been updated, edited and partially rewritten, the remaining nine chapters have been only lightly edited, where appropriate, since the first edition.

The next three chapters focus on aspects of classroom behaviour. Chapter 11 was originally published in the *Australasian Journal of Special Education*, volume 31, Chapter 12 comprises an expanded and updated version of an article first published in *Educational Psychology*, volume 20, while Chapter 13 is published for the first time in this collection. The final chapter (Chapter 14) reviews research on teacher judgement of reading performance and is also published for the first time in this collection.

Finally, it should be noted that the vast majority of texts in this field tend to be *general introductions* to educational psychology for education undergraduates or *more specialised* volumes and monographs written at an advanced level on *specific topics* within the field. This is an overview of research and ideas on selected topics over recent years, written at a level appropriate for graduates and professionals – postgraduate students of educational psychology and special education in training; educational psychologists; teachers; special educators; education academics; education bureaucrats, etc. As such, it may be seen as a bridge between the introductory text and the academic monograph.

Kevin Wheldall,
Sydney, 2009

Chapter 1

When will we ever learn? Or the elephant in the classroom

Kevin Wheldall

Preamble

> *Nul n'aura de l'esprit, hors nous et nos amis*
> [No one shall have wit save we and our friends]
> > (Molière, *Les Femmes Savantes*, III, 2 1672)

> The very powerful and the very stupid have one thing in common. Instead of altering their views to fit the facts, they alter the facts to fit their views which can be very uncomfortable if you happen to be one of the facts that needs altering.
> > (Doctor Who, '*The Face of Evil*' 1977)

In his play *Les Femmes Savantes* ('The Wise Women'), the seventeenth-century French dramatist, Molière, satirised the contemporary cult of *la préciosité* (or 'preciousness'). It had become the fashion in learned society to speak in an extravagant and prolix manner as a means of demonstrating erudition. Instead of referring to one's teeth, for example, the pretentious, fashionable elite would instead talk of *l'ameublement de la bouche* (literally, 'the furniture of the mouth').

I am reminded of this famous play, with embarrassing frequency, when I read much contemporary educational 'research', especially that emanating from a supposedly postmodernist perspective. Rhetoric appears to have replaced reason and assertion appears to have replaced the need for empirical fact. It is apparent to almost everyone, except to many educational researchers themselves, that much contemporary educational research has little relevance to, or has little potential to inform, educational practice. I believe passionately that we shall only make progress in education when we base educational decision making on the findings from empirical, and where possible *experimental*, educational psychological research. I welcome this opportunity to provide a personal perspective on developments in educational psychology over recent years and to comment on the contemporary state of affairs.

How has the discipline of educational psychology developed?

More than 25 years ago, in 1981, Richard Riding and I, both then working in the Department of Educational Psychology at the University of Birmingham, established and became joint editors of a new journal: *Educational Psychology: An International Journal of Experimental Educational Psychology*. In this collection of chapters, contributed by members of the Editorial Board of *Educational Psychology* and others, a series of perspectives is provided on progress in key areas within the discipline over the past 20–30 years. In the first issue of *Educational Psychology* in 1981, Richard Riding and I (as the founding joint editors) nailed our colours to the mast in our opening editorial article entitled 'Effective Educational Research' (Riding and Wheldall 1981). In that article, we spelled out our hopes and aspirations for educational psychology, the discipline, as well as for the journal. The aim of this introductory chapter is to reconsider some of these issues, to question the progress made in educational psychology, and to explore the interface between research and practice in education.

The journal was dedicated to the 'rapid dissemination of *experimental* psychological research which has a direct bearing on educational topics and problems' (Riding and Wheldall 1981: 5). Riding and I (1981: 8) wrote:

> Teachers frequently complain that educational psychology has little to offer them that is of real value in the classroom. We think that it is important to admit that, to some extent, they are right. Experimental studies, in the true sense of the term, are in the minority in educational psychology.

We argued that effective educational research necessarily entails the predominant use of traditional experimental psychological methods and designs. The main founding aim of the journal was to provide a forum for and to encourage experimental research in educational psychology. It seemed to us, working in two separate fields and from two very different theoretical perspectives (behavioural and cognitive psychology), that there was a clear need for a vehicle to promote a rigorous, experimentally based educational psychology which would directly inform educational practice. This view was based on our belief that the balance between experimental and non-experimentally based research had been seriously tilted in favour of the latter, and that far fewer truly experimental studies were being carried out, or at least reported. Has this situation changed?

Before answering this question directly, it is only fair to comment on the achievements of *Educational Psychology* in helping to redress the balance. A perusal of the contents over the years provides clear testimony to the variety and quality of the experimental research in educational psychology being carried out internationally. This is true for both cognitive and behavioural perspectives and also for the developmental perspective. Many important experimentally based studies have been reported, which have clear implications for practice, for immediate application in the real world of education. From this, we could begin to conclude that clear progress was being made in the right direction. Without wishing to play down these achievements, however, it must also be said that one journal does not make a movement. To take a camping analogy, it is not enough to make sure that life is warm and cosy inside the tent. It is even more important to look at what is happening outside.

It would be foolish to pretend that there has been much of a change of research climate in this direction within educational research generally. In fact, there has been an increasing preference for manifestly non-experimental research and widespread disenchantment with empirical educational research methodology altogether.

First the good news. There is evidence that single-subject and small-N methodology, pioneered by behaviour analysts, has become more generally accepted as a means by which the effectiveness of interventions in applied settings can be experimentally assessed. In some field settings it is certainly difficult, if not impossible, to run fully randomised control group designs with large sample sizes. On the other hand, small-N designs using single subjects as their own controls by means of reversal and/or multiple baseline designs allow rigorous evaluation of treatment effectiveness for a wide range of educational innovations. The manifest major disadvantage of such methods, weak generalisability, is at least partially overcome by the accumulation of clear replications of the effect over a number of subjects and over replicated studies by different research groupings. It is important, however, not to overemphasise the applicability of small-N methodology; it is neither feasible nor appropriate for all experimental studies.

The bad news is the 'crisis of confidence' by not a few academics and researchers in traditional, statistically based methodology. In a desperate search for immediate and manifest relevance, some have been seduced by the apparent charms of action research, ethnographic methodology, postmodernist theorising, and so-called qualitative approaches. These are, of course, by no means the same thing, but have become increasingly frequent bedfellows. One student, quizzed as to the nature of his proposed research, responded by saying: 'It's action research really. It's phenomenological.' When the bemused academic asked him what he meant by this, the student replied: 'Well, I'm only doing it in one school.' Amusing howlers aside, however, this points up a very real danger.

The impression has gained ground that qualitative research is necessarily more relevant, avoids the problems of carrying out research based on traditional methodologies, and is altogether easier to do. As a consequence, we are left with the curious notion that a more subjective approach is preferable to a more objective approach with known and acknowledged limitations. Without wishing to minimise the contribution that such research might conceivably make to sociological analyses of educational processes, or to deny the valuable service action research can perform in demonstrating the practical utility and applicability of new initiatives in schools and classrooms, neither of these methodologies can possibly do more than serve as informal pilot or pre-pilot studies to properly conceived psychological evaluations of essentially psychological phenomena relevant to educational practice. *Teaching and learning are essentially psychological phenomena.*

Again, perhaps one should stress that what has gone before is not meant to ignore the possible value of qualitative or action research in suggesting relevant testable hypotheses for future empirical research. It is whether such methods *alone* can unequivocally demonstrate scientific truths that is in doubt. How and why educational innovations work is and must be the legitimate concern of research in educational psychology – not because it affords the luxury of sterile model building, but because an empirically determined psychology of pedagogy and related educational processes is the only way we can achieve long-term progress. As Wheldall and Carter (1996: 133) put it:

> We would support the great value of qualitative methodology, particularly in providing rich insight into the processes in naturalistic situations. However, qualitative methodology is equally unsuitable to other research tasks such as providing unambiguous evidence of causal relationships. Notwithstanding the problems of artificiality and socially valid outcome measures that can arise with quantitative methodology, many questions in education are fundamentally quantitative in nature. Rational and incremental progress should be informed by the research methods which are appropriate to the questions being forwarded. Qualitative methods are both different and complementary.

Finally, it is instructive to reflect on whether true experimental designs are any more prevalent today in educational research than they were when *Educational Psychology* (the journal) was founded. Seethaler and Fuchs (2005) suggest that this is unlikely on the basis of their analysis of the content of five peer-reviewed special education journals over the past five years. Of the articles published, only 5.46 per cent reported a reading or maths intervention using a group design and only 4.22 per cent employed random allocation to groups. It is, then, perhaps rather harsh to criticise teachers for not recognising the value of evidence-based practice by employing teaching methods and programmes validated by 'gold-standard' randomised control group designs when so very few articles published by educational researchers actually report findings from such studies! Moreover, special education has a far stronger tradition than regular education for hard-nosed, data-driven educational psychological approaches to both instruction and research. If this is the case for special education, what must the situation be like for regular educators keen to be guided by gold-standard evidence-based practice?

The rise of constructivism

Alongside and sometimes in consort with an increasing preference for qualitative educational research methodology, within educational psychology per se, as well as in educational research more generally, we have also witnessed the rise of what has come to be known as 'constructivism' as a dominant force within the discipline (see Chapter 2 and Chapter 9). But while constructivism, in its many forms and guises, appears to be the current 'flavour of the month' in educational psychology, perhaps the enthusiasm with which it is being advocated (if not always so readily adopted) should be tempered with a more rigorous concern with its evidential basis.

Wheldall and Carter (1996) commented that some aspects of constructivism appear to be little more than 'old wine in new bottles'. Moreover, much of the apparent research literature promoting constructivist pedagogy appears to be more descriptive or exhortative than evidence-based. Apps and Carter (2006), for example, refer to a pilot study they conducted in which they searched the ERIC database from 1982 to 1999 for the terms 'constructivism' and 'discovery learning', and also for the term 'direct instruction' as a comparison reference point. According to Apps and Carter, the search revealed that, while discovery learning produced 1,871 hits and constructivism 1,170 hits, direct instruction produced fewer than half as many, 409 hits. More important, however, was their subsequent more detailed analysis of the abstracts of the first 50 and the last 50 articles within each category. As Apps and Carter (2006: 8) comment, their results:

> illustrated the increase in constructivist literature and revealed a tendency for this literature to be primarily of a non-empirical nature. For example, 51% of articles addressing direct instruction were empirical and examined student learning outcomes, compared with 2% of articles addressing discovery learning and 4% addressing constructivism.

(In a subsequent study specifically addressing constructivist approaches to special education, they examined all 114 peer-reviewed articles up to October 2004 on this topic revealed by searches of both ERIC and PsychINFO and found that only 6 [5.3 per cent] were experimental in nature.) These findings suggest that there is considerably more empirical work to be done before the evidence can match the rhetoric advocating constructivist approaches to teaching.

This lack of reliance on empirical evidence is not confined to constructivists, however. The idea of advocating the use of programmes of proven effectiveness sounds like 'teaching one's grandmother to suck eggs': who would use an ineffective programme? But teachers and educators often do. This leads to an important point regarding the way in which educational practice is advanced.

Programmes of proven effectiveness

It is quite commonplace in education to see methods, programmes, and techniques employed for which the data on effectiveness is minimal, non-existent, or even contrary. The late American educator Jeanne Chall (2000: 3) addressed this very issue:

What is particularly striking about educational innovations is that most were considered successes long before they were actually sufficiently tried and tested. Seldom were they presented together with a rationale based on educational theory and research. Nor had they been tried first in small pilot studies before being offered as solutions to national education problems.

She subsequently laments: '[P]ractice often went in a direction opposite from the existing research evidence' (2000: 180). My own experience as an educational psychological researcher bears testimony to Chall's observations. Specifically, I am referring to educational innovations, for which there was limited or no evidence of efficacy, being adopted. In New South Wales, Australia (where I have lived and worked since 1990), the state educational bureaucracy embraced and implemented at least three disparate programmes or innovations, without sufficient or sufficiently strong evidence of their effectiveness in improving student outcomes in schools. Reading Recovery, 'accelerative learning', and a behaviour management approach called W.I.N.S. (Working Ideas for Needs Satisfaction) were all enthusiastically adopted by the state education department and all three exemplified at least one of Chall's criticisms. I shall resist the temptation to dwell on accelerative learning, the treatment for which there was no known disease, since I was not involved with it in any way, but I will mention briefly the other two.

I was commissioned to evaluate the behaviour management package, W.I.N.S., following a wide-scale 'train the trainer' implementation programme across the state. We found that, in spite of the positive evaluations it received in our surveys from trainers and others, there was no empirical evidence to testify to its efficacy in terms of bringing about substantial change in either teacher or student behaviour or, indeed, on any other measure we employed. Fortunately, as it turned out, very few schools were actually using it (Wheldall and Beaman 1994).

The case of Reading Recovery is even more tragic since it is still widely employed in New South Wales schools (and in some other Australian states and many other countries). Again, we were commissioned to evaluate the programme but, even before we reported, a decision was taken to expand its use throughout the state. In short, the findings from our carefully controlled, *experimental* evaluation showed that Reading Recovery was effective for only about one in three students who experienced it: one was 'recovered', one would have recovered anyway without intervention, and one was not helped much at all. Moreover, those students for whom Reading Recovery appeared to be effective tended to be the students with less intransigent phonological problems. Our report was basically ignored and never officially released in spite of the findings of our evaluation being published in arguably the most respected reading research journal in the world, the *Reading Research Quarterly* (Center *et al.* 1995), and being described by eminent American researchers Shanahan and Barr (1995) as one of the 'more sophisticated studies'. Moreover, they concluded, on the basis of their systematic review of the available literature on the efficacy of Reading Recovery (Shanahan and Barr 1995: 959):

> It is less effective and more costly than has been claimed, and does not lead to systemic changes in classroom instruction, making it difficult to maintain learning gains. This is discouraging given program claims and its great expense.

Reading Recovery is far too expensive a model to be advocated given its relatively limited efficacy. This probably accounts for the increasing disenchantment with Reading Recovery in the United States as confirmed by Snow, Burns, and Griffin, editors of the highly influential report of the Committee on the Prevention of Reading Difficulties in Young Children (Snow *et al.* 1998). In their synthesis of the relevant research into reading, based on the contributions of an impressive array of 'the great and the good' in reading research in the United States, they offered little support for either the effectiveness or the cost-effectiveness of Reading Recovery. State politicians, however, seem determined to continue providing high levels of funding to support Reading Recovery implementations.

My research student, Meree Reynolds, and I have recently published a review of the research evidence on Reading Recovery (Reynolds and Wheldall 2007). We concluded that Reading Recovery is simply not effective enough, for enough students, to warrant the very high costs involved in implementing it.

More generally, imagine the outcry if new miracle wonder drugs were released to an unsuspecting public without extensive, experimental clinical trials testifying to their efficacy. But in education, this is precisely what typically happens. And so we see them pass, fad after fad, guru following guru, educational disaster after educational disaster. The result is that in education we do not make progress, we merely see changes of fashion. Half-baked ideas are conceived, promoted, and inflicted on a beleaguered teaching profession with only rarely a hint of carefully controlled experimental evaluation.

Thankfully there are, however, programmes, methods and innovations in education for which there are proven efficacy data. It is just that, as Chall (2000) says, teachers prefer not to use them. Conceptually, positive reinforcement, mastery learning, direct (systematic and intensive) instruction, and 'phonics' are all good examples of approaches or methods for which there is considerable, not to say (arguably) unequivocal empirical support testifying to effectiveness. Programmes based on such approaches and methods are available. The task is to persuade teachers to employ them.

In the sections that follow, I will explore in a little more detail two of the examples from the list above. Over the past 25 years, my research has focused primarily on classroom behaviour management employing contingent teacher praise as positive reinforcement, and on effective reading instruction for low-progress readers.

Praise as positive reinforcement for appropriate classroom behaviour

Most teachers have heard about positive reinforcement and the importance of praise and reward for academic learning. Moreover, most teachers probably sincerely believe that, on the whole, they are reasonably positive in their interactions with students. The reality is, however, a little more complicated.

In company with other research groups in the United States and elsewhere, I have been involved, over the years, in collecting data on teachers' classroom use of praise and reprimand (approval and disapproval), both in the UK and in Australia. In 2000, we reviewed the research literature on this topic (Beaman and Wheldall 2000; updated as Chapter 12 of this book), which was remarkably consistent (Beaman and Wheldall 2000: 431):

> There is a considerable degree of agreement across the studies reviewed, carried out in the United States, Canada, the United Kingdom, Australia, New Zealand, Hong Kong and St Helena, regarding the ways in which teachers typically deploy approval and disapproval, with some interesting variations. There is little evidence to suggest that teachers, universally, systematically deploy contingent praise as positive reinforcement in spite of the considerable literature testifying to its effectiveness. In particular, praise for appropriate classroom social behaviour is only rarely observed.

In spite of a huge research base testifying to the efficacy of contingent praise (e.g. Wheldall (1987); Wheldall and Glynn (1989); Wheldall *et al.* 1986), it is hardly ever used by teachers to reinforce students for behaving appropriately in the classroom. In Australia and in the UK, we found that primary teachers, for example, typically praised academic work three to four times as much as they expressed disapproval, but disapproval/reprimand for inappropriate classroom behaviour was three to five times more common than approval for behaving well, which was very uncommon. A very similar pattern was observed for high-school teachers.

The rates of approval were also typically very low. The group of Australian primary teachers observed had a total approval rate of only 0.61 responses per minute (only about half that of their British peers). This means that, on average, teachers praise at a rate of 36 responses per hour and thus each student in the class will typically receive just over one positive comment per hour. To be effective in keeping students motivated, praise needs to be far more abundant than this and in a ratio of three or more times more praise than reprimand. The research clearly shows that praising students for behaving well leads to reductions in inappropriate behaviour and increases in the amount of time students spend on-task or appropriately engaged (Merrett and Wheldall 1990; Wheldall and Glynn 1989; Wheldall and Merrett 1989). In spite of the overwhelming evidence, however, not only is praise not practised effectively, its very utility is in question.

At a recent education conference, I was informed in all seriousness, 'Everyone knows that praise is out of fashion'. It sometimes seems as if the more empirical evidence there is to support a teaching method, the less likely it is to be widely employed, and the more likely it is to be derided.

Teaching reading effectively using phonics

If there is one area, in particular, in which psychologists addressing educational issues have made huge gains in knowledge over the past 30 years or so, it has to be in the areas of how the reading process works and how it may best be taught. Unfortunately, the vast body of scientific research evidence notwithstanding, it also remains one of the most controversial topics since it appears to have divided psychologists and educationists into two warring sides: 'whole language' versus 'phonics'. This debate has occupied considerable space in both the educational literature and the popular media.

One of my main areas of research interest has been the study of low-progress readers and how best to help them to acquire more developed reading and related skills (Wheldall and Beaman 2000, 2009). Many, if not most, of these students, however, would not need remedial reading intervention at all if they had been offered adequate and effective initial instruction in reading in the first place.

The model of initial (and remedial) reading instruction provided in schools should be based on scientifically validated best practice. Over the past 30 years, we have seen the growth of a considerable body of scientific research literature internationally, illuminating both how reading works and how it should best be taught. Moreover, a number of comprehensive reports have been produced collating, summarising, and consolidating these researches and drawing inevitable conclusions. De Lemos (2002) has produced for the Australian Council of Educational Research an excellent digest of these more extensive reports and their implications for practice, including that of the National Reading Panel in the United States (National Institute for Child Health and Human Development 2000). More recently, we have seen similar reports from both Australia (Department of Education, Science and Training 2005) and the UK (Rose 2006), reaching very similar conclusions.

It is now universally acknowledged by the scientific community researching reading and related skills that reading is quintessentially phonologically based – that is, that the ability to decompose the word stream of human speech into its component sounds is an essential prerequisite of learning to read (Pogorzelski and Wheldall 2005). Children who experience difficulties in so doing typically experience problems in learning to read if these difficulties are not specifically addressed by appropriate instruction.

The development of phonological sensitivity, however, is a necessary but not sufficient condition for learning to read to take place. The beginning readers must also understand that the decomposed letter sounds of speech may be associated with graphic symbols or letters. This letter–sound correspondence is best taught overtly and systematically in the early stages of learning to read. Learning to read by this so-called 'phonics' method has been shown to be the most effective method of teaching reading, a conclusion reached by the National Reading Panel in the United States (National Institute of Child Health and Human Development, 2000), the National Inquiry into the Teaching of Literacy in Australia (Department of Education, Science and Training 2005) and the 'Rose Report' in the UK (Rose 2006).

Reading instruction based on the body of scientific research referred to above should replace the far less effective practices of many teachers, even though these are commonly advocated in many teacher education establishments and by state education departments. It is recognised that the views of those advocating a 'whole-language philosophy' towards reading instruction are sincerely held and, indeed, did much to correct a previous preoccupation with sub-skills teaching to the neglect of a need for, and an appreciation of, reading meaningful connected text. The fact remains, however, and regardless of how well meaning its adherents, that whole-language-based teaching will continue to fail an unacceptable and substantial minority of students (20–30 per cent) in our schools if it is not supplemented with programmes of explicit and systematic phonics instruction.

The introduction of such evidence-based practices into the initial training of teachers and professional development courses for serving teachers would lead to immediate and considerable improvements in the overall literacy standards of young school students in their early years of schooling. This would reduce the need for very expensive (and not always very satisfactory) large-scale remedial reading programmes in schools. (Reading Recovery, for example, as already mentioned, consumes a large part of state education budgets, but has been shown to be only mildly effective for only the less disabled readers.) More effective initial reading instruction would drastically reduce the number of students in need of remedial reading instruction, perhaps to less than 5 per cent.

By ensuring that the vast majority of students learn to read quickly and easily, as a result of employing the evidence-based best practice teaching methods referred to above, students with more intractable reading difficulties could be afforded more time and resources. Remedial reading specialists would welcome the opportunity to restrict their remit to serving the needs of such a small minority of students rather than continuing to attempt to stem the tide of low-progress readers emerging from our schools.

The elephant in the classroom

It was in his 'Introductory Lectures on Psychoanalysis', if I recall correctly, that Freud related the anecdote of a young woman being interviewed for the post of nanny who, when asked if she had had any experience with children, responded with words to the effect of, 'Why yes, I was a child once myself!' So it appears to be with education. Everyone has been to school and so everyone fancies him or herself as somewhat of an expert on education. While relatively few laypersons seem inclined to take up positions on preferred techniques for brain surgery, nuclear fission, or rocket science, society is not short of pundits on matters educational. How best to teach reading and how to maintain classroom discipline effectively are both educational issues upon which politicians, parents, and the person in the street all feel fully qualified to venture an opinion. A considered appraisal of the relevant scientific evidence is not seen as a necessary prerequisite to enter into this debate. Why should this be so? Is it perhaps connected to the fact that the education profession itself eschews such an approach?

Similarly, we would be surprised, if not somewhat perplexed, if our physician were to declare that, contemporary best practice notwithstanding, his preference was to employ leeches or exorcism to effect a cure of our malady. We are reluctant to employ legal representatives who decide not to rely on precedent or case law, but to try an operatic rendition of a plea of mitigation instead. Our confidence in the firm of architects we employed would be shaken if they declared that scale drawings of our proposed new house were very old hat and that a dialectical materialist critique of the concept of property would be an altogether more interesting and intellectually stimulating exercise. And yet we are only mildly surprised when teachers and other educators choose methods and adopt positions on the basis of personal preference, ideology, or convenience. We do not expect the same standards of reason, rigour, and responsibility that we take for granted in other professions.

We are not surprised that teachers, after leaving college, read few if any books or journals on research and developments in education (Rudland and Kemp 2004), and yet we expect all other professionals to keep up to date. In many professions we expect practitioners to demonstrate continuing competence through the mandatory professional development requirements demanded for continuing membership of professional bodies; such requirements are only just beginning to be expected of teachers. Other professionals are held morally, if not always legally, accountable for the quality of their service delivery; no such accountability is required of teachers.

In fact, we might seriously ask how the occupation of teacher/educator qualifies for the epithet 'professional' other than by casual assertion. Surely, to be a profession there should, at the very least, be some commonly agreed notion of what the job actually entails, a body of shared agreed knowledge of best practice which can withstand critical scrutiny, a body of key skills learned to a high level of competence if not mastery, and agreed criteria by which it can readily be seen that progress toward completion of the job is being made.

After so many years of educational psychological research, then, it would seem that there is little evidence to suggest that we are very much closer to real progress in educational endeavour. Important advances have undoubtedly been made, advances with enormous practical potential for improved teaching and learning, but they have yet to be seriously translated into educational practice per se. The role of educational psychology as an applied discipline must certainly be to provide teachers with the means by which they can inform their practice based on coherent theory and empirical research findings. Perhaps an even more important task remains, however: to research, and then to implement, the most effective methods of convincing teachers and educators of the value of basing their teaching on educational psychological research.

What, then, is the elephant in the classroom? The unspoken (or rarely admitted) truth is that educational progress is not being delayed because of a shortage of funding for schools. Children's school performance is not being impeded by there being too few teachers. Educational standards are not slipping because parents do not care and students are lazy these days. The elephant in the classroom, that many educationists claim not to see, is that the quality of teaching in our schools is simply not good enough. It is not good enough because it is largely based on educational theory and methods for which there is little or no supporting empirical evidence for efficacy or which have been discredited. The education provided to children in our schools is largely ineffective because the education system ignores the extant scientific research evidence on what we know to constitute effective instruction and best teaching practice.

Acknowledgements

I would like to thank the numerous research colleagues, research assistants, and research students who have worked with me over the years and, in particular, Robyn Beaman, who also provided valuable feedback on earlier drafts of this essay.

References

Apps, M. and Carter, M. (2006). When all is said and done, more is said than done: Research examining constructivist instruction for students with special needs. *Australasian Journal of Special Education*, *30*: 107–25.

Beaman, R. and Wheldall, K. (2000). Teachers' use of approval and disapproval. *Educational Psychology*, *20*: 431–6.

Center, Y., Wheldall, K., Freeman, L., Outhred, L. and McNaught, M. (1995). An evaluation of Reading Recovery. *Reading Research Quarterly*, *30*: 240–63.

Chall, J. S. (2000). *The achievement challenge*. New York: Guilford Press.

de Lemos, M. (2002). *Closing the gap between research and practice: Foundations for the acquisition of literacy*. Camberwell, Victoria: Australian Council for Educational Research.

Department of Education, Science and Training. (2005). *Teaching reading*. Canberra: Department of Education, Science and Training.

Merrett, F. and Wheldall, K. (1990). *Positive teaching in the primary school*. London: Paul Chapman.

National Institute of Child Health and Human Development. (2000). *Report of the National Reading Panel: Teaching children to read*. Washington, DC: U.S. Government Printing Office.

Pogorzelski, S. and Wheldall, K. (2005). The importance of phonological processing skills for older low-progress readers. *Educational Psychology in Practice, 21*: 1–22.

Reynolds, M. and Wheldall, K. (2007). Reading Recovery twenty years down the track: Looking forward, looking back. *International Journal of Disability, Development and Education, 54*: 199–223.

Riding, R. J. and Wheldall, K. (1981). Effective educational research. *Educational Psychology, 1*: 5–11.

Rudland, N. and Kemp, C. (2004). The professional reading habits of teachers: Implications for student learning. *The Australasian Journal of Special Education, 28*: 4–17.

Rose, J. (2006). *Independent review of the teaching of early reading: Final Report.* London: Department for Education and Skills.

Seethaler, P. M. and Fuchs, L. S. (2005). A drop in the bucket: Randomised controlled trials testing reading and maths interventions. *Learning Disabilities Research and Practice, 20*: 98–102.

Shanahan, T. and Barr, R. (1995). Reading Recovery: An independent evaluation of the effects of an early instructional intervention for at-risk learners. *Reading Research Quarterly, 30*: 958–6.

Snow, C. E., Burns, M. S. and Griffin, P. (eds). (1998). *Preventing reading difficulties in young children.* Washington, DC: National Academy Press.

Wheldall, K. (ed.). (1987). *The behaviourist in the classroom.* London: Allen and Unwin.

Wheldall, K. and Glynn, T. (1989). *Effective classroom learning: A behavioural interactionist approach to teaching.* London: Basil Blackwell.

Wheldall, K. and Merrett, F. (1989). *Positive teaching in the secondary school.* London: Paul Chapman.

Wheldall, K. and Beaman, R. (1994). *An evaluation of the WINS (Working Ideas for Need Satisfaction) training package* (Report submitted to the New South Wales Department of School Education, 1993). Sydney: Macquarie University Special Education Centre. *Collected Original Resources in Education, 18*(1), fiche 4 E01.

Wheldall, K. and Carter, M. (1996). Reconstructing behaviour analysis in education: A revised behavioural interactionist perspective for special education. *Educational Psychology, 16*: 121–40.

Wheldall, K. and Beaman, R. (2000). *An evaluation of MULTILIT: 'Making Up Lost Time In Literacy'.* Canberra: Department of Education, Training and Youth Affairs.

Wheldall, K. and Beaman, R. (2009). Effective instruction for older low-progress readers: Meeting the needs of indigenous students. In C. Wyatt-Smith, J. Elkins and S. Gunn (eds), *Multiple perspectives on difficulties in learning literacy and numeracy.* New York: Springer.

Wheldall, K., Merrett, F. and Glynn, T. (eds). (1986). *Behaviour analysis in educational psychology.* London: Croom Helm.

Chapter 2

Educational psychology – theory, research, and teaching

Dennis M. McInerney

There is, or should be, a strong link between educational psychology theorising and research and teaching-learning processes. Best practice in classrooms, whether at school or in post-compulsory schooling, should reflect what the best theorising and research has to offer. But 'best' is context specific and often time limited. What was considered 'best practice' 30, 20, or even 10 years ago is not necessarily considered best practice today. Some practices have stood the test of time and are still in vogue, either directly or through some sort of metamorphosis. Other practices have been relegated to history's dustbin as misguided, not useful, or based upon flawed research.

The learning worlds of today are far more complex and multilayered than they were 30 years ago. And by this I mean not only in terms of the variety and complexity of information that individuals need to learn, but also in terms of the availability of learning pathways that were only dreamed of and experienced through *The Jetsons* cartoons. Today the digital world and the internet have revolutionised both what we learn and how we learn. Naturally this new context has made some old approaches and theorising about learning and teaching obsolescent. In other ways, the new context has enabled us to scrutinise old theories more closely and breathe new life into them through research, theory, and practice that capitalises on this new technology.

In this review I do not pretend to cover all theoretical and research issues that have been part of the history of educational psychology over recent decades. I want to take a rather idiosyncratic view as a teacher, researcher, theoretician, and author of educational psychology texts and research. My analysis is also based on a review of the contents of the journal *Educational Psychology* since its inception.

I have been teaching and researching in educational psychology for more than 30 years and tremendous changes have occurred in both its content and emphases, as well as in the themes that characterise the research that underpins teaching. While my short review could never be comprehensive, it will attempt to give an overview of significant developments over that period from both a researcher's and a teacher's perspective, particularly in the Australian context. I go back to a little before 1980 to give a context for where research has come from.

Curriculum emphasis on educational psychology has declined

Educational psychology formed a greater part of the basics (what we called the foundations) of teacher training and education 25–30 years ago – in other words, a greater percentage of student time at university, particularly for people training as educators or for related fields, was spent studying educational psychology. At my institution, for example, we have had to fight a continuing battle over the years to preserve an identifiable presence in course structures.

The battle has been fought on two fronts. First, there have been competing demands for curriculum space from a whole raft of contemporary 'key areas' such as technology, and at the same time there was a diminution in total available teaching time for all subjects. Second, the battle was against the consistently argued case that educational (and developmental) psychology should be integrated with other foundation and curriculum areas in composite subjects. In this latter case, the identity and quality of educational psychology offerings have often been compromised. Ironically, as teaching time for educational psychology diminished, the depth of theorising and range of topics explored through research increased, and there has been a burgeoning of research and scholarly journals related to educational psychology.

Range of topics has expanded

The range of topics covered by educational psychology courses 25–30 years ago, as well as the range of research areas of interest, was considerably narrower than today, and the emphases were also different. The currently increasing range of topics reflects the growth of new theoretical and research interest and a phenomenon whereby kernel research and theoretical interests exploded into a range of new but related interests. I deal with this 'explosion' later in this review. However, it is interesting to see concepts that were key to educational psychology a quarter of a century ago recycled in much of the research and theorising of today.

Four basic emphases

There were four basic emphases in educational psychology research 25 years ago (e.g. Joyce *et al.* 1987). These are each covered in turn below.

Cognitive psychology

Cognitive psychology encompassed the work of Gagné, Ausubel, Bruner, and others, and a whole raft of cognitive processing topics such as the transfer of learning (then referred to as 'training'); the role of prior knowledge; massed versus distributed practice; the 7 ± 2 rule (cognitive load); serial position effect; whole and part learning; mnemonics, and so on (e.g. Eysenck (1984); Shuell (1986); Wessells (1982); earlier resources that are of historical interest are Kingsley and Garry (1957); Seagoe 1972). Many of these constructs had great similarity to, and were precursors of, what we now call metacognition and metacognitive processes, but were then not labelled as such; many, such as transfer of learning and the relevance of prior learning, were conceptually more simple than in today's theorising and research.

Over recent years the amount of research reported on metacognitive strategies and training (often in the areas of reading and mathematics education) has increased considerably, with specific examinations of the nature of effective skills and strategies, their development, and whether skills and strategies should be trained independent of content or embedded in content.

Related to investigations of metacognition was a growing interest in learning style and cognitive style research. Early volumes of the journal *Educational Psychology*, for example, had little on metacognition, learning styles, and cognitive styles. Learning and cognitive styles, in particular, subsequently became an increasingly dominant area of research interest in this and other journals.

Behavioural psychology

The second basic emphasis, behavioural psychology, and mechanistic views of learning in which individuals were seen more as bundles of operants shaped by reinforcement than active thinking and perceiving processors of information, while still strong at the beginning of the 1980s, was in decline. While the father of behaviourism, Skinner, acknowledged that people (and higher primates) thought, deliberated, felt, and so on, these cognitive and affective processes could not be observed, and hence did not provide a path to a science of behaviour which the observance and manipulation of operants did. During the 1970s and early 1980s much research was reported on individualised behaviourally-oriented teaching programmes, such as the Personalised System of Instruction (PSI) (Keller and Sherman 1974), but the radical behaviourism which dominated previous decades was dead.

Early volumes of *Educational Psychology* published articles with a behavioural emphasis in which teaching was seen as a process of transmitting external knowledge to students through demonstration, reinforcement, and controlled and sequenced practice (see Wheldall 1987). There were articles on praise and punishment, task analysis, direct instruction, precision teaching, contingency programmes, behavioural checklists, and the like. By the end of the 1980s there were fewer articles with this orientation.

Behavioural psychology is still a force reflected in practice if not in research (McInerney and McInerney 2006). Positive teaching and applied behaviour analysis approaches receive some continuing research attention. In particular, technology has allowed for many of the principles of behavioural teaching to be re-explored with state-of-the-art computer equipment and programs.

Sophisticated modern computer programs not only allow realistic simulation of learning situations, but provide opportunities for immediate correction and feedback, many alternative learning paths, and 'intelligent' reactions to choices made by the learner, although these important developments are still not fully realised and more research and development needs to be done.

Social cognitive theory

A third emphasis, social learning theory, largely identified with Bandura and derived from behavioural theory, was prominent in the early 1980s (Bandura 1977, 1986). This theory was relabelled social cognitive theory in later years to take into account the 'thinking' component of modelling. Social learning theory was seen, in many ways, as a logical marriage of cognitive and behavioural approaches. Considerable research was reported on the effects of modelling, and, indeed, even today there are significant research articles based on social cognitive theory. In particular, it has seen a resurgence of theoretical and research interest more recently through self-efficacy and self-regulation research, which are major areas of research reported in journals such as the *Journal of Educational Psychology*, *Contemporary Educational Psychology*, and the *American Educational Research Journal*.

Humanism

A fourth emphasis covered in those early days, sometimes referred to as the 'third psychology', was humanism, originally identified with Rogers (1961, 1969, 1983) and Maslow (1968). Humanism was seen by many as an antidote to many of the overly mechanistic approaches to learning and teaching being promulgated at the time, as well as to some of the overly cognitive theories of learning and motivation, sometimes labelled as 'cold' (e.g. Silberman *et al.* 1976). In some ways the humanistic theoretical approach to education and learning has seen a rebirth in research in the 1990s into caring schools and communities of learners, and still acts as an antidote to overly 'cold' theoretical approaches to motivation and learning (e.g. McInerney and McInerney (2006); Noddings 1992, 1995).

In general, the first three (cognitive, behavioural, and social learning) theories emphasised a skills-based approach to teaching and learning (what we might loosely call a science of teaching and learning) that was teacher dominated. In the late 1970s and 1980s, the micro-skills of teaching took centre stage in much teacher preparation, and if you review micro-skills material you will see an interesting blend of early cognitive, social learning, and behavioural principles espoused (e.g. Turney 1985a, 1985b). Micro-skills programmes (there were a number of these internationally) were buttressed by research represented in contemporaneous journal literature. At the same time there was considerable research into teachers, teaching, school learning, and school curricula. Although there is not such an emphasis on these topics today, there is periodically an article related to teacher motivation, teacher efficacy, teacher strategies, teacher values and beliefs, and so on. What is around is more likely to be located in practitioner journals than in research journals. An area that is attracting considerable contemporary attention these days in journals is teacher efficacy, school/classroom efficacy, and collective efficacy.

The growth of cognitive psychology research

As suggested above, over the last 25 years cognitive psychology has come to dominate educational psychology theorising and research. Early cognitive models looked at the most effective ways of structuring learning so that it could be effectively assimilated in a relatively final form by the learner. This approach is reflected in the schema theories of Gagné and Ausubel. An alternative approach was presented by Bruner, who emphasised discovery learning – a process of learning through which learners were expected to discover or 'construct' their own understandings and knowledge from challenging problems. The word 'construct' was not generally in the lexicon of educational psychology at the time. Considerable research in the 1970s and 1980s was conducted into the effects and benefits of discovery learning, open discovery, and guided discovery. Every now and then articles still pop up today which examine the relative values of guided and free discovery approaches to learning (e.g. De Jong and Van Joolingen 1998).

Today we see a vastly increased range of research based on cognitive psychology. Interestingly, social learning theory and a number of behaviourally based theories, such as positive teaching and direct instruction, have increasingly included a cognitive element (perhaps to make the theory and practices more attractive in an academic world largely critical of such approaches). Furthermore, beneath the surface of many cognitive approaches to learning (such as strategy instruction à la metacognition, and situated cognition), you may see some behavioural principles in cognitive clothing (e.g. Pressley *et al.* 1992).

Much of this recent cognitive emphasis, such as information processing, schema theory, and cognitive load, has its roots in the work of people such as Gagné and Ausubel, as well as in computer science. Information processing frameworks have characterised much research in mathematics, science, and reading over recent years, and in many ways have lent themselves more effectively to experimental studies than a number of other research themes and models. Considerable interest has been shown in examining the effectiveness of various learning and study strategies, again often in the context of mathematics, science, and reading.

Cognitive development and educational practice

During the 1970s and 1980s Piaget's work was being introduced to English-speaking countries. Indeed, for a number of years at my college there was a two-hour subject solely dedicated to Piaget (this had nothing to do with the fact that our director at the time had written one of the early books on Piaget and the application of his theory to teaching and learning and that this was the prescribed text!; McNally 1977).

The study of Piaget was of immense importance and still is today; however, the emphasis has changed considerably. In the 1970s and 1980s the research and teaching emphasis was on the structuralist elements of Piaget's theory, dealing with children growing through a discrete set of cognitive stages – sensori-motor, pre-operational, concrete operational, and formal operational – whereby they develop increasingly sophisticated ways of handling the world of knowledge. Indeed, this emphasis on the structuralist elements of the theory led educators to design what have been termed developmentally appropriate curricula based on Piaget's stages (see Fleer (1996); Forman 1980). There was considerable research to test out this theorising, and much of it took place in cross-cultural settings. Increasingly, the structuralist elements of Piaget's theory were challenged (Halford 1989).

In the 1980s, little time was spent on researching, or indeed teaching, Piaget's notion that learners construct their own schemas through personal interaction with the world of experience – referred to as personal or cognitive construc- tivism. Indeed, I cannot recall that this notion was paid much attention until recently – probably as a result of neo-Piagetians fine-tuning the balance of the theory, especially as research evidence for the structuralist component of the theory became less definitive (Bidell and Fischer 1992). Nevertheless, the important point here is that this component of Piaget's theory has formed a foundation for much of the constructivist theorising that we see reflected today in research and theoretical publications in educational psychology (McInerney and McInerney 2006).

Additionally, very little time was spent in educational psychology research on the social dimensions of learning. Usually research was on the individual learner and what the teacher/instructor did to or for the learner to make him or her learn, or the cognitive processing that characterised individual learning. One exception to this general pattern was social learning/cognitive theory which dealt with social interactions, but here the focus was on social interaction as a source of modelling through which learned behaviour was acquired via the observation of others and reinforcement. Over the past 25 years the social dimensions of learning have become a major focus of theory and research in educational psychology. This development included increasing attention to the social elements of Piaget's theory (DeVries 1997) and increasing focus on the theorising of Vygotsky.

The name Vygotsky and the term 'social constructivism' did not appear much in the educational research journals and textbooks of the 1970s and 1980s in Australia and the United States. However, as time moved on, Vygotsky became a strong focus of attention. Vygotsky's theorising clearly threw emphasis on the social dimensions of learning; he believed that learners construct their own meanings within social environments – a notion that has been termed social constructivism in contrast to Piaget's personal constructivism (Kozulin and Presseisen 1995; Moll 1990).

An important theoretical element of Vygotskian theory that received considerable research attention is the zone of proximal development (ZPD) (Smagorinsky 1995). The ZPD is typically thought of as each person's range of potential for learning, where that learning is culturally shaped by the social environment in which learning takes place. The ZPD has been, and still is, researched through studies on scaffolding and mediated learning, reciprocal teaching, distributed learning, collaborative learning, and learning communities (Alfassi, 1998; Hart and Speece 1998; King et al. 1998; McInerney et al. 1997). These types of study have given us new and valuable perspectives on the nature and processes of learning which are far removed from the didactic teaching-learning processes prevalent in the 1970s.

A related concept of increasing importance in educational psychology is sociocultural constructivism, which emphasises the wider social, cultural, and historical contexts of learning and the reciprocal interaction of these contexts with the individual's learning in order to construct shared knowledge (John-Steiner and Mahn 1996; Marshall 1996). Considerable theoretical and empirical advances have been made examining both social and sociocultural constructivism. And so constructivism as a major force in educational psychology was born (although of course somewhat belatedly in the United States and Australia, as Vygotsky died in the last century – and had had a much earlier impact in Europe).

As well as Vygotskian theorising emphasising the importance of the social construction of learning, there was a growing interest in the social dimensions of learning generally, which led to considerable research into co-operative and group learning, with research investigating various programmes such as STAD, TGI, Jigsaw, and Group Investigation (e.g. Johnson et al. (2000); Kagan (1994); Qin et al. (1995); Slavin 1991), the effectiveness of peer modelling techniques such as reciprocal teaching (Hart and Speece 1998), and the use of learning networks of various kinds such as the computer-supported intentional learning environment (CSILE) approach which was researched in the 1990s (e.g. Hewitt and Scardamalia (1998); Scardamalia and Bereiter 1995). These efforts, while beginning in the late 1970s, became more prominent in the 1980s and early 1990s.

Constructivism

When my co-author and I were developing the first edition of our text in the early 1990s, we opted for the catchy title *Educational Psychology: Constructing Learning* (McInerney and McInerney 1994). It seemed to reflect some of what we had read in the research and theoretical literature at the time. Constructivism was still somewhat on the fringe of educational psychology and was not even included in some of our competitor texts at the time. For our second edition

(McInerney and McInerney 1998) we made a thorough revision and opted to expand the constructivist elements. We did this with some trepidation, as we were not sure that constructivism would continue to be a dominant psychology and we didn't want our book to be tied to a fad. Indeed, there were many debates about the fruitfulness or otherwise of constructivism at meetings such as the American Educational Research Association, with competing metaphors of learning vying for attention. When revising the book for its third edition (McInerney and McInerney 2002), we were concerned to investigate how constructivism had fared over the intervening years. Much to our relief the amount of journal space spent on constructivism and approaches to learning and teaching based on constructivism had multiplied enormously. As I revised the fourth edition of the text (McInerney and McInerney 2006), constructivism seemed firmly established in the theoretical and research literature, as evidenced by a large range of educational psychology and related journals such as *Journal of Educational Psychology*, *British Journal of Educational Psychology*, *Contemporary Educational Psychology*, *Educational Researcher*, and *Review of Educational Research*.

Constructivism underlies many contemporary research themes such as information processing, metacognition, self-regulation, self-efficacy, peer tutoring, scaffolding, learning strategies and study skills, and a range of research themes related to mathematics. It has been something of an iconoclastic force in educational psychology and psychology in general, particularly radical constructivism, which asserts that all knowledge is individually constructed and equally valid (von Glaserfield 1995). Constructivism certainly dented ideas that knowledge was fixed and immutable and could be passed on from teacher to learner in a transmission mode. I am not sure how this theory would sit with Skinner, Ausubel, or Gagné, let alone with the recent information processing theorists, but I do know we would have had difficulty with the notion 30 years ago when the dominant teaching technique was transmission of knowledge.

Motivation theory

Motivation theory and research was still highly influenced, 25–30 years ago, by reinforcement theory (or biological versions of it), with a pinch of intrinsic motivation and variability theory thrown in to leaven the process. Considerable research was directed towards examining the effects of intrinsic versus extrinsic rewards on motivation, and whether the use of extrinsic rewards was positive or negative (e.g. Ryan and Deci 2000). At times this issue flares up again, with conflicting research demonstrating either that extrinsic rewards undermine intrinsic motivation and performance or that they do not (e.g. Cameron and Pierce 1996). Theorising about which motivators determined action was relatively elementary and never satisfactorily explained complex motivated human behaviour effectively. Nevertheless, research based on elementary approaches, such as reinforcement theory, provided educators with a battery of motivational skills that worked.

However, there was growing interest in cognitive models of motivation (Ames and Ames 1984). So over the 25-year period to the present a vast range of cognitive theories of motivation, and in particular ones reflecting constructivist theorising, have been developed and explored through research – many with underlying similarities, but still providing different and important perspectives on what motivates learners (McInerney 2005a). Among these are attribution theory, expectancy-value theory, goal theory, self-determination theory, personal investment theory, self-worth theory, and self-related constructs such as self-concept, self-regulation, and self-efficacy theories, as well as situated cognition.

To my mind the growth in cognitive theories of motivation is one of the most significant of any area in educational psychology over the last 25 years, and is strongly reflected in the increasing number of articles dedicated to motivation that are published in educational psychology journals. This shift from elementary and basic theories of motivation based on behavioural models to cognitive interpretations has had a strong impact on the ways in which we look at classrooms and schools, and in particular their structures vis-à-vis learning. Today there is considerable research evidence to support the view that:

- teachers, schools, and classrooms should emphasise mastery goals and de-emphasise performance goals;
- students should be encouraged to be origins rather than pawns in their approaches to learning;
- feelings of personal worth directly relate to learning and achievement;
- self-determination and choice may be key elements of effective motivation and learning;
- attributions for success and failure to internal and controllable causes such as effort are more likely to enhance motivation and achievement than attributions to external and uncontrollable causes such as luck; and
- expectations for success and valuing success are important ingredients of school achievement.

These insights from cognitive motivation theories and research give rise to many suggestions for reinventing schools so that they become places of success for all students. Unfortunately there is evidence that many schools are still stuck in a time warp more characteristic of the 1970s and 1980s.

Multicultural and cross-cultural perspectives

It is quite apparent that there has been a surge of interest in cross-cultural issues and the application of theories and research to heterogeneous groups. Schools and educational institutions were relatively homogeneous in their approach to teaching 25 and more years ago, even if the student body was anything but homogeneous. In other words, a one-size-fits-all approach to theory, research, and application was common. Over the 25-year period there has been an increasing recognition of the great diversity that characterises learners culturally, socially, geographically, and linguistically, and of the need to take this into account in our theorising, research, and practice (McInerney 2005a, 2005b). So we see increasingly reflected in mainstream educational journals articles related to diversity which take a cross-cultural approach (see also McInerney and Van Etten (2001), and later volumes in the series).

It was probably the close and increasingly methodologically sophisticated scrutiny of blockbuster theories such as those of Piaget, Vygotsky, Kohlberg, and others in societies characterised by diversity that began the cross-cultural trend in educational psychology. The introduction of cross-cultural perspectives has been enormously important. There is an increasing number of cross-cultural articles in educational psychology journals, particularly articles related to validating measuring instruments and methodologies among diverse groups. This emergence of the relevance and importance of cross-cultural studies is well reflected in articles published in *Educational Psychology*, probably reflecting the international spread of contributors to the journal. The journal is not North American-dominated. This shift from a monocultural research perspective to a multicultural one has had an important effect on the way in which we think about the universality of Western theorising and practice, and challenges us constantly to avoid a one-size-fits-all paradigm for research and classroom practice.

While not related to cross-cultural issues per se, there has been an increasing interest in looking at psychological phenomena from a male/female perspective, and the interaction of sex and culture. While many of these studies are labelled studies in gender, they do not effectively tease out the differences between sex (a biological imperative) and gender (a sociocognitive construction). Typically, early research examined the nature and causes of differences between the sexes on a raft of outcomes (such as reading, mathematics, and science), initially centring more specifically on the need to improve the performance of girls in traditionally male areas (e.g. Halpern and LaMay 2000). Today there is considerable interest in investigating why males appear to have slipped behind girls on a number of major educational criteria.

Other research themes

Clearly the dominant research theme after learning styles and cognitive styles research is reading research. Along with learning and cognitive styles research it swamps other areas. Major research themes were, and still are, concerned with demonstrating the relative effectiveness of whole-word approaches and phonics. It is fascinating to see how particular themes and emphases go around and come back again in reading research.

A number of other themes received a good airing at times in *Educational Psychology*. For example, educational assessment got a special issue in 1988 (Volume 8, Issue 4) when it was a reasonably hot topic of research. Bullying and self–concept have also received exposure since about 1995, but not much prior to that. Research related to special education has been consistently represented in the journal from the earliest issues. While the focus of a number of articles was mainstreaming, the range of topics covered under the banner of special needs education was quite broad.

Methodological developments

It is quite apparent when one does a broad sweep of the educational psychology research literature over the last 25 years that the methodological and statistical sophistication required of researchers has increased enormously and, indeed, it appears at times that the sophistication demanded by journals for publication of articles outstrips, in general, the skills of most practitioners and many research- ers. The methodological skills needed to stay on top of the game are growing exponentially. One of the developments of note over this period of time has been the increasing representation of qualitative research methodologies or combinations of qualitative with quantitative methods.

Five paradoxes

In conclusion and in the context of the above brief overview, I would like to discuss five paradoxes and ask you to reflect on them.

1. Constructivism

There appears to be a paradox in the new emphasis on constructivism as the route to effective learning. Research into learning certainly suggests the im- portance of the active, transforming role of the learner. Research into teaching, however, demonstrates the importance of direct instruction, which is largely based on behavioural principles. Indeed, the strongest finding from research into teaching and learning appears to be that the only approach that clearly and un- ambiguously works is direct instruction, albeit with some cognitive components in recent models (Rosenshine, 1986; Rosenshine and Meister 1995; Swanson and Hoskyn 1998; Weinert and Helmke 1995). This paradox has yet to be resolved. This is not to say that there is not significant research support for various other models of instruction such as cooperative and group-learning models.

I would like to see more research examining the positive effects of construc- tivist approaches to teaching and learning relative to the clearly demonstrated positive effects of techniques based on behavioural approaches. Perhaps one solution to the paradox lies in what is determined to be the appropriate outcome of learning. Perhaps outcome measures tested are low-level knowledge and skills that are relatively easy to reproduce through direct instruction methods. If we devised research that effectively measured more complex and deeper learning outcomes, as well as attitudes and the relationships between various elements of learning, and related these to either constructivist or behavioural approaches, we might see a different set of findings.

2. Impact on policy and practice

As the field of educational psychology has become more complex and rich, offering much to the policy maker and practitioner, there is seemingly less impact on the world of teaching. Many practices in classrooms still reflect the transmission and reinforcement dogmas of the 1970s and 1980s. In other words, recent theory and research seem to have had a disappointing impact on educational policy and practice. Why is this so? For example, new approaches to understanding motivation such as goal theory, and new approaches to teaching such as constructivism, appear to have limited impact. Perhaps teachers find it too difficult to implement constructivist approaches because they do not have sufficient training and expertise, are confused by the varieties of constructivism (personal, social, sociocultural, radical), are under-resourced for such 'open' techniques, or are constrained by accountability strictures. Perhaps teachers fail to make use of the wealth of information coming from cognitive motivation research because the area is so clouded by a plethora of similar yet conflicting theoretical and research paradigms, as well as an overload of information. Or perhaps teacher socialisation overwhelms whatever research practices and findings that teachers were exposed to during their training. Maybe we do an inadequate job of educating teachers, and their on-the-job situation precludes there being enough opportunity for them to fine-tune general findings from research to their local context.

3. Cross-cultural dimensions

While the study of sociocultural influences on cognition, learning, and motivation has burgeoned, and cross-cultural psychology has much to say about cognition, learning, and motivation, little of this finds its way into mainstream educational psychology textbooks. Why is this the case when we are preparing educators for educational settings characterised by diversity?

It is also of note that many cross-cultural studies show that there is less variation between groups than within groups, so we need to de-emphasise stereotypes based on ethnicity and culture, yet such stereotypes still abound in both the research and the applied literature. Indeed, one still reads in texts and research literature that such-and-such a group has such-and-such learning and motivational characteristics based on some dated anthropological, sociological, or psychological research conducted 40 or 50 years ago. Why is this so?

4. Teaching time

In inverse proportion to the growth in educational psychology research and theorising, the amount of time made available to it in tertiary education programmes for professionals such as teachers and counsellors has diminished (in my personal experience). The more educational psychology has to offer, the less time it has in which to offer it.

5. Research training

While journals demand growing methodological and statistical sophistication in research articles, the time available to teach these skills in postgraduate courses in psychology and related areas is declining. This situation is made even more odd by the fact that there is great pressure today to publish in top-rate journals while completing one's doctorate. How can we address this problem?

Conclusion

A review such as this can never be complete, and other writers would perhaps have taken another approach. Indeed, one reviewer of this chapter suggested that I tackle more fundamental issues – such as changes in the criteria by which people judge scientific evidence; the impact of other disciplines such as sociology on educational psychology; the politicisation of educational research; research that is undertaken for funding rather than scientific reasons, and the impact of educational psychology on other fields such as social work, counselling, and medical and paramedical practices. Another reviewer suggested that I look at the field by dividing research into different categories to the ones I chose, namely pure research, applied research, interdisciplinary research, and policy research. These alternative approaches are worth considering and in your personal survey of the field, as you mull over 20–30 years of educational psychology, you might like to take one or other of these approaches. I wish you well!

Acknowledgements

I would like to thank sincerely Ray Debus, Martin Dowson, Herb Marsh, Andrew Martin, Mike Pressley, Phil Winne, and the anonymous reviewers for helpful comments on earlier drafts of this paper. They kept my historicity in order and my idiosyncrasies in check.

References

Alfassi, M. (1998). Reading for meaning: The efficacy of reciprocal teaching in fostering reading comprehension in high school students in remedial reading classes. *American Educational Research Journal*, 35: 309–32.

Ames, R. A. and Ames, C. (eds). (1984). *Research on motivation in education: Student motivation, 1.* Orlando, FL: Academic Press.

Bandura, A. (1977). *Social learning theory.* Morristown, NJ: General Learning Press.

Bandura, A. (1986). *Social foundations of thought and action.* Englewood Cliffs, NJ: Prentice Hall.

Bidell, T. R. and Fischer, K. W. (1992). Beyond the stage debate: Action, structure, and variability in Piagetian theory and research. In R. J. Sternberg and C. A. Berg (eds), *Intellectual development.* New York: Cambridge University Press (pp. 252–94).

Cameron, J. and Pierce, W. D. (1996). Reinforcement, reward, and intrinsic motivation: A meta-analysis. *Review of Educational Research, 64*: 363–423.

De Jong, T. and Van Joolingen, W. R. (1998). Scientific discovery learning with computer simulations of conceptual domains. *Review of Educational Research, 68*: 179–201.

DeVries, R. (1997). Piaget's social theory. *Educational Researcher, 26*: 4–17.

Eysenck, M. W. (1984). *A handbook of cognitive psychology.* Hillsdale, NJ: Lawrence Erlbaum.

Fleer, M. (ed.). (1996). *DAPcentrism: Challenging developmentally appropriate practice.* Watson, ACT: Australian Early Childhood Association.

Forman, G. E. (1980). Constructivism: Piaget. In G. M. Gazda and R. J. Corsini (eds), *Theories of learning.* Itasca, IL: F. E. Peacock (pp. 252–94).

Halford, G. S. (1989). Reflections on 25 years of Piagetian cognitive developmental psychology, 1963–1988. *Human Development, 32*: 325–57.

Halpern, D. F. and LaMay, M. L. (2000). The smarter sex: A critical review of sex differences in intelligence. *Educational Psychology Review, 12*: 229–46.

Hart, E. R. and Speece, D. L. (1998). Reciprocal teaching goes to college: Effects for postsecondary students at risk for academic failure. *Journal of Educational Psychology, 90*: 670–81.

Hewitt, J. and Scardamalia, M. (1998). Design principles for distributed knowledge building processes. *Educational Psychology Review, 20*: 75–96.

Johnson, D. W., Johnson, R. T. and Stanne, M. B. (2000). *Cooperative learning methods: A meta-analysis.* Available online at: http://www.cooplearn.org/pages/cl-methods.html (accessed 10/2005).

John-Steiner, V. and Mahn, H. (1996). Sociocultural approaches to learning and development: A Vygotskian framework. *Educational Psychologist, 31*: 191–206.

Joyce, B., Showers, B. and Rolheiser-Bennett, C. (1987). Staff development and student learning: A synthesis of research on models of teaching. *Educational Leadership, 45*: 11–22.

Kagan, S. (1994). *Cooperative learning.* San Juan Capistrano, CA: Kagan Cooperative Learning.

Keller, F. S. and Sherman, J. G. (1974). *The Keller plan handbook.* Menlo Park, CA: W. A. Benjamin.

King, A., Staffieri, A. and Adelgais, A. (1998). Mutual peer tutoring: Effects of structuring tutorial interaction to scaffold peer learning. *Journal of Educational Psychology, 90*: 134–52.

Kingsley, H. L. and Garry, R. (1957). *The nature and conditions of learning* (2nd ed.). Englewood Cliffs, NJ: Prentice Hall.

Kozulin, A. and Presseisen, B. Z. (1995). Mediated learning experience and psychological tools: Vygotsky's and Feuerstein's perspectives in a study of student learning. *Educational Psychologist, 30*: 67–75.

Marshall, H. H. (1996). Implications of differentiating and understanding constructivist approaches. *Educational Psychologist, 31*: 235–40.

Maslow, A. H. (1968). *Toward a psychology of being*, 2nd ed. Princeton, NJ: Harper and Row.

McInerney, D. M. (2005a). *Helping kids achieve their best: Understanding and using motivation in the classroom*. Greenwich, CT: Information Age Publishing.

McInerney, D. M. (2005b, September). 'The role of sociocultural factors in enhancing student engagement'. Invited keynote address at the 3rd International Seminar on Learning and Motivation: Enhancing Student Engagement (ISLM2005). Universiti Utara Malaysia, Langkawi.

McInerney, D. M. and McInerney, V. (1994, 1998, 2002, 2006). *Educational psychology: Constructing learning*, 1st to 4th eds. Frenchs Forest, NSW: Pearson.

McInerney, D. M. and Van Etten, S. (2001). *Research on sociocultural influences on motivation and learning, 1*. Greenwich, CT: Information Age Publishing.

McInerney, D. M., McInerney, V. and Marsh, H. W. (1997). Effects of metacognitive strategy training within a cooperative group learning context on computer achievement and anxiety. *Journal of Educational Psychology, 89*: 686–95.

McNally, D. W. (1977). *Piaget, education and teaching*. Sussex, UK: Harvester Press, Hassocks.

Moll, L. C. (ed.). (1990). *Vygotsky and education*. Cambridge, UK: Cambridge University Press.

Noddings, N. (1992). *The challenge to care in schools: An alternative approach to education*. New York: Teachers College Press.

Noddings, N. (1995). Teaching themes of care. *Phi Delta Kappan, 76*: 675–9.

Pressley, M., Harris, K. R. and Marks, M. B. (1992). But good strategy instructors are constructivists. *Educational Psychology Review, 4*: 3–31.

Qin, Z., Johnson, D. W. and Johnson, R. T. (1995). Cooperative versus competitive efforts and problem solving. *Review of Educational Research, 2*: 129–43.

Rogers, C. R. (1961). *On becoming a person*. Boston, MA: Houghton Mifflin.

Rogers, C. R. (1969). *Freedom to learn*. Columbus, OH: Charles E. Merrill.

Rogers, C. R. (1983). *Freedom to learn: For the 80's*. Columbus, OH: Charles E. Merrill.

Rosenshine, B. V. (1986). Synthesis of research on explicit teaching. *Educational Leadership, 43*: 60–9.

Rosenshine, B. and Meister, C. (1995). Direct instruction. In L. W. Anderson (ed.), *International encyclopedia of teaching and teacher education*, 2nd ed. Tarrytown, NY: Pergamon, 143–9.

Ryan, R. M. and Deci, E. L. (2000). Intrinsic and extrinsic motivations: Classic definitions and new directions. *Contemporary Educational Psychology, 25*: 54–67.

Scardamalia, M. and Bereiter, C. (1995, April). 'CSILE and progressive discourse: Evolving designs'. Paper presented at the annual meeting of the American Educational Research Association, San Francisco.

Seagoe, M. V. (1972). *The learning process and school practice*. Scranton, PA: Chandler.

Shuell, T. J. (1986). Cognitive conceptions of learning. *Review of Educational Research, 56*: 411–36.

Silberman, M. L., Allender, J. S. and Yanoff, J. M. (eds). (1976). *Real learning. A sourcebook for teachers*. Boston, MA: Little, Brown and Co.

Slavin, R. E. (1991). Group rewards make groupwork work. *Educational Leadership, 48*: 71–82.

Smagorinsky, P. (1995). The social construction of data: Methodological problems of investigating learning in the zone of proximal development. *Review of Educational Research*, *65*: 191–212.

Swanson, H. L. and Hoskyn, M. (1998). Experimental intervention research on students with learning disabilities: A meta-analysis of treatment outcomes. *Review of Educational Research*, *68*: 277–332.

Turney, C. (1985a). *Sydney micro skills redeveloped, Series 1 handbook*. Sydney: Sydney University Press.

Turney, C. (1985b). *Sydney micro skills redeveloped, Series 2 handbook*. Sydney: Sydney University Press.

von Glaserfeld, E. (1995). *Radical constructivism: A way of knowing and learning*. London: Falmer Press.

Weinert, F. E. and Helmke, A. (1995). Interclassroom differences in instructional quality and interindividual differences in cognitive development. *Educational Psychologist*, *30*: 15–20.

Wessells, M. G. (1982). *Cognitive psychology*. New York: Harper and Row.

Wheldall, K. (1987). *The behaviourist in the classroom*. London: Allen and Unwin.

Chapter 3

Intelligence and IQ

Ted Nettelbeck and Carlene Wilson

Why might teachers be interested in IQ? Even in special education one en-counters the argument that IQ testing, initially invented to identify children likely to encounter educational difficulties and to facilitate decision making about them, serves little purpose because it lacks prescriptive utility. According to this line of argument, IQ can describe someone as more or less able in some general way, but, that established, the IQ score provides few leads about what to do next – which is what an educator will be most concerned with. And is there any point, in any case, in attempting to define intelligence? Can't it mean many different things? Some certainly think that IQ testing serves no useful purpose, can cause harm, and should be abandoned (Strydom and Du Plessis 2000). Arguments along these lines commonly point to misuses of IQ testing, with particular emphasis on inappropriate practices in the past, especially early during the twentieth century when these new measures were first being enthusiastically taken up on a large scale (Gould 1981). That misuse has occurred and continues to occur is undeniable and, clearly, procedures for reducing this must be applied. But IQ tests can be useful; for an investment of no more than an hour or two, it is possible to gain insights into a child's capacities that would otherwise be hard won by detailed observation over very much longer periods of time.

Researchers into the nature of intelligence have certainly not yet achieved consensus about how to define or measure it. Twenty years ago, definitions from several experts working in the field revealed unresolved differences of opinion (Sternberg and Detterman 1986). That outcome would probably be much the same today. Nonetheless, such differences are more related to detail than substance and there is now wide agreement within the field that, at least in part, 'intelligence' is an 'ability to understand complex ideas, to adapt effectively to the environment, to learn from experience, [and] to engage in various forms of reasoning to overcome obstacles by taking thought' (Neisser *et al.* 1996: 77).

In this chapter, we argue that intelligence should be of interest to teachers and that IQ provides a useful, albeit somewhat limited, proxy for aspects of intelligence immediately relevant to academic and other important life achievements. As we shall see, IQ should not be viewed as a pure measure of intelligence, but it does tap a general ability that predicts success to a useful extent in cultures like ours.

A review of test validity commissioned by the American Psychological Association during 1996–99, and based on more than 125 meta-analytic reviews, found that, contrary to long-held assumptions in some quarters, IQ and other psychological tests compared very favourably with the validity of medical tests (Meyer *et al.* 2001). This is a point worth emphasising; we would be surprised if those so opposed to IQ testing held similar concerns about, for example, home pregnancy testing or mammogram screening for breast cancer – tests that are less precise as predictors of expected outcomes than IQ.

On the other hand, it should be recognised that opposition to IQ testing has not been limited to issues of validity. As previously noted, there has also been considerable concern about ethical considerations, like the misapplication of testing and the effects of labelling an individual on the basis of an IQ score.

Reviewing what is known about intelligence and IQ and the relevance of these constructs to education, we revisit controversies that have characterised the field of individual differences in abilities for a century: whether 'intelligence' exists as a useful scientific construct, how many different kinds of intelligence exist, whether creative talents represent something different, whether 'emotional intelligence' predicts something about future achievement that IQ or personality traits do not, and whether IQ can be improved by education.

The attempt to improve understanding of human intelligence has thus far predominantly been limited to the field of psychometrics – essentially the development and validation of mental tests. The main method has sought to reduce performance on many variables to a smaller number of underlying psychological domains (language, number, divergent thinking, memory, and so on). These domains, and structures that link them together somehow, have been inferred from patterns of individual differences in scores from a broad, representative sample of persons performing a wide range of activities. This approach to defining intelligence has always struggled to avoid the tautological circularity of relying on a descriptive term to explain the thing described, but, in our opinion, modern tests have overcome this dilemma to an appreciable extent and do have good construct validity.[1]

To clarify our position from the outset, our opinion is that IQ and similar aptitude/achievement tests for assessing abilities can inform decisions about children's capabilities.[2] They therefore have a useful role in educational settings. Past uses have been more to do with screening and diagnosis than with prescribing appropriate educational interventions, but more recently tests have become available that can be used for treatment planning. Besides standardised testing, assessment certainly involves other information-gathering activities – qualitative as well as quantitative. Thus, interpreting an individual's IQ score continues to require both art and science because of validity limitations. As a consequence, it should not be assumed that a given IQ score or profile of scores provides more than a guide to a relatively narrow range of capabilities for that individual at that point in time.

Is 'intelligence' a useful scientific construct?

The Frenchman Alfred Binet developed the first IQ test at the beginning of the twentieth century, successfully demonstrating that his test could identify schoolchildren who could be expected to encounter learning problems within the normal curriculum. However, the test was rapidly refined by others to permit distinctions among those with average and above-average abilities. The early success of the IQ test in predicting academic performance led to its widespread use and, within the community at large, it is now probably psychology's most widely familiar innovation. Tests have revolutionised educational policies and employment selection procedures, based on the proposition that a person's intellectual capabilities can be identified in advance and therefore matched to work requirements or appropriate educational practices. There is considerable evidence to support both of these assertions.

Nevertheless, almost since its invention, IQ has remained a controversial tool. In part, this has reflected poor consensus among 'experts' about the nature of intelligence. First, intelligence is defined in terms of observable behaviours that are valued by the relevant culture, so that intelligent behaviours can vary across cultures or subcultures, or even between different groups residing within a majority culture. It is widely accepted that some universal biological substrate must underpin intelligence, irrespective of the particular ways in which it is culturally defined and, as far as is known, all cultures value 'being clever', regardless of how that is culturally defined. But recent advances in researching the neurological bases of intelligence notwithstanding, current theories are couched in terms of performance on ability tests, which reflect cultural priorities.

Second, there continues to be debate about whether intelligence is a general trait or whether it is more useful to think in terms of different kinds of intelligences. This issue is considered further in the section after next. Third, there has also been debate about whether we can use intelligence to explain other behaviours, rather than merely as description. Concluding that a child is successful at school because s/he is intelligent may provide a useful description, but this lacks scientific explanatory value if 'being intelligent' can only be defined in terms of success at school. Howe (1988, 1997), for example, has advocated that intelligence as explanation is tautological and extended his views to argue that achievement differences in all domains are principally the consequence of application (Howe *et al.* 1998).

At a trivial level, Howe was correct to insist that an IQ score is descriptive and without explanatory value; earlier IQ tests that relied on a single global score usually reveal little about underlying cognitive processes. Nonetheless, providing that test usage does not extend beyond the population on whom test development has been based, IQ scores derived either wholly or in part from items that do not directly test school-based knowledge do predict educational achievement to a remarkable extent, and occupational success and other social and well-being outcomes reasonably well. Differences in IQ account for about 25 per cent of variance in school performance and somewhat less for work performance and social outcomes (Neisser *et al.* 1996), although Hunter (1983) has pointed to evidence that there is no single better predictor of job success than IQ. Most usefully, IQ measured even prior to commencing school predicts subsequent learning achievements with reasonable accuracy, the more so as children become older. Moreover, it identifies a highly stable individual characteristic. Although individual IQs can change up or down for reasons that generally appear to be idiosyncratic, as Deary *et al.* (2004) have recently reported, the uncorrected correlation between IQs from a very large sample of Scottish schoolchildren, initially estimated at age 11 in 1932 and remeasured at age 80 in 2001, was .7.[3]

Of course, these results also underscore that substantial residual variance in these activities will be explained by other kinds of important individual differences – personality traits, motivation, and environmental influences and opportunities among them. But it does not follow from accepting this that IQ differences reveal nothing about underlying differences in fundamental abilities or that testing is a waste of time. As we will argue below, despite shortcomings and important caveats on its application, the IQ score has good construct validity as an estimate for general intelligence. Beyond predicting achievements in life events and longitudinal stability, individual differences in IQ certainly reflect genetic variation. IQ scores, which obviously rely on complex, learned techniques of problem solving, also correlate to a remarkable extent with performance on extremely simple speeded tasks and other indices of brain activities that require little prior knowledge or acquired skills (Deary 2000). Thus, IQ continues to be a useful tool for assessing intelligence, and psychology has already developed falsifiable theories, which include variables besides those drawn directly from educational settings, that will continue to guide future research into the nature of intelligence.

Is IQ the same as intelligence?

On grounds already outlined, IQ is an acceptable proxy for intelligence, but it should not be regarded as meaning the same thing, for two main reasons.

First, as will be clarified in the next section, intelligence is best defined in terms of multiple domains configured within a hierarchical structure that accounts for different degrees of commonality among and specificity between those domains. IQ, on the other hand, has until fairly recently amounted to little more than an average outcome from an abridged range of those domains. A principal and justifiable criticism from educators has been that diverse alternative combinations of answers to test items will achieve the same average outcome (i.e. IQ) and that IQ has consequently provided little guidance for educational intervention.

Second, Flynn (1999) has now firmly established that, in all countries where IQ tests have been used, mean IQ has risen steadily throughout the past

100 years. IQ gains are cohort effects; they represent average trends across time and there has been no evidence that distributions of IQ have become broader or changed in any way. Nor is there any evidence that individual IQ improves as a person becomes older. On the contrary, beyond the early 20s test performance begins to deteriorate, a trend that accelerates appreciably during old age. However, this decline is hidden by age-related norms and, because individual differences within age cohorts tend to be consistent, individual IQ remains remarkably stable. Similarly, although children obviously become smarter as they develop, in general terms, they pass through similar stages of development and within cohort differences remain stable, so that individual IQ tends not to change much, at least beyond about the age of 7 years.

The cross-generational increases in average IQ identified by Flynn have been disguised by periodical restandardisations of the tests, but are revealed either by cross-generational comparisons on tests unchanged for very long periods, like Raven's Progressive Matrices, or by superior contemporary performance compared with earlier norms for tests that have been revised occasionally, like the Wechsler scales and the Stanford-Binet. The time frame for improved performance is too short for the causes to be anything other than environmental. Thus, assuming that intelligence derives from brain capacities that are inborn and evolved over very long periods of time, it must follow that, because IQ is influenced by relatively short-term adaptation, IQ is not the same thing as intelligence. Abstract problem-solving ability is plausibly a necessary component of intelligence as defined for our culture but, as discussion in the next section will demonstrate, falls well short of providing a sufficient explanation.

Suggested causes of rising IQ have included wider adoption of education as a high priority, improved educational opportunities, increased competition linked to population increases, higher employment demands, technological advancements, better prenatal care and improved obstetric methods, better nutrition and other health factors, changes in child rearing practices, and more flexible and better quality parent–child interactions. Thus far, however, the causes are not understood, although it seems improbable that there is one single common cause, and any combination of the foregoing appears plausible. Improvement is not limited to those aspects of the tests most obviously associated with educational curricula, such as vocabulary, arithmetic, and general knowledge and, in fact, is most pronounced for abstract problem solving.

Levels of improvement across all abilities represented in the tests are apparently uniform across the IQ range 70–115, but may be a little larger in the lower range, although the proportion of persons with intellectual disability has probably not been affected (Flynn 2000). The extent of improvement has varied across nations and at different times, but, on average, amounts to a steady, continuous gain of about two standard deviations across the twentieth century. Even if gains are now beginning to tail off, as Flynn believes, this change is massive. It translates into 30 IQ points, which, if taken literally, would mean that 50 per cent of the population 100 years ago would have had intellectual capabilities consistent with intellectual disability as defined by current IQ norms. Obviously, this proposition is absurd. Although we have continuously improved in our capacity to solve the kind of problems that IQ tests have been designed to measure, there is no evidence that people 100 years ago were less intelligent than people now.

Flynn has proposed that, for reasons yet to be explained, people in cultures like ours have learned across at least 100 years to invest their mental capacities better into abstract problem solving, in a way that represents a shift from how mental capacities were previously invested. Moreover, to address the paradox that such a large environmental effect can occur despite strong evidence that IQ is highly heritable, Dickens and Flynn (2001) have successfully developed a mathematical feedback model that demonstrates that small environmental changes can produce a large impact on IQ. The key to the effectiveness of their model is that reciprocal genetic and environmental influences on behaviour generate multiplier mechanisms that operate at both the individual and social levels and act to magnify reciprocal causality between genetic endowment and environmental opportunities. Essentially, Dickens and Flynn's model is a formalised version of the widely accepted intuition that IQ can be improved by intellectual challenges (Ceci and Williams 1997; Vygotsky 1978). What is new, however, and what makes their argument so powerful, is their explication of how, despite large genetic influences, very large environmental effects can arise from iterative processes whereby a small improvement leads to more challenge, which leads to further improvement resulting in higher challenges, which leads to more improvement, and so on.

Clearly, tests that are too far out-of-date will significantly overestimate IQ and can therefore cause poor decisions. Unlike the situation 20 years ago, test publishers are now well aware of the issue and tests have been more frequently revised in recent years. Frequent recalibration will be required for as long as IQ continues to rise. It is important to recognise, however, that the practical utility of IQ tests applied within generations remains unaffected by IQ gains over time.

Are there many different kinds of intelligence?

Throughout much of the twentieth century the theoretical challenge to psychometricians has been how to integrate two age-old intuitions about human intelligence within a single coherent theory.

On the one hand, numerous studies using exploratory factor analysis have demonstrated considerable commonality among a large and diverse range of tests of apparently different abilities. This observation, first made by Spearman (1927) and termed by him a 'positive manifold', has widely been accepted as evidence for a general mental ability (Spearman's g). This idea has been longstanding in Western European–North American cultures, including Australia, and the idea is embedded in many languages.

On the other hand, the relative specificity of different abilities is also a commonplace observation. That individuals with savant syndrome can develop extraordinary, very high levels of competence in music, mathematics and number manipulation, language, artwork, mechanical dexterity, and so on, despite low IQ consistent with an intellectual disability, has sometimes been interpreted as challenging the validity of a general mental ability, although Nettelbeck and Young (1999) have argued otherwise. Most recently, Gardner (1983, 1999) has been foremost among theorists arguing that human cognitive abilities are best envisaged as several independent forms of intelligence.

Theories of multiple intelligences have a long history stretching back to the seminal work of Thorndike (1926) and Thurstone (1938), especially in educational psychology, presumably because an assessment system that can identify relative strengths and weaknesses in a profile describing a child's cognitive performance has the potential to generate practical interventions, whereas a global IQ score offers little opportunity for this.

Consistent with this approach, Gardner has stressed that human abilities encompass a much broader range of domains than the language, spatial, and logical problem-solving activities sampled by most IQ tests. His theory includes these three abilities but also extends to musical, bodily-kinesthetic (athleticism), personal, social, and naturalistic intelligences, derived from speculation about the existence in the brain of putative modules, each responsible for a different kind of intelligence. Gardner does not deny that Spearman's g has been demonstrated to exist, but he considers it to be essentially limited to school classroom activities and of less significance for explaining other salient real-life achievements. This perspective usefully emphasises that cognitive activities unrelated to academic achievement can be important for real-life performance but, given the high value afforded academic success within our culture, we would argue that he 'throws out the baby with the bathwater' by devaluing general ability. In any case, consistent with a long history of failed attempts by many other investigators to demonstrate the existence of independent, domain-specific cognitive abilities, Gardner's separate intelligences do show considerable overlap – they share variance across domains and are not as neatly independent as Gardner and others have thought. A person doing well in one domain tends to do well in others. And from a practical perspective, the theory has not been validated and there has been little attempt to develop tests consistent with the theory.

Carroll (1993) has provided the most detailed description yet available of the psychometric structure of human intelligence, as derived from meta-analyses of IQ-type test performance. He considered virtually every significant investigation into the structure of intelligence published during the twentieth century, identifying 461 very large data sets that met strict inclusion criteria. His analyses have convincingly defined intelligence as a hierarchical structure involving three 'strata', identified by factor analysis. The first stage of his analysis of a very diverse range of ability tests identified some 69 relatively narrow, specific abilities. Nonetheless, these could not be regarded as independent; residual commonality among these defined some nine broad abilities – essentially those consistently identified across some three decades of research by Gf-Gc theory

(Cattell 1971; Horn and Noll 1997).[4] These are 'fluid' reasoning, 'crystallised' acculturated knowledge acquired by the application of fluid reasoning, short-term memory, long-term memory, visual processing, auditory processing, quantitative knowledge, processing speed for less difficult tasks, and speed of decision for more intellectually demanding problems. Again, commonality among these in turn defined a single general factor, which Carroll equated with Spearman's g. Debate continues about whether this general factor is better conceptualised as Cattell's fluid ability – essentially the capacity to cope with novelty and abstract problems by thinking flexibly (Gustafsson 1984).

However, irrespective of how this matter is eventually determined, the conclusion that we draw from Carroll's research is that an adequate description of human intelligence in psychometric terms requires a complex model that encompasses a strong general ability, together with eight or nine additional broad forms of different intelligences. Moreover, the range of different abilities to be taken into account is more diverse than can be derived from a single IQ test in the Binet/Wechsler tradition; an adequate psychometric description of intelligence is therefore dependent on a large array of tests for all known cognitive abilities. However, just as importantly, the general ability is certainly more powerful in an explanatory sense, when accounting for childhood and adulthood outcomes, than any other single factor – and may account for as much variance in test and real-life outcomes as all of the other broad abilities combined (Kline 1991).

It follows from this theory that IQ tests, like the Wechsler scales or the Stanford Binet that were developed principally on the basis of their inventors' intuitions, have covered only limited aspects of cognitive abilities. This can readily be seen by comparing the factor structures of these tests with that for the Woodcock-Johnson Psycho-Educational Battery-Revised (WJ-R) (McGrew 1997), which was designed to provide an operational representation of Gf-Gc theory. McGrew's analysis showed that the Stanford Binet (fourth edition) covers only three or four (depending on the age of the examinee) of the required nine broad factors and only one subtest tested fluid ability. Earlier Wechsler scales delivered even fewer domains; considerable research has demonstrated the inadequacy of assumed test structure and this test has essentially been a measure of acculturated knowledge, visual processing, and speed when processing less demanding tasks. The most recent revisions of these tests (Stanford Binet fifth edition; the Wechsler Intelligence Scale for Children fourth edition) have attempted to align with current hierarchical, multifactorial theory about intelligence and to provide wider factor coverage, but it will be some time before these new versions are subjected to rigorous research evaluation. On the other hand, consistent with the theory from which it was developed, WJ-R has been confirmed as providing wide coverage of all factors defined by Gf-Gc theory except speed of more demanding decisions. Although the older omnibus IQ tests have a long history of application that has placed them at the forefront of tests most preferred by practising psychologists for assessment purposes, we recommend that practitioners give careful consideration to including the most recent version of the Woodcock-Johnson test battery (WJ-III) in the future.

One further comment on Gardner's theory is warranted because this theory underscores the problem of how to decide which specific abilities to include in a comprehensive descriptive model of intelligence and which not to include. Clearly, having only eight domains to assess avoids the practical difficulties that Guilford encountered; Guilford ended up with an unworkably large number of domains, with expansion limited only by the will to conceive more (Guilford and Hoepfner 1971). The accepted guideline among psychometricians has been to include those activities that strengthen the general factor but also add specificity – that is, information relevant only to the specific ability. This, of course, is the approach that Gardner eschews, but we do not agree. Bodily kinesthetic (athletic) and musical achievements are obviously important forms of expression that are valued within our culture. They are relatively independent from general problem-solving ability, but not entirely. Music is more correlated with the general factor than athletic ability; but neither strongly predicts academic success at school. Whether definition of intelligence should extend to activities beyond those relevant to survival in an adaptive sense can only be a matter of opinion. Early in the twentieth century, achievement in classical Greek or Latin was found to correlate highly with general ability, although these days these areas of learning are outside most educational curricula. Although presumably appropriate indicators of intelligence among the educationally privileged in a bygone age, they are scarcely used now. Computer literacy, however, may not be far from inclusion. Most psychometricians have held that musical or sporting abilities are better regarded as domains separate from intelligence. When advancing his theory of successful intelligence (see below), Sternberg (2003) advocated reserving the term intelligence for abilities 'needed to succeed by adapting to, shaping, and selecting environments' (Sternberg 2003: xvi); he makes clear that he would exclude musical activities from this definition. However, as is clear from the wide acceptance of Gardner's theory in some quarters, not everyone agrees.

Sternberg has advocated a different approach to Gardner's – one that also has sought to extend conceptions of intelligence beyond the traditional association with academic achievement. Whereas Gardner's theory describes different domains of activities, Sternberg has set out to explain intelligence in terms of underlying psychological processes. Initially concerned with identifying basic components of information processing and how these combine to support problem solving, his early research forced him to confront the conundrum central to cognitive psychology of having to invoke higher executive functions ('metacomponents') to accommodate the observation that problem solvers make choices and develop strategies to accomplish them (Sternberg 1977).

This earlier work was incorporated within his 'triarchic theory of human intelligence' (Sternberg 1985) as a componential subtheory that described processes underpinning the analytical abilities principally drawn on in traditional academic settings. The other two arms of the triarchic theory were the experiential subtheory and the contextual subtheory. The former recognised that repeated activities that begin as requiring conscious control tend to become over-learned and automatic and that, as a consequence, they are less dependent on intelligent monitoring. It is principally when confronting novelty that components and metacomponents of information processing are required; the experiential subtheory was therefore largely concerned with how creative abilities and the processes that support them are applied to novel situations. The contextual subtheory sought to explain adaptive behaviours in real-life settings – how these shape existing environments and how new ones are chosen. This subtheory focused on how tacit knowledge (i.e. procedural knowledge learned incidentally without formal tuition) comes to be applied to everyday practical situations.

Sternberg's productivity in research and scholarship has been prodigious, involving extensive collaboration with other researchers. He has generated considerable research in support of these subtheoretical distinctions so that, for example, creative and less creative thinkers can be reliably distinguished in terms of different underlying processes, and analytical and creative abilities have been shown to be separate entities. Practical abilities have also been shown to be different from creativity and those domains tapped by IQ. Sternberg and others have emphasised that, in some everyday situations, practical intelligence will be much more important to survival and success than academic abilities. Moreover, Sternberg and his co-workers have already developed a wide range of tests to measure these different constructs.

Recently, Sternberg (2003) expanded the triarchic theory in terms of his 'theory of successful intelligence', the 'propulsion theory of creative contributions', and the 'balance theory of wisdom'. The former is an overarching theory that starts from the point that different individuals will have relative strengths and weaknesses in analytical, creative, and practical abilities. However, most people can be successful in their own terms, provided they can shape their environments so as to capitalise on their strengths. This idea has potential for educational environments because children can be taught to use their specific aptitudes more effectively, which will be more motivating for the child, assuming of course that teachers can be helped by the test procedures devised by Sternberg to identify these.

Having noted that some kinds of creative idea tend to be taken up whereas others are not, Sternberg has outlined his propulsion theory of creative contributions as an attempt to define the circumstances under which creative ideas become translated into reality. The balance theory of wisdom is as yet scarcely more than a sketch, drawn from Sternberg's observation that successfully intelligent individuals can nonetheless behave in ways that can be sociopathic and harmful to others. Drawing on concepts of morality, he regards wisdom as the application of tacit knowledge to issues of common benefit. Most importantly, consistent with Vygotsky's (1978) ideas about a reciprocal link between cognitive development and education, Sternberg insists that tools can be – and have already been – developed to measure abilities other than analytical, be they creative thinking or practical, including wisdom. He also emphasises that improvement is possible and that teaching programmes can be devised to achieve this.

Sternberg acknowledges that abilities including creativity will rely to some degree on inherited characteristics and we agree, seeing useful purpose in recognising that inheritance does constrain levels of achievement. In our opinion, talents exist, particularly for creative activities like music, art, literature, and mathematics. By this we mean that there are brain capacities that are probably inborn, specialised for particular knowledge that is usually domain-specific and largely independent from IQ, that may include a strong motivational component, and that are capable of operating at very high levels of proficiency (Nettelbeck and Young 1999). Although substantial practice is required for outstanding accomplishment, this alone cannot provide a sufficient explanation for exceptional skill because of evidence that a talent is apparent before there has been prolonged opportunity for practice. Exceptional capabilities typically emerge at an early age and are qualitatively superior to skills that the majority of people develop over much longer periods of time.

Sternberg's ideas about intelligence are far-reaching and challenging, with potential to impact beyond areas of assessment available via current mental tests. His ideas also extend beyond current limits to scientific knowledge. He is determined to ensure that every means be explored to expand intelligence theory beyond what predicts academic achievement and to admit possible environmental influences to theory about how intelligence develops. We have no argument with that.

Does emotional intelligence improve predictions about academic achievement?

Precursors to Salovey and Mayer's (1990) proposal that emotional intelligence (EI) moderates behaviour are found in earlier theories of social intelligence (Greenspan 1981; Thorndike 1926) and similar constructs like personal intelligence (Wechsler 1940) and both interpersonal and intrapersonal intelligences (Gardner 1983). Theory initially focused on issues around social competence and judgement, but attempts to define social intelligence proved problematic, with disagreement among researchers about what was involved. Consequently, research failed to deliver procedures for distinguishing social intelligence from other forms of ability and this line of work stalled for some time (Jones and Day 1997; Keating 1978).

Payne (1986, cited by Mayer *et al.* 2000) has been credited with first use of the term 'emotional intelligence'; but current high interest in EI stems from the research of Salovey, Mayer, and their colleagues and from popular books for lay audiences by Goleman (1995, 1998). Goleman has enthusiastically proselytised about EI (also referred to as EQ, by analogy with IQ) as critically important to achievement within educational settings and in the workplace, particularly at management levels. Salovey and Mayer, on the other hand, have been more circumspect, preferring to promote their ideas as work in progress.

A definition of EI attracting wide acceptance as a working definition has been provided by Mayer and Salovey (1997: 10): 'the ability to perceive emotions, to access and generate emotions so as to assist thought, to understand emotions and emotional knowledge, and to reflectively regulate emotions so as to promote emotional and intellectual growth'. However, EI has been conceptualised in other ways and at present there is considerable confusion about the nature of EI and the best ways to measure it (Roberts *et al.* 2001). Two broad categories of EI have been developed, with EI defined either as a form of intelligence based on cognitive processing of emotions (termed 'ability' EI) or, alternatively, as including intelligence together with personality and motivational and affective dispositions ('mixed' EI). These alternative conceptions have influenced the different ways researchers have explored the best way to measure EI. Attempts to measure ability EI, which presumably should be located within a psychometric model like Carroll's (1993, see above) as an additional broad factor sharing variance with general intelligence, have focused on developing putatively objective measures of peak performance, analogous to IQ items. Predictably, such measures have therefore tended to correlate with IQ. On the other hand, mixed forms of EI have generally been assessed by self-report questionnaires, which have correlated more with personality dimensions, particularly extraversion and openness.

The promise of EI to improve our understanding of why there are wide individual differences in classroom and workplace performance has clearly resonated among teachers, parents, and managers. Intuitively these ideas appear to make sense because it is well established that IQ and other personal factors cannot fully account for these performance differences. Moreover, considerable research has already found that measures of EI do predict important life outcomes, like academic achievement, the avoidance of deviant behaviours (Petrides *et al.* 2004), workplace success, and family and interpersonal relations (Schutte *et al.* 2001) moderately well.

However, from both theoretical and practical perspectives, the relevance of EI as a useful construct must depend on whether it adds something unique to knowledge about what influences real-life outcomes, over and above what can already be attributed to IQ and personality. This question addresses what the psychometricians refer to as incremental predictive validity. In this sense, a balanced conclusion is that the jury is still out. Recent research (Bastian *et al.* 2005; Gannon and Ranzjin 2005) has found that, after effects from IQ and personality have been controlled for, EI accounts for only very little of the extent to which individual differences exist in academic achievement, problem solving, social coping, and life satisfaction. In other words, because EI also correlates with IQ and personality and these are more effective predictors of real-life behaviours, EI may provide at best only modest incremental predictive validity.

It is, however, early days yet; EI research only has a 15-year history, compared with 100 years of research into intelligence and IQ. Known problems with current EI measures limit their adequacy (Warwick and Nettelbeck 2005), but improved tests are being sought. It is possible too that EI operates more like a threshold variable, with little incremental improvement beyond a level that defines adequate competence. If so, then EI may be relevant in less highly selected and relatively uniform samples than those that have participated in much of the research to date, drawn predominantly from university students. In any case, given uncertain understanding of EI and how it might impact the real-life achievements of schoolchildren, teachers are unlikely to be readily persuaded to abandon such ideas without considerably more opportunity to test them thoroughly. Nor should they embrace rhetoric unsupported by empirical evidence.

Can new technologies provide new ways of assessing intelligence?

The possibility that parameters of information processing can be developed to replace current IQ tests can be traced back to ideas that Sir Francis Galton published during the last half of the nineteenth century. Much more recently, when reflecting on the future of psychological testing and assessment in general during the first two decades of the twenty-first century, the prominent psychometrician Joseph D. Matarazzo predicted at the time of his retirement as President of the American Psychological Association that current laboratory-based measures of information processing could soon be developed to replace today's individually administered tests of cognitive abilities. These views were published in the prestigious *American Psychologist* (Matarazzo 1992). Matarazzo has been a highly distinguished and influential psychometrician who has published extensively on testing and assessment. He is the author of a highly successful textbook on the Wechsler scales. One can expect, therefore, that his opinions will have attracted considerable interest.

Much of what Matarazzo said was uncontroversial. For example, he concluded on the basis of their reasonably good predictive validity for educational and work achievement that well-established tests like the Wechsler and Stanford Binet will continue to be used, but be revised in accordance with ever-improving theory. We can be confident too about his prediction that computer-assisted technology will result in new ways of administering and scoring tests. However, Matarazzo (1992: 1012) also predicted the practical application of what he termed 'biological indices of brain function and structure'. In our opinion, this conclusion may have been premature. We certainly agree that some of these measures are already valuable tools for advancing theoretical understanding about the psychological nature of cognitive abilities and some may, moreover, have potential as adjuncts to currently available tests. However, the newer procedures currently fall too far short of the very high standards of reliability developed within the psychometric tradition to permit accurate assessment of individual differences and, as yet, there has been only limited success in validating these putative biological indices in terms of the brain functions that they have been assumed to measure.

Future discoveries about the biological bases of intelligence will certainly impact on future procedures for cognitive assessment and, ultimately, an adequate theory of intelligence must derive from what is known about brain functions. New technologies like structural and functional magnetic resonance imaging, which measures parameters of the active brain, are already profoundly influencing how researchers go about trying to improve our understanding of human intelligence. However, such knowledge currently falls short of what would be required for adequate theorising and strong predictive validity.

The tasks to which Matarazzo referred rely more on psychological than biological capabilities. They are therefore not necessarily independent of personal factors, including mood, motivation, and culture. Sometimes referred to as 'elementary cognitive tasks' (ECTs), they are only elementary in the sense that they involve relatively low knowledge requirements for participants, compared with most items in traditional tests of cognitive abilities. That such easy-to-learn tasks correlate moderately well with much more intellectually demanding IQ tests is consistent with Galton's idea that individual differences in intelligence must in some way depend on difference in lower-level sensory processes. However, on the other hand, it is not the case that ECTs require only basic mental capacities and exclude the operation of more complex intellectual functions, and there is not, as yet, wide agreement about the nature of the processes that must underpin performance on reaction time tasks or inspection time,[5] or the many different measures of latency and amplitude that can be extracted from scalp (electroencephalogram) recordings of brain activity. Moreover, although these procedures have been designed to measure the speed or efficiency of different aspects of information processing, Roberts and Stankov (1999) have demonstrated that mental speed is not a single construct. The main contributions from research with ECTs thus far have improved understanding of a subset of components identified by psychometric theory as essential to a broad account of intelligence.

Moreover it seems unlikely, given the multifactorial complexity of Carroll's psychometric model, that simply the speed of brain processes can provide a sufficient explanation for intelligence, even though the capacity for quick thought is certainly a marker of higher IQ. If functions additional to processing speed are involved, it is improbable that ECT-type measures can replace psychometrically derived tests in the foreseeable future, although these procedures have certainly proved to be useful scientific tools for testing hypotheses about the nature of human intelligence and we expect that they will continue to be so. It is also possible that, provided the relevant predictive validity has first been established, such methods will have potential as adjuncts to, or additional procedures included within, psychometric tests of cognitive abilities. For example, preliminary evidence suggests that accelerated slowing of inspection time within a short period of time may predict abnormal cognitive decline during old age at a preclinical stage (Gregory *et al.* 2008).

For these reasons we have concluded that the foreseeable future of cognitive testing will be directed towards applying theory to the improvement of existing instruments, as well as developing new tests. A primary characteristic of future tests will be that they will assess a wide range of cognitive domains as well as general ability.

Can IQ be improved by education?

As described above, Deary *et al.* (2004) have shown that IQ scores tend to be constant across the life span. Similarly, Moffitt *et al.* (1993) followed children longitudinally for each year from 7–14 years, and found that individual differences in IQ remained remarkably stable. In summary, there is now considerable evidence that, beyond about 5–6 years of age, IQ does remain about the same for most people, despite idiosyncratic change for some. This is not to say, however, that IQ could not be changed. The situations described by Moffitt *et al.* (1993) and by Deary and his colleagues (2004) have not involved attempts to improve IQ by intervention.

On the other hand, during the past 25 years, behavioural genetics has firmly established that individual differences in IQ are substantially influenced by genetic variation in the general population (Plomin and Petrill 1997). This research has therefore challenged the empiricist/associationist tradition that has dominated psychology, particularly North American psychology, which holds that mental growth follows appropriate sensory experience and that, given the same opportunities, equal mental development will eventuate. This tradition has tended to regard higher IQ as resulting from better opportunities to access culture-relevant knowledge. A corollary of this tradition has been that appropriate educational intervention can restore intelligent capacities to children who have previously suffered socio-cultural disadvantage that has put them at risk for those with low IQs. However, some 40 years of experience with compensatory preschool programmes in the US has shown that, although initial substantial IQ gains are possible, these fade within a few years when children move beyond the intervention programmes. Such programmes have had other positive results, like improved school readiness, higher numbers of socially disadvantaged children staying longer in school, fewer numbers in special education, and improved parental involvement in children's education (Zigler and Styfco 2005). But IQ has certainly proved very resistant to improvement by such training (Spitz 1986). Is it the case, therefore, that IQ is fixed and unchangeable from a very early age?

Several large kinship studies comparing IQs from identical and fraternal twins, and from adopted children and adopting and natural parents, have demonstrated that the broad heritability of IQ is high.[6] For Western European–North American cultures, including Australia, in the later decades of the twentieth century, broad heritability of IQ has been around 40 per cent during childhood; it rises to about 50 per cent during early adulthood and may be as high as 80 per cent during old age (Plomin and Petrill 1997). This change reflects diminishing variance in environmental influences across the lifespan.

Surprisingly, behavioural genetics has found that major environmental influences have not been located in the main between-family differences defining socio-economic status (although IQ does correlate moderately with socio-economic status (SES)). Instead, idiosyncratic within-family differences have now been identified as the main contributors to environmental influences. In short, the environmental circumstances that children are exposed to within families are different because the siblings are born at different times, parents react differently at different times, friendship groups are different, school experiences are different, and so on. This line of evidence might appear at first sight to limit severely the opportunity for environmental impact on IQ; this has been the position taken by some (Jensen 1998). However, despite these high levels of broad heritability, Flynn has shown that such impact does take place across generations, as already described above. Moreover, Dickens and Flynn (2001) have been able to show that, because genes and environment interact through a number of selective mechanisms, relatively small initial environmental changes can be magnified into very large effects by feedback mechanisms that utilise social multipliers.

Flynn's findings have clearly demonstrated that the average IQ within a population has increased across generations. Although an average improvement across generations is not the same thing as positively impacting an individual's IQ, Flynn's research reinforces the possibility that the latter might be achieved if the causes of rising average IQ could be identified.

A number of intensive training programmes have been developed with the aim of improving cognitive skills, particularly for children with an intellectual disability. One widely publicised has been the Instrumental Enrichment programme devised by Feuerstein (1980), based on his theory that the development of intelligence relies heavily on the effectiveness of parents and others in helping children to understand environmental experiences. Although widely applied and accepted as a programme capable of improving thinking skills, its efficacy has been strongly challenged by some (e.g. Spitz 1986).

Ceci (Ceci 1991; Ceci and Williams 1997) has been foremost in developing the argument that education has a direct beneficial effect on childhood IQ. Duration of schooling – particularly the highest grade completed successfully – has long been known to correlate fairly strongly with adult IQ, income, and occupational level. However, these outcomes do not prove that school has a positive developmental impact on IQ because, alternatively, smarter children may choose to stay longer in education. Ceci has not disputed that this may be so, but he has insisted that such effects are likely to be bi-directional and he has assembled convincing evidence to support his contention that education moderates IQ. He has also shown that both schooling and IQ independently influence financial income.

Ceci has examined several sources of evidence, including the impact of intermittent schooling for children from remote communities and from itinerant families, which results in marked cumulative deficits beyond about age 6; delayed start, which can cost about 5 IQ points a year beyond about age 5; and dropping out of school early, which, starting from age 13, can reduce IQ by age 18 by about 8 IQ points. There is also strong evidence from cross-generational research in previously remote areas that higher levels of average IQ accompany improved community accessibility and improved educational resources. Moreover, there is good evidence of smaller effect sizes associated with circumstances like the influence on IQ of the long summer vacation and cohort-related differences reliably linked to different dates for starting school. These effects are typically small and not permanent but their existence adds support to Ceci's theory. Taken as a whole, such evidence does suggest that education has beneficial effects on IQ.

Ceci (1991) also considered ways in which schooling might influence IQ, pointing to the possibility that school could provide IQ-relevant knowledge and inculcate the modes of thought and attitudes that should help to foster better test performance. He also emphasised that parental and family attitudes about supporting education, and parents' and children's expectations for academic achievement, are important determinants of successful outcomes. Thus, early preschool years may be as critical as early school years because long-term attitudes towards and early strategies to guide learning are learned then.

It is important to note, however, that although IQ may be influenced by schooling and by family attitudes to education, better academic performance will not always be attributable to higher IQ. There is certainly evidence to support this assertion, not least from the much remarked higher academic achievements of the children of Asian immigrants into countries like the US and Australia. Consistent with Flynn's (1998) analysis of Asian-American achievements, which discounted higher average IQ as an explanation and pointed, instead, to heavier cultural investment in education as the means to upward mobility, Dandy and Nettelbeck (2002a) found that Asian-Australian children across primary school grades 6 and 7 reported spending much more time on homework than their Anglo-Celtic-Australian peers and were more likely to aspire to occupations that required tertiary qualifications. Furthermore, a follow-up investigation confirmed stronger commitment among Asian parents to education as providing opportunities for the future economic success of their children (Dandy and Nettelbeck 2002b). These differences may have reflected cultural factors but could also be due to the commitment to social advancement that tends to characterise all immigrant groups.

Uses for IQ tests

We intend that the foregoing account of current theories about intelligence and of practices for measuring the range of cognitive abilities that define intelligence should help to persuade those previously sceptical about whether IQ-type tests can be useful in educational settings. First, intelligence tests can be used to verify or clarify the existence of some 'exceptionality' suspected by a teacher in some areas of a child's academic functioning. Initial screening of this kind is unlikely to identify appropriate remediation, which will better be advanced by problem-directed procedures, but it can help quickly to identify those whose school performance diverges significantly from their intellectual potential, or children with high abilities who may benefit from exposure to more challenging opportunities, or those with special support needs. Second, modern tests, particularly the Woodcock-Johnson battery (WJ-III), can also be used to diagnose difficulties encountered by an individual (e.g. intellectual disability, learning disability) and to improve instruction and curriculum planning, for example by assisting in resource planning for remedial or advanced educational activities. However, in general, intelligence tests are not used to determine individual programming needs or to evaluate teaching outcomes, given the divergence between test and curriculum content.

Difficulties with intelligence tests used in these ways will occur if screening results in either a high level of false positives or misses. The former may lead to a labelling problem that, because teachers' future expectations for a student may be influenced by impressions based on IQ, could serve to disadvantage individuals in the school context. The latter could result in someone being denied access to special resources, either remedial or extending, thereby compromising educational outcomes. Problems associated with poor diagnosis can also occur, especially when inappropriate or out-of-date tests are used, or test administration and scoring are less than optimal, or the person being assessed is unwilling to attend to the test demands or to comply with instructions.

To guard against and reduce such shortcomings, assessment should always involve other activities additional to testing. Assessment should always include background personal history, information about current functioning from medical and school records, information from interviews with the child, parents, and others familiar with the child, direct observation, including during the test session, and additional tests. Thus, testing is only one part of a larger assessment process because testing cannot be entirely objective. A multiple assessment approach will better place the psychologist to engage in hypothesis testing, which, on the basis of information gathered before testing begins, can help to sharpen the focus of referral questions. These in turn should guide decisions about exactly what tests to include in the assessment. Hypothesis testing proceeds by considering which aspects of evidence converge on a possible conclusion and which do not. As a general rule of thumb, any interpretation should be supported by at least two pieces of corroborating evidence and careful consideration should always be given to discrepancies that might challenge a tentative conclusion. In particular, parents are commonly better placed than anyone to provide the assessor with accurate relevant information; an assessment that proves not to accord with parental impressions should be reconsidered very carefully indeed.

Ultimately IQ-type tests provide only samples of a child's behaviour and they must not be over-interpreted. However, such tests do provide the opportunity, within only an hour or two, to learn something of significance to future academic achievements, from a wide range of a child's cognitive abilities. What an IQ test reveals can be garnered in a classroom, but this would typically require a much longer period of time. For these reasons we continue to advocate the use of IQ and similar aptitude/achievement tests because, given current knowledge limitations, they are the best tools available for predicting important future educational and other significant life outcomes. Our support for these tests is contingent on two provisos. First, they must be consistent with current hierarchical, multifaceted theory that includes a general ability. Second, the child's cultural background must be the same as that within which the tests were developed.

Notes

1 Over the past 20 years there has been a growing trend to regard all forms of validity as subsumed under 'construct validity', which is concerned with confirming the theory that IQ measures intelligence (Messick, 1980). Ultimately, validity can only be demonstrated in concrete terms by a correlation coefficient, and it makes little sense to rely on just one coefficient as the validity for a test. Thus, construct validity embraces all other types, principally predictive (correlates with future performance) and concurrent (simultaneous measurement). The American Psychological Association's standards manual combines these as 'criterion validity'. Various forms of validity must first be determined in order to establish construct validity. It is important, too, to appreciate that even a low validity coefficient has potential benefit. In the general sense that a test measures to some extent what it has been designed to measure, the test will improve on random, chance procedures. As discussed throughout this article, omnibus IQ tests have long developmental histories and they have convincing construct validity because IQ tests intercorrelate with each other but not with tests that are not IQ tests; they predict academic and other life achievements after partialling out social class; they discriminate occupational groups defined in terms of intelligence requirements; factor analysis establishes a strong general factor, correlated with IQ, on which all subtests load; IQ is stable across the lifetime; and IQ has high heritability (see Note 5), particularly beyond childhood.
2 Although theoretically distinguishable, the practical differences between so-called 'aptitude' and 'achievement' tests are frequently confused. Educational selection tests like the Scholastic Aptitude Test in the US have frequently been described as achievement tests. Similarly, the Woodcock-Johnson battery, the content of which is consistent with other IQ tests, has been so described.
3 This result has not been corrected upwards to take account of either test unreliability or restricted range of scores. The correlation therefore means that, at minimum, about 50 per cent of variability in later scores was accounted for across most of the lifespan by individual differences in the initial measure.
4 Gf stands for 'general fluid ability'. Similarly Gc stands for 'general crystallised ability'. Cattell initially proposed that these two broad group factors should substitute for Spearman's g. In later versions of the theory, expanded primarily by J. L. Horn, these two factors have remained paramount.
5 Inspection time (IT) is a measure of processing speed unconfounded by motor speed because it is a threshold estimate of the time required by an individual to

make a simple judgement with specified high accuracy. Thus, speed of reaction is irrelevant. Individual differences in IT are highly reliable, moderately heritable, and share genetic influences on IQ. Teachers reliably identify individual differences in IT. Unlike IQ, childhood estimates of IT are also stable across generations. IT and IQ among both children and adults correlate about −0.5 (slower times with lower IQs). For further details see contributors to *Intelligence* (2001, Vol. 29, Special Issue: Inspection time).

6 Broad heritability is the proportion of total variation in IQ in a population that is explained by genetic variation. Heritability will vary across time because of changed circumstances, diminishing where environmental influences rise and increasing where environmental influences fall. It is possible to partition broad heritability, which includes all sources of genetic variation, into narrow ('additive') influences and 'non-additive' sources. Additive influences are genes critical to the expression of the parental trait in the offspring. Non-additive sources include genetic-environmental confounding, indirect genetic influences on IQ from personality variables, and differences in mood and motivation. Including such non-additive sources therefore inflates estimates of broad heritability.

References

Bastian, V. A., Burns, N. R. and Nettelbeck, T. (2005). Emotional intelligence predicts life skills, but not as well as personality and cognitive abilities. *Personality and Individual Differences, 39*: 1135–45.

Carroll, J. B. (1993). *Human cognitive abilities: A survey of factor-analytic studies.* New York: Cambridge University Press.

Cattell, R. B. (1971). *Abilities: Their structure, growth and action.* Boston, MA: Houghton Mifflin.

Ceci, S. J. (1991). How much does schooling influence general intelligence and its cognitive components? A reassessment of the evidence. *Developmental Psychology, 27*: 703–22.

Ceci, S. J. and Williams, W. M. (1997). Schooling, intelligence, and income. *American Psychologist, 52*: 1051–8.

Dandy, J. and Nettelbeck, T. (2002a). The relationship between IQ, homework, aspirations and academic achievement for Chinese, Vietnamese and Anglo-Celtic Australian school children. *Educational Psychology, 22*: 267–75.

Dandy, J. and Nettelbeck, T. (2002b). Parents' academic standards and educational aspirations for their children: A cross-cultural study. *Educational Psychology, 22*: 621–7.

Deary, I. J. (2000). *Looking down on human intelligence.* Oxford: Oxford University Press.

Deary, I. J., Whiteman, M. C., Starr, J. M., Whalley, L. J. and Fox, H. C. (2004). The impact of childhood intelligence on later life: Following up the Scottish mental surveys of 1932 and 1947. *Journal of Personality and Social Psychology, 86*: 130–47.

Dickens, W. T. and Flynn, J. R. (2001). Heritability estimates versus large environmental effects: The IQ paradox resolved. *Psychological Review, 108*: 346–69.

Feuerstein, R. (1980). *Instrumental enrichment: An intervention program for cognitive modifiability.* Baltimore: University Park Press.

Flynn, J. R. (1998). IQ gains over time: Toward finding the causes. In U. Neisser (ed.), *The rising curve: Long-term gains in IQ and related measures.* Washington, DC: American Psychological Association, 25–66.

Flynn, J. R. (1999). Searching for justice: The discovery of IQ gains over time. *American Psychologist, 54*: 5–20.

Flynn, J. R. (2000). IQ gains, WISC subtests and fluid g: G theory and the relevance of Spearman's hypothesis to race. In Novartis Foundation Symposium 233 (ed.), *The nature of intelligence*. Chichester, UK: Wiley, 202–27.

Gannon, N. and Ranzjin, R. (2005). Does emotional intelligence predict unique variance in life satisfaction beyond IQ and personality? *Personality and Individual Differences*, *38*: 1353–64.

Gardner, H. (1983). *Frames of mind: the theory of multiple intelligences*. New York: Harper and Row.

Gardner, H. (1999). *Intelligence reframed: Multiple intelligences for the 21st century*. New York: Basic Books.

Goleman, D. (1995). *Emotional intelligence*. New York: Bantam.

Goleman, D. (1998). *Working with emotional intelligence*. New York: Bantam.

Gould, S. J. (1981). *The mismeasure of man*. London: Penguin.

Greenspan, S. (1981). Defining childhood social competence: A proposed working model. In B. K. Keogh (ed.), *Advances in Special Education*, *3*. Greenwich, CT: JAI Press, 41–82.

Gregory, T., Nettelbeck, T., Howard, S. and Wilson, C. (2008). Inspection Time: A biomarker for cognitive decline. *Intelligence*, *36*: 664–671.

Guilford, J. P. and Hoepfner, R. (1971). *The analysis of intelligence*. New York: McGraw-Hill.

Gustafsson, J. E. (1984). A unifying model for the structure of intellectual abilities. *Intelligence*, *8*: 179–203.

Horn, J. L. and Noll, J. (1997). Human cognitive capabilities: Gf-Gc theory. In D. P. Flanagan, J. Genshaft and P. L. Harrison (eds), *Contemporary intellectual assessment: Theories, tests and issues*. New York: Guilford Press, 53–91.

Howe, M. J. A. (1988). Intelligence as explanation. *British Journal of Psychology*, *79*: 349–60.

Howe, M. J. A. (1997). *IQ in question: The truth about intelligence*. London: Sage.

Howe, M. J. A., Davidson, J. W. and Sloboda, J. (1998). Innate talents: Reality or myth? *Behavioral and Brain Sciences*, *21*: 399–442.

Hunter, J. E. (1983). A causal analysis of cognitive ability, job knowledge, and supervisor ratings. In F. Landy, S. Zedeck and J. Cleveland (eds), *Performance measurement and theory*. Hillsdale, NJ: Erlbaum, 257–66.

Jensen, A. R. (1998). *The g factor: The science of mental ability*. Westport, CT: Praeger/Greenwood.

Jones, K. and Day, J. D. (1997). Discrimination of two aspects of cognitive-social intelligence from academic intelligence. *Journal of Educational Psychology*, *89*: 486–97.

Keating, D. P. (1978). The search for social intelligence. *Journal of Educational Psychology*, *70*: 218–13.

Kline, P. (1991). *Intelligence: The psychometric view*. London: Routledge.

Matarazzo, J. D. (1992). Psychological testing in the 21st century. *American Psychologist*, *47*: 1007–18.

Mayer, J. D. and Salovey, P. (1997). What is emotional intelligence? In P. Salovey and D. Sluyter (eds), *Emotional development and emotional intelligence: Implications for educators*. New York: Basic Books, 3–31.

Mayer, J. D., Salovey, P. and Caruso, D. (2000). *Test Manual for the MSCEIT v. 2: The Mayer, Salovey and Caruso Emotional Intelligence Test*. Toronto, ON: Multi Health Systems.

McGrew, K. S. (1997). Analysis of the major intelligence batteries according to a proposed comprehensive Gf-Gc framework. In D. P. Flanagan, J. Genshaft and P. L. Harrison (eds), *Contemporary intellectual assessment: Theories, tests and issues*. New York: Guilford Press, 151–80.

Messick, S. (1980). Test validity and the ethics of assessment. *American Psychologist, 35*: 1012–27.

Meyer, G. J., Finn, S. E., Eyde, L. D., Kay, G. G., Moreland, K. L. and Dies, R. R. (2001). Psychological testing and psychological assessment: A review of evidence and issues. *American Psychologist, 56*: 128–65.

Moffitt, T. E., Caspi, A., Harkness, A. R. and Silva, P. A. (1993). The natural history of change in intellectual performance: Who changes? How much? Is it meaningful?. *Journal of Child Psychology and Psychiatry, 34*: 455–506.

Neisser, U., Boodoo, G., Bouchard Jr., T. J., Boykin, A. W., Brody, N. and Ceci, S. J. (1996). Intelligence: Knowns and unknowns. *American Psychologist, 51*: 77–101.

Nettelbeck, T. and Young, R. (1999). Savant syndrome. In L. M. Glidden (ed.), *International research in mental retardation, 22*. San Diego, CA: Academic Press, 137–73.

Petrides, K. V., Frederickson, N. and Furnham, A. (2004). The role of trait emotional intelligence in academic performance and deviant behaviour at school. *Personality and Individual Differences, 36*: 277–93.

Plomin, R. and Petrill, S. A. (1997). Genetics and intelligence: What is new? *Intelligence, 24*: 53–78.

Roberts, R. D. and Stankov, L. (1999). Individual differences in speed of mental processing and human cognitive abilities: Towards a taxonomic model. *Learning and Individual Differences, 11*: 1–120.

Roberts, R. D., Zeidner, M. and Matthews, G. (2001). Does emotional intelligence meet traditional standards for an intelligence? *Emotion, 1*: 196–231.

Salovey, P. and Mayer, J. D. (1990). Emotional intelligence. *Imagination, Cognition and Personality, 9*: 185–211.

Schutte, N. S., Malouff, J. M., Bobik, C., Coston, T. D., Greeson, C. and Jedlicka, C. (2001). Emotional intelligence and interpersonal relationships. *Journal of Social Psychology, 141*: 523–36.

Spearman, C. (1927). *The abilities of man*. London: Macmillan.

Spitz, H. H. (1986). *The raising of intelligence: A selected history of attempts to raise retarded intelligence*. Hillsdale, NJ: Erlbaum.

Sternberg, R. J. (1977). *Intelligence, information processing, and analogical reasoning: The componential analysis of human abilities*. Hillsdale, NJ: Lawrence Erlbaum.

Sternberg, R. J. (1985). *Beyond IQ: A triarchic theory of human intelligence*. New York: Cambridge University Press.

Sternberg, R. J. (2003). *Wisdom, intelligence and creativity synthesized*. New York: Cambridge University Press.

Sternberg, R. J. and Detterman, D. K. (1986). *What is intelligence? Contemporary viewpoints on its nature and definition*. Norwood, NJ: Ablex.

Strydom, J. and du Plessis, S. (2000). *IQ test: Where does it come from and what does it measure?* Available online at: http://www.audiblox2000.com/dyslexia_dyslexic/dyslexia014.htm (accessed 19 May 2005).

Thorndike, E. L. (1926). *The measurement of intelligence*. New York: Teachers College, Columbia University.

Thurstone, L. L. (1938). *Primary mental abilities*. Chicago: University of Chicago Press.

Vygotsky, L. S. (1978). *Mind in society: The development of higher psychological processes*. Cambridge, MA: Harvard University Press.

Warwick, J. and Nettelbeck, T. (2005). Emotional intelligence is ? *Personality and Individual Differences*, *37*: 1091–100.

Wechsler, D. (1940). Non-intellective factors in general intelligence. *Psychological Bulletin*, *37*: 444–5.

Zigler, E. and Styfco, S. J. (eds). (2005). *The Head Start debates.* Baltimore: Brookes.

Chapter 4

Trends in peer learning

Keith J. Topping

Peer learning has a long history. It is possibly as old as any form of collaborative or community action and probably has always taken place, sometimes implicitly and vicariously. In this review, however, we are concerned with explicit and deliberate peer learning.

Peer learning can be defined as the acquisition of knowledge and skill through active helping and supporting among status equals or matched companions. It involves people from similar social groupings who are not professional teachers helping each other to learn and learning themselves by so doing.

Even this can be traced back over centuries in the written record. So what can have changed significantly in the last 25 years or so? In fact, quite a lot.

Archaic perceptions of peer learning considered the peer helper as a surrogate teacher in a linear model of the transmission of knowledge, from teacher to peer helper to learner. There was an assumption that peer helpers should be among the 'best students' (i.e. those who were most like the professional teachers). However, the differential in levels of ability and interest in such a situation could prove under-stimulating for the helper, who was unlikely to gain cognitively from the interactions. More recently, it was realised that the peer helping interaction is qualitatively different from that between a professional teacher and a child or young person, and involves different advantages and disadvantages.

Most recently, there has been a great deal more interest in deploying helpers whose capabilities are nearer to those of the helped, so that both members of the pair find some cognitive challenge in their joint activities. The helper is intended to be 'learning by teaching' and also to be a more proximate and credible model.

Types of peer learning, implementation, and effects

The longest established and most intensively researched forms of peer learning are peer tutoring and cooperative learning. Both have been researched more in schools than in other contexts.

Peer tutoring (PT) is characterised by specific role-taking as tutor or tutee, with high focus on curriculum content and usually also on clear procedures for interaction, in which participants receive generic and/or specific training. Some peer-tutoring methods scaffold the interaction with structured materials, while others prescribe structured interactive behaviours that can be effectively applied to any materials of interest.

Confusion between 'tutoring' and 'mentoring' is evident in the literature. Mentoring can be defined as an encouraging and supportive one-to-one relationship with a more experienced worker (who is not a line manager) in a joint area of interest. It is characterised by positive role modelling, promotion of raised aspirations, positive reinforcement, open-ended counselling, and joint problem solving. It is often cross-age, always fixed-role, quite often cross-institution, and often targeted to disadvantaged groups.

Cooperative learning (CL) is more than 'working together' – it has been described as 'structuring positive interdependence' (Slavin 1990) in pursuit of a specific shared goal or output. This is likely to involve the specification of goals, tasks, resources, roles, and rewards by the teacher, who facilitates or more firmly guides the interactive process. Typically operating in small groups of about six heterogeneous learners, CL often requires previous training to ensure equal participation and simultaneous interaction, synergy, and added value. Having all group members work with the same information might heighten cognitive conflict but risks intra-group comparison and 'competence threat'. This can be avoided by a 'jigsaw' arrangement for informational interdependence (Buchs *et al.* 2004). Higher effect sizes tend to be associated with approaches which combine group goals and individual accountability. At its worst CL can result in 'the blind leading the blind' or 'pooling ignorance', or one person doing all the work – hence the need for structure.

However, many schools might think they are implementing peer tutoring or cooperative learning, when all they are really doing is putting children together and hoping for the best. Bennett *et al.* (1984) found that, while children were often placed in groups, mostly they worked as individuals. Only one-sixth of the time was spent interacting with other pupils, and most of this was not related to the task. Little of the talk between pupils in groups enhanced the task in hand.

Sometimes hoping for the best works for some children, but typically not for those most in need. Spontaneous (untrained) tutoring behaviours can tend to be primitive (e.g. Person and Graesser 1999), often characterised by questioning limited both in frequency and level of cognitive demand, coupled with infrequent correction of errors and the giving of positive feedback when not appropriate. Accordingly, one of the most important changes over the last 25 years has been a greater focus upon implementation integrity. This has involved sharpening awareness of the organisational variables in the delivery of peer learning.

Organisational variables

Methods for peer learning (PL) can vary on at least 13 organisational dimensions:

1 Curriculum content – that is, the knowledge or skills or combination to be covered. The scope of PL is very wide and projects are reported in the literature in virtually every imaginable subject.

2 Contact constellation – some projects operate with one helper working with a group of peers, but the size of group can vary from two to 30 or more. Sometimes two or more helpers take a group together. PL in pairs (dyads) is more intensive – there is less opportunity to drift into token participation in a pair.

3 Within or between institutions – while most PL takes place within the same institution, it can also take place between different institutions, as when young people from a high school tutor in their neighbourhood elementary (primary) school, or university students help in regular schools.

4 Year of study – helpers and helped may be from the same or different years of study, and/or be the same or different ages.

5 Ability – while many projects operate on a cross-ability basis (even if they are same-age/year), there is increasing interest in same-ability PL. In this, the helper might have superior mastery of only a very small portion of the curriculum, or all might be of equal ability but working towards a shared, deeper, and hopefully correct understanding. Failures in 'meta-ignorance' can be a problem – the helper doesn't know that they don't know the correct facts.

6 Role continuity – roles need not be permanent, especially in same-ability projects. Structured switching of roles at strategic moments (reciprocal PL) can have the advantage of involving greater novelty and a wider boost to self-esteem, in that all participants get to be helpers.

7 Time – PL might be scheduled in regular class contact time, outside of this, or as a combination of both, depending on the extent to which it is substitutional or supplementary for regular teaching.

8 Place – correspondingly, PL can vary enormously in location of operation.

9 Helper characteristics – if helpers are those who are merely average (or even less), all partners should find some challenge in their joint activities. Although the gain of the helped might not be so great, the aggregate gain of both combined may be greater.

10 Characteristics of the helped – projects may be for all or for a targeted subgroup, such as the especially able or gifted, those with disabilities, those considered at risk of under-achievement, failure, or dropout, or those from ethnic, religious, linguistic and other minorities.

11 Objectives – projects may target intellectual (cognitive) gains, formal academic achievement, affective and attitudinal gains, social and emotional gains, self-image and self-concept gains, or any combination. Organisational objectives might include reducing dropout, increasing access, etc.

12 Voluntary or compulsory – some projects require participation, while in others helpers self-select. This can have marked effects on the quality of what ensues.

13 Reinforcement – some projects involve extrinsic reinforcement for the helpers (and sometimes also the helped), while others rely on intrinsic motivation. Beyond simple social praise, extrinsic reward can take the form of certification, course credit, or more tangible reinforcement such as money. Extrinsic reward is much more common in North America than elsewhere, and this has led to some debate about possible excess in this regard. The availability of extrinsic reinforcement can have effects on recruitment in voluntary projects, which might be good or bad.

Recent years have seen much more emphasis upon equal-opportunity involvement in peer learning, engaging all members of the educational community without exception (as in class-wide tutoring; e.g. Greenwood *et al.* 1989). Interest in reciprocal tutoring has also greatly expanded (e.g. Fantuzzo *et al.* 1989), since this enables all involved to function as both helper and helped, avoiding any social divisiveness according to perceived ability and status, and offering a richer apprenticeship for future involvement.

When planning peer learning, the following aspects of organisation need to be considered (Topping 2001a):

1   Context – there will be problems and opportunities specific to the local context.
2   Objectives – consider what you hope to achieve, and in what domains.
3   Curriculum area.
4   Participants – who will be the helpers, who will be the helped, and how will you match them? There will also have to be trainers and quality assurers.
5   Helping technique – will the method used be packaged or newly designed?
6   Contact – how frequently, for how long, and where will the contact occur?
7   Materials – what resources will be required, and how will they need to be differentiated?
8   Training – this will be needed for staff first, then for helpers and helped.
9   Process monitoring – the quality assurance of the process must be considered.
10 Assessment of students – the product and the process should be assessed; consider whether any of this should be self- and/or peer assessment.
11 Evaluation – you will need to find out whether it worked.
12 Feedback – this should be provided to all participants, to improve future efforts.

Effects

When peer tutoring or cooperative learning is implemented with thoughtfulness about what form of organisation best fits the target purpose, context, and

population, and with reasonably high implementation integrity, results are typically very good (Topping 2001a;Topping and Ehly 1998).The research evidence
is clear that both peer tutoring and cooperative learning can yield significant
gains in academic achievement in the targeted curriculum area. In the case of
CL, this can be for all members of the group. In the case of PT, both tutees and
tutors can gain – if the organisation is appropriate.This latter finding helps dispel
concerns that engagement in peer tutoring might be a 'waste of time' for more
able tutors – but with the caveat about organisation.

Additionally, both CL and PT can simultaneously yield gains in transferable
social and communication skills and in affective functioning (improvements in
self-esteem, liking for partner or subject area; regarding CL, see Johnson and
Johnson (1986); Slavin (1990, 1995); regarding PT see Cohen *et al.* (1982);
Rohrbeck *et al.* (2003); Sharpley and Sharpley 1981). Although these are more
elusive to measure and are not found as reliably as academic gains, they represent
considerable added value for no more input.

Peer learning has also been noted to be among the most cost–effective of
learning strategies (e.g. Levine *et al.* 1987). Some studies certainly demonstrate
high effect size at low delivery cost. However, even in the research literature there
are occasional reports of peer learning programmes which did not show significant effects. Additionally, the average effect size across many studies is generally
modest, again emphasising the importance of appropriate selection of method
for purpose and context, and the need to quality-assure implementation.

A theoretical model of peer learning

So, peer learning works. At least, it does if you organise and implement it well.
But how does it work?This is not merely a matter of obscure academic interest,
since a deeper understanding of how peer learning obtains its positive effects
should enable both researchers and practitioners to design ever more adaptive
and effective forms of peer learning. For many years, peer learning was under-
theorised, supported by old sayings such as 'to teach is to learn twice'. In the last
25 years, a number of researchers have conducted work with strong implications
for building theory in peer learning (e.g. Chi *et al.* (2001); King 1998). However,
a plethora of theories does not help the hard-pressed practitioner.

Accordingly, Topping and Ehly (2001) synthesised existing research into a
single theoretical model (Figure 4.1). This initially assigns some of the main
sub-processes into five categories.

The first of these categories includes organisational or structural features
of the learning interaction, such as the need and press inherent in PL toward
increased time on task (t.o.t.) and time engaged with task (t.e.t.), the need for
both helper and helped to elaborate goals and plans, the individualisation of
learning and immediacy of feedback possible within the small group or one–on-
one situation, and the sheer excitement and variety of a novel kind of learning
interaction.

Cognitively, PL involves conflict and challenge (reflecting Piagetian schools of thought, and necessary to loosen blockages formed from old myths and false beliefs). It also involves support and scaffolding from a more competent other, necessitating management of activities to be within the zone of proximal development of both parties (reflecting Vygotskian schools of thought, and necessary to balance any damaging excess of challenge; Vygotsky 1978).

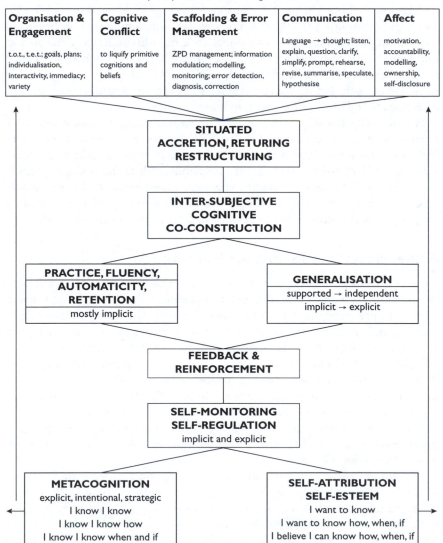

Figure 4.1 Theoretical model of peer-assisted learning.

The helper seeks to manage and modulate the information processing demands upon the learner to maximise the rate of progress – neither too much nor too little. The helper also provides a cognitive model of competent performance. However, the cognitive demands upon the helper in terms of monitoring learner performance and detecting, diagnosing, correcting, and otherwise managing misconceptions and errors are even greater – and herein lies much of the cognitive exercise and benefit for the helper.

PL also makes heavy demands upon the communication skills of both helper and helped, and in so doing develops those skills. A participant might never have truly grasped a concept until having to explain it to another, embodying and crystallising thought into language – another Vygotskian idea, of course. Listening, explaining, questioning, summarising, speculating, and hypothesising are all valuable skills which should be transferable.

The affective component of PL might also prove very powerful. A trusting relationship with a peer who holds no position of authority might facilitate self-disclosure of ignorance and misconception, enabling subsequent diagnosis and correction. The helper's modelling of enthusiasm, competence, and the possibility of success can influence the self-confidence of the helped, while a sense of loyalty and accountability to each other might help to keep the pair motivated and on-task.

These five categories or sub-processes feed into a larger onward process of the helper and helped extending each other's declarative knowledge, procedural skill, and conditional and selective application of knowledge and skills by adding to and extending current capabilities (accretion), modifying current capabilities (re-tuning), and (in areas of completely new learning or cases of gross misconception or error) rebuilding new understanding (restructuring). These are somewhat similar to the Piagetian concepts of assimilation and accommodation. This leads to the joint construction of a shared understanding between helper and helped – which is firmly situated within the current authentic context of application, and adapted to the idiosyncrasies in their perceptions (i.e. is inter-subjective), so might not represent absolute truth, but form a foundation for further progress.

Subsequently, PL enables and facilitates a greater volume of engaged and successful practice, leading to consolidation, fluency, and automaticity of core skills. Much of this might occur implicitly – without the helper or helped being fully aware of what is happening. Simultaneously or subsequently, PL can lead to generalisation from the specific situated example through which a concept is learned, extending the ability to apply that concept and its developmental variants to an ever-widening range of alternative and varied contexts in multiple communities of practice.

As this occurs, both helper and helped give feedback to each other, implicitly and/or explicitly. Indeed, implicit feedback is likely to have already occurred spontaneously in the earlier stages. PL increases the quantity and immediacy of feedback to the learner very substantially.

Explicit reinforcement might stem from within the partnership or beyond it, by way of verbal and/or non-verbal praise, social acknowledgement and status, official accreditation, or even more tangible reward. However, reinforcement which is indiscriminate or predominantly for effort risks over-weighting the significance of the reinforced concept in the network of understandings of the learner.

As the learning relationship develops, both helper and helped should become more consciously aware of what is happening in their learning interaction, and more able to monitor and regulate the effectiveness of their own learning strategies in different contexts.

This development into fully conscious explicit and strategic metacognition not only promotes more effective onward learning, it should make helper and helped more confident that they can achieve even more, and that their success is the result of their own efforts. These affective and cognitive outcomes feed back into the originating five sub-processes – a continuous iterative process and a virtuous circle. As the PL relationship develops, the model should continue to apply as the learning moves from the surface level to the strategic and on to the deep level, and from the declarative into the procedural and conditional.

Simplistic forms of peer tutoring, focusing on drill and practice, seem likely to utilise only a few of the possible channels or sub-processes (typically only organisation, perhaps some communication, scaffolding and error management, practice, and reinforcement – fewer than half of the total possibilities). More elaborate and cognitively demanding forms of peer tutoring, such as peer tutoring in thinking skills (e.g. Topping 2001b), aim to utilise all the channels, with both tutor and tutee operating and benefiting in every channel. This might be enhanced and assured by role reciprocation. The greater the differential in ability or experience between helper and helped, the less cognitive conflict and the more scaffolding might be expected. Too great a differential might result in minimal cognitive engagement (let alone conflict) for the helper, and unthinking but encapsulated acceptance (with no retuning or co-construction) by the helped. Of course, if the helper is older, more experienced, and therefore more credible, but actually has no greater correct knowledge or ability than the helped, then a mismatch and faulty learning might occur in a different way.

Teachers are likely to need to be particularly attentive to the channels in the lower and later parts of the chart: the development of generalisation, self-regulation, metacognition, and enhanced self-esteem and motivation; the progression from implicit to explicit, and from dependency on support to increasing independence; the shift from simple thinking to higher-order and more abstract thinking, moving from the surface level to the strategic and on to the deep level, and from declarative knowledge into the procedural and conditional; and the completion of the loop, the joining of the circle, the acceleration of the dynamic spiral, for both helper and helped.

Extension of peer learning to more challenging subjects

Much peer learning in schools originally targeted core skill areas, such as reading (Topping 1987) and mathematics (Topping and Bamford 1998). Where peer tutoring was deployed specifically for practice and consolidation purposes, this sometimes resulted in narrow 'drill and skill' approaches (especially in the United States). However, teachers became more confident and trusting in children, and slowly moved to using peer learning in a less mechanistic way and in more challenging subject areas. Peer learning extended to spelling and writing (e.g. Nixon and Topping 2000), and then moved onwards to science (Topping 1998a; Topping *et al.* 2004). More recently, peer learning has extended to thinking skills (an area in which some teachers feel under-confident; Topping 2001b; Topping and Bryce 2004). Most recently, peer learning in thinking skills has shown compelling effects on cognitive modifiability (Topping and Trickey 2007). As peer learning began to take hold in college and university education, PL was increasingly applied to a very wide range of subjects.

Extension of forms of peer learning

While peer tutoring and cooperative learning remain the most widely used and best evaluated forms of peer learning, other forms have developed and are used increasingly. Unfortunately, in some cases new forms have been widely adopted before being adequately evaluated, and the implementation quality of some new forms has been extremely variable. A classic example is 'circle time' – very popular with teachers and widely adopted in elementary schools in the United Kingdom, but completely devoid of robust evidence of effectiveness until recently, and then found to be no more effective than untrained intuitive teacher behaviour (Miller and Moran 2007). Similarly, various forms of peer mediation and peer befriending schemes have been implemented, often in the hope that angry conflict and bullying will be reduced, but with highly varying quality and results (insofar as the largely descriptive nature of the literature in these areas permits such interpretation). There is good evidence that problem-solving strategies can be effectively taught to children as young as four, but that is not quite the same thing.

Peer counselling and education

Mediation and befriending schemes might have elements of peer counselling within them, and there is some limited evidence that peer counselling can be at least as effective as adult counselling, but this is not a high benchmark. Equally, such schemes might be construed as containing elements of peer education (peers offering credible and reliable information about sensitive life issues and the opportunity to discuss this in an informal peer-group setting). Again, evidence of effectiveness is limited, although some well-structured programmes delivered to high-quality standards have shown measurable effects (Topping 1996a).

Peer monitoring

Another interesting area of development is peer monitoring (peers observing and checking the behaviours of others in the group with respect to appropriateness and effectiveness). For some years the literature has contained occasional reports of peer monitoring of unwanted behaviour (often in locations difficult for adults to supervise). More recently peer monitoring has been extended to learning behaviours (which is less contentious for participants) and operated on a class-wide basis, with excellent results (e.g. Brown *et al.* 1999).

Peer assessment

However, the area which has seen most growth in widespread use and in development of the evidence base is peer assessment (peers evaluating the products or outcomes of learning of others in the group). Having learners 'mark', 'grade', or quantitatively assess the products of their peers places them too much in a teacher-like role, and the result can be learner social discomfort and a central tendency in the assessments – everyone is rated 'average'. Much more cognitively demanding for the assessor is giving formative and qualitative feedback, which is likely to be both more socially comfortable and more useful to the assessee. The benefits for both parties have been extensively documented, more in higher education (Topping 1998b) than in schools (Topping 2003a), but the latter is growing. Peer assessment can enhance self-assessment, and both can yield metacognitive gains.

Peer learning in other contexts

Much research into peer learning has been conducted in schools, where it has come to be used with increasingly improbable learner groups. For example, peer tutoring has been found effective on a large scale with tutors as young as kindergarten or first grade (5 to 6 years old; e.g. Fuchs *et al.* (1997); Mathes *et al.* 1998). Peer learning is increasingly found in colleges and universities (Topping 1996b, 1998b). All of these are relatively controlled contexts which are somewhat amenable to systematic measurement.

However, peer learning has increasingly also been used in other contexts, some more challenging because of longer-standing learning failure in those to be helped (as in peer learning with adults of restricted literacy in domestic or community contexts; e.g. Scoble *et al.* 1988), some because of greater transience and fluidity (voluntary organisations, after-school clubs, libraries, churches), some because learning is not the primary goal of the organisation (as in workplace learning), and some because the population involved as helpers and helped have their own considerable intrapersonal challenges (as in peer tutoring in prisons).

Peer learning with exceptional learners

It might be thought that regular students would have difficulty delivering tutoring to peers with learning disabilities, developmental delay, or other exceptional needs. However, in recent years the literature has gone beyond this to demonstrate that learners who themselves have educational challenges can act effectively as tutors to other learners (e.g. Scruggs and Osguthorpe 1986). For example, Shanahan *et al.* (1994) described reciprocal peer tutoring between regular elementary school students and students from a school for children with severe learning disabilities. Spencer and Balboni (2003) reviewed 52 studies in which elementary and secondary school-age students with mental retardation served as tutors and/or tutees in academic, social, and daily living/self-help skills.

The gains for the tutors themselves have been increasingly emphasised. Maher *et al.* (1998) found deploying disruptive students as peer tutors effective in improving the tutors' achievement and behaviour, as well as advantageous for the tutees. However, Sutherland *et al.* (2000) reviewed eight experimental studies on the effectiveness of cooperative learning for students with emotional and behavioural disorders, and concluded that results were mixed.

Scruggs and Mastropieri (1998) reviewed the effectiveness of peer tutoring with tutors and tutees with special needs, and concluded:

1 Students with special needs benefit academically whether tutees or tutors.
2 Tutors benefit less academically if there is no cognitive challenge for them.
3 Participants benefit more if carefully selected and trained.
4 Participants benefit more if progress is continuously monitored.
5 Improved attitudes to the curriculum area are frequent.
6 Improved interactions with partners outside tutoring sessions are frequent.
7 More generalised attitudinal or interactive gains are less consistent.

Socio-emotional and transferable skill gains

Even in programmes principally targeting cognitive/academic gain, social and other transferable skill gains might accrue. Affective changes in attitude to school, the teacher, the subject, peers, and to the self might also be found. Schunk and Zimmermann (1994) argue that such changes are important for sustainability and generalisation, since they enhance self-belief, internal attribution for success, and consequently self-regulation of subsequent learning behaviour. They can help develop 'educational resilience', which might sustain the learner through transitions to less optimal learning environments.

For example, in one cross-age peer tutoring project in reading in 34 classrooms, only three teachers did not observe gains in student motivation, confidence, enjoyment, and relating during the tutoring sessions. Only seven teachers did not observe these and self-esteem gains generalising outside the tutoring sessions, although these wider effects tended to be less strong (Topping 2003b). A recent study of cooperative learning in science found that gains in transferable cooperative learning skills predicted social gains both in and out of class. Urban single-age classes tended to start lower in social cohesiveness, but made the biggest gains in this and in self-esteem as a result of CL (Tolmie *et al.* 2009). Gumpel and Frank (1999) successfully deployed direct peer tutoring of social skills to social rejectees.

Information technology and peer learning

In recent years, information technology has begun to permeate peer learning in various ways. First, peer learning at a distance in online communities has been extensively explored. Graham (2002) reviewed the research into creating effective cooperative learning in face-to-face and virtual environments for distance education, with particular emphasis upon creating the groups, structuring learning activities, and facilitating group interactions. Davies (2000) researched computerised peer assessment in university. McLuckie and Topping (2004) defined and devised means of assessing the transferable skills needed for effective peer learning in online contexts, identifying the advantages and disadvantages of the online context.

Second, software has been developed that is intended to help manage peer learning, thereby providing a management information system for the coordinator or facilitator of a programme (e.g. I-Help) (Bull and McCalla 2002). This is particularly necessary in cross-age or cross-institution peer learning in complex distributed environments.

Third, formative computer-aided assessment has been linked to tutoring systems, so that both helpers and helped receive regular, frequent, and timely feedback on the effectiveness of their learning together (e.g. Topping 1999).

Finally, systems have been devised for tutoring by artificial intelligences (e.g. Merrill *et al.* 1992), but these have some way to go before approaching the skill levels and adaptability of human tutors.

Embedding: Systemic approaches

Peer learning has moved from a method perceived as being only for a few selected learners, to a method used on a class-wide equal-opportunity and inclusive basis. Some schools have developed whole-school approaches to the deployment of various forms of peer learning. However, greater critical mass does not ensure sustainability. Where the main driver and/or organiser is one person, their departure can lead to the collapse of the initiative. Abrami *et al.* (2004) found that expectation of success was the most significant factor distinguishing users and non-users of CL, suggesting a need for implementation support that impacts upon both teacher organisation skills and self-efficacy. It is important that several colleagues are engaged in a peer learning programme, and that embedding the programme across the learning organisation and succession planning are carefully considered well in advance.

Arguably, there is no better apprenticeship for being a helper than being helped. Many schools with cross-year class-wide peer tutor programmes actively promote the equal-opportunity and apprenticeship advantages of this model. Every student who is helped in a lower grade fully expects from the outset to become a helper when in a higher grade. As students are helped in preparation for becoming helpers, any ambivalence about receiving help decreases. The asymmetry between helper and helped is reduced, and the stigma often otherwise associated with receiving help disappears. All the students have the chance to participate and the opportunity to help, which makes them all feel equally valuable and worthwhile. Sometimes students who are helped in one subject are simultaneously helpers to students in a lower grade in the same subject. Those who are helped in one subject might be helpers to their own age peers in another subject. Even the most able student in any grade can be presented with problems that require the help of an even more capable student from a higher grade, and thereby can learn that no one is as smart as all of us.

Over time a critical mass of teachers who support peer learning can develop in the school. PL builds on individuals' strengths and mobilises them as active participants in the learning process – this is true for teachers as well as students. Not only do helpers learn the subject better and deeper, but they also learn transferable skills in helping, cooperation, listening, and communication. PL encourages personal and social development. All of this influences the school ethos, developing a cultural norm of helping and caring. PL can contribute to a sense of cohesive community.

References

Abrami, P. C., Poulsen, C. and Chambers, B. (2004). Teacher motivation to implement cooperative learning: Factors differentiating users and non-users of cooperative learning. *Educational Psychology, 24*: 201–16.

Bennett, S. N., Desforges, C. W., Cockburn, A. and Wilkinson, B. (1984). *The quality of pupil learning experiences.* London: Lawrence Erlbaum.

Brown, C. C., Topping, K. J., Henington, C. and Skinner, C. H. (1999). Peer monitoring of learning behaviour: The case of 'Checking Chums'. *Educational Psychology in Practice, 15*: 174–82.

Buchs, C., Butera, F. and Mugny, G. (2004). Resource interdependence, student interactions and performance in cooperative learning. *Educational Psychology, 24*: 291–314.

Bull, S. and McCalla, G. (2002). Modelling cognitive style in a peer help network. *Instructional Science, 30*: 497–528.

Chi, M. T. H., Siler, S. A., Jeong, H., Yamauchi, T. and Hausmann, R. G. (2001). Learning from human tutoring. *Cognitive Science, 25*: 471–533.

Cohen, P. A., Kulik, J. A. and Kulik, C. C. (1982). Educational outcomes of tutoring: A meta-analysis of findings. *American Educational Research Journal, 19*: 237–48.

Davies, P. (2000). Computerized peer assessment. *Innovations in Education and Training International*, 37: 346–55.

Fantuzzo, J. W., Riggio, R. E., Connelly, S. and Dimeff, L. A. (1989). Effects of reciprocal peer tutoring on academic achievement and psychological adjustment: A componential analysis. *Journal of Educational Psychology, 81*: 173–7.

Fuchs, D., Fuchs, L. S., Mathes, P. G. and Simmons, D. C. (1997). Peer-assisted learning strategies: Making classrooms more responsive to diversity. *American Educational Research Journal, 34*: 174–206.

Graham, C. R. (2002). Factors for effective learning groups in face-to-face and virtual environments. *Quarterly Review of Distance Education, 3*: 307–19.

Greenwood, C. R., Delquadri, J. C. and Hall, R. V. (1989). Longitudinal effects of class-wide peer tutoring. *Journal of Educational Psychology, 81*: 371–83.

Gumpel, T. P. and Frank, R. (1999). An expansion of the peer-tutoring paradigm: Cross-age peer tutoring of social skills among socially rejected boys. *Journal of Applied Behavior Analysis, 32*: 115–18.

Johnson, D. W. and Johnson, R. T. (1986). *Learning together and alone*, 2nd ed. Englewood Cliffs, NJ: Prentice Hall.

King, A. (1998). Transactive peer tutoring: Distributing cognition and metacognition. *Educational Psychology Review, 10*: 57–74.

Levine, H. M., Glass, G. V. and Meister, G. R. (1987). A cost-effectiveness analysis of computer-assisted instruction. *Evaluation Review, 11*: 50–72.

Maher, C. A., Maher, B. C. and Thurston, C. J. (1998). Disruptive students as tutors: A systems approach to planning and evaluation of programs. In K. J. Topping and S. Ehly (eds), *Peer-assisted learning*. Mahwah, NJ: Lawrence Erlbaum Associates, 145–63.

Mathes, P. G., Howard, J. K., Allen, S. H. and Fuchs, D. (1998). Peer-assisted learning strategies for first-grade readers: Responding to the needs of diverse learners. *Reading Research Quarterly*, 33: 62–94.

McLuckie, J. and Topping, K. J. (2004). Transferable skills for online peer learning. *Assessment and Evaluation in Higher Education, 29*: 563–84.

Merrill, D. C., Reiser, B. J., Ranney, M. and Trafton, J. G. (1992). Effective tutoring techniques: A comparison of human tutors and intelligent tutoring systems. *Journal of the Learning Sciences, 2*: 277–305.

Miller, D. and Moran, T. (2007). Theory and practice in self-esteem enhancement. Circle-time and efficacy-based approaches: A controlled evaluation. *Teacher and Teaching: Theory and Practice, 13*(6): 603–17.

Nixon, J. and Topping, K. J. (2000). Emergent writing: The impact of structured peer interaction. *Educational Psychology, 21*: 41–58.

Person, N. K. and Graesser, A. G. (1999). Evolution of discourse during cross-age tutoring. In A. M. O'Donnell and A. King (eds), *Cognitive perspectives on peer learning*. Mahwah, NJ: Lawrence Erlbaum, 69–86.

Rohrbeck, C. A., Ginsburg-Block, M. D., Fantuzzo, J. W. and Miller, T. R. (2003). Peer-assisted learning interventions with elementary school students: A meta-analytic review. *Journal of Educational Psychology, 95*: 240–57.

Schunk, D. H. and Zimmermann, B. J. (eds). (1994). *Self-regulation of learning and perform-ance*. New York: Lawrence Erlbaum.

Scoble, J., Topping, K. J. and Wigglesworth, C. (1988). Training family and friends as adult literacy tutors. *Journal of Reading (Journal of Adolescent and Adult Literacy)*, *31*: 410–17.

Scruggs, T. E. and Mastropieri, M. A. (1998). Tutoring and students with special needs. In K. J. Topping and S. Ehly (eds), *Peer-assisted learning*. Mahwah, NJ: Lawrence Erlbaum, 165–82.

Scruggs, T. E. and Osguthorpe, R. T. (1986). Tutoring interventions with special educa-tion settings: A comparison of cross-age and peer tutoring. *Psychology in the Schools*, *23*: 187–93.

Shanahan, K., Topping, K. J. and Bamford, J. (1994). Cross-school reciprocal peer tutor-ing of mathematics and Makaton with children with severe learning difficulty. *British Journal of Learning Disabilities*, *22*: 109–12.

Sharpley, A. M. and Sharpley, C. F. (1981). Peer tutoring: A review of the literature. *Collected Original Resources in Education*, *5*(3): 7–C11.

Slavin, R. E. (1990). *Co-operative learning: Theory, research and practice*. Englewood Cliffs, NJ: Prentice Hall.

Slavin, R. E. (1995). Research on cooperative learning and achievement: What we know, what we need to know. Baltimore, MD: Center for Research on the Education of Students Placed at Risk, Johns Hopkins University. Available online at: http://www.successforall.com/resource/research/cooplearn.htm (accessed 28 March 2005).

Spencer, V. G. and Balboni, G. (2003). Can students with mental retardation teach their peers? *Education and Training in Mental Retardation and Developmental Disabilities*, *38*: 32–61.

Sutherland, K. S., Wehby, J. H. and Gunter, P. L. (2000). The effectiveness of cooperative learning with students with emotional and behavioral disorders: A literature review. *Behavioral Disorders*, *25*: 225–38.

Tolmie, A., Topping, K. J., Christie, D., Donaldson, C., Howe, C., Jessiman, E., Livingston, K. and Thurston, A. (2009). Social effects of collaborative learning in primary schools. Learning and Instruction (in press).

Topping, K. J. (1987). Peer tutored paired reading: Outcome data from ten projects. *Educational Psychology*, *7*: 133–45.

Topping, K. J. (1996a). Reaching where adults cannot: Peer education and counselling. *Educational Psychology in Practice*, *11*(4): 23–9.

Topping, K. J. (1996b). The effectiveness of peer tutoring in further and higher education: A typology and review of the literature. *Higher Education*, *32*: 321–45.

Topping, K. J. (1998a). *The paired science handbook: Parental involvement and peer tutoring in science*. London: Fulton.

Topping, K. J. (1998b). Peer assessment between students in college and university. *Review of Educational Research*, *68*: 249–76.

Topping, K. J. (1999). Formative assessment of reading comprehension by compu-ter. Reading OnLine. Available online at: http://www.readingonline.org/critical/topping/ (accessed 4 November 2004).

Topping, K. J. (2001a). *Peer assisted learning: A practical guide for teachers*. Cambridge, MA: Brookline Books.

Topping, K. J. (2001b). *Thinking reading writing: A practical guide to paired learning with peers, parents and volunteers*. New York: Continuum International.

Topping, K. J. (2003a). Self and peer assessment in school and university: Reliability, validity and utility. In M. S. R. Segers, F. J. R. C. Dochy and E. C. Cascallar (eds), *Optimizing new modes of assessment: In search of qualities and standards*. Dordrecht, Netherlands: Kluwer Academic, 55–87.

Topping, K. J. (2003b). Read On evaluation. Available online at: http://www.dundee.ac.uk/fedsoc/research/projects/readon/evaluation/ (accessed 29 March 2005).

Topping, K. J. and Bamford, J. (1998). *The paired maths handbook: Parental involvement and peer tutoring in mathematics*. London: Fulton.

Topping, K. J. and Ehly, S. (eds). (1998). *Peer-assisted learning*. Mahwah, NJ: Lawrence Erlbaum.

Topping, K. J. and Ehly, S. W. (2001). Peer assisted learning: A framework for consultation. *Journal of Educational and Psychological Consultation, 12*: 113–32.

Topping, K. J. and Bryce, A. (2004). Cross-age peer tutoring of reading and thinking: Influence on thinking skills. *Educational Psychology, 24*: 595–621.

Topping, K. J. and Trickey, S. (2007). Collaborative philosophical enquiry for school children: Cognitive effects at 10–12 years. *British Journal of Educational Psychology*, 77: 271–88.

Topping, K. J., Peter, C., Stephen, P. and Whale, M. (2004). Cross-age peer tutoring of science in the primary school: Influence on scientific language and thinking. *Educational Psychology, 24*: 57–75.

Vygotsky, L. S. (1978). *Mind in society: The development of higher psychological processes* (M. Cole, V. John-Steiner, S. Scribner and E. Souberman (eds)). Cambridge, MA: MIT Press.

Chapter 5

Family environments and children's outcomes

Kevin Marjoribanks

It is generally agreed that if parents are involved positively in activities associated with children's learning then the school outcomes of those children are likely to be enhanced. As a result, teachers are increasingly encouraged to recognise the importance of parents as partners in the education of children. Coleman (1993) observed, however, that with the changing nature of societies, schools now interact more than ever with particularly varied groups of families. He suggested that some parents 'are deeply involved and have the skills to be effective. Others are involved, but in ways that are ineffective or harmful. And still others take little time to inculcate in their children those personal traits that facilitate the school's goals' (Coleman 1993: 6).

While parent-teacher programmes are constructed to be supportive of children's learning, Lareau and Shumar (1996) reflected on some of the potential unintended outcomes of such programmes. They indicated that parents from different social and cultural contexts approach schools with quite diverse expectations and interpretations of what it means for them to be educationally helpful when interacting with their children. In addition, they suggested that the nature and intellectual quality of parent–teacher interactions might be affected quite significantly by teachers' perceptions of parents' backgrounds. If qualitatively different family–school relationships do develop for parents from contrasting backgrounds then it is possible, perhaps likely, that a school's attempt to promote partnerships with parents might actually be associated with an increased divergence in children's learning outcomes.

It is the purpose of this chapter to indicate some of the theoretical orientations that have provided the frameworks for examining relationships between family learning environments and children's outcomes, and to present some of the findings from that family research. Then, suggestions are made about possible future directions for family learning environment research if concerns such as those expressed by Coleman, Lareau, and Shumar are to be addressed.

Theoretical orientations

Much of the development of family environment research relates to Murray's (1938) theory of personality, which suggested that if the behaviour of individuals is to be understood then it is necessary to devise a method of analysis that 'will lead to satisfactory dynamical formulations of external environments' (Murray 1938: 16). He proposed that an environment should be classified by the kind of benefits or harms that it provides. If the environment has a potentially beneficial effect, Murray suggested that individuals typically approach the environment and attempt to interact with it. In contrast, if the environment has a potentially harmful effect, individuals attempt to prevent its occurrence by avoiding the environment or defending themselves against it.

The directional tendency of the environment implied in Murray's framework was designated as the press of the environment. Each press is defined as having a qualitative aspect which is the kind of benefit that the environment has or might have upon an individual. In addition, each press has a quantitative aspect which is assessed by the power an environment has either to benefit or harm different individuals or the same individual at different times. Murray (1938: 122) distinguished between the alpha press of the environment 'which is the press that actually exists, as far as scientific discovery can determine it,' and an environment's beta press 'which is the subject's own interpretation of the phenomena that is perceived.'

It was not until Bloom (1964) and a number of his doctoral students examined the family correlates of children's affective and cognitive outcomes that a school of research emerged to assess the alpha press of family environments. Bloom defined environments as the conditions, forces, and external stimuli that impinge on individuals. He proposed that these forces, which may be physical or social as well as intellectual, provide a network that surrounds, engulfs, and plays on the individual. Bloom (1964: 187) suggested that 'such a view of the environment reduces it for analytical purposes to those aspects of the environment which are related to a particular characteristic or set of characteristics.' That is, the total context surrounding an individual may be defined as being composed of a number of sub-environments. If the development of a particular characteristic is to be understood then it becomes necessary to identify that sub-environment of press variables which is potentially related to the characteristic.

In what might be considered an extension of the sub-environment approach, Bronfenbrenner and Ceci (1994) proposed that children's school outcomes are related to proximal processes, which are enduring forms of interaction that occur in immediate settings such as families, and to more remote situations in which the immediate settings are embedded. They indicated:

> The form, power, content and direction of the proximal processes affecting development vary systematically as a joint function of the characteristics of the developing person, of the environment – both immediate and more

remote – in which the processes are taking place, and the nature of the developmental outcome under consideration.

(Bronfenbrenner and Ceci 1994: 572)

The nature of the relations between distal contexts and outcomes was emphasised by Ceci *et al.* (1997: 311) who stated:

[T]he efficacy of a proximal process is determined to a large degree by the distal environmental resources. Proximal processes are the engines that actually drive the outcome but only if the distal resources can be imported into the process to make it effective.

Similarly, in the development of a general family theory, Coleman (1988, 1990) examined the concept of family social capital when he addressed the complexity of relationships among family background, immediate family settings, and children's school outcomes. He suggested that family influences are analytically separable into components such as economic, human, and social capital. Human capital provides parents with resources to create supportive proximal learning settings and it can be measured by indicators such as parents' educational attainment. In contrast, family social capital is defined by the resources individuals may access through social ties. It is the amount and quality of academically oriented interaction between parents and children that provides children with access to parents' human capital. Coleman (1997) suggested that, if the human capital possessed by parents is not complemented by strong and positive social relations in families, then it is irrelevant to children's educational outcomes whether parents have a great deal or small amount of human capital.

Family social capital may be considered, therefore, to have two elements: the social relationships that allow individuals to obtain possible access to economic, human, and cultural resources; and the amount and quality of those resources. In families, the potentially valuable social capital related to a child's successful schooling includes: (a) the amount and quality of interest in, support of, encouragement of, and knowledge about education that parents and other family members have; and (b) the extent to which such resources are transmitted to the child in interactions with family members.

In an early attempt to identify important family proximal processes or family social capital dimensions, Rosen (1956, 1973) developed the concept of the family achievement syndrome. He proposed that achievement-oriented families may be characterised by variations in the interrelated components of achievement training, independence training, achievement-value orientations, and educational–occupational aspirations. Rosen suggested that achievement and independence training act together to generate achievement motivation, which provides children with the psychological impetus to excel in situations involving standards of excellence. It was proposed that the learning of achievement-oriented values can be quite independent of the acquisition of the achievement motive. While value orientations are probably acquired when verbal communications in families are quite complex, it was considered that achievement motivation is generated from parent–child interactions early in the child's life when many of the interactions are emotional and non-verbal. Within the achievement syndrome, therefore, achievement values help to shape children's behaviour so that achievement motivation can be translated into successful school outcomes.

Rosen stated, however, that while achievement motivation and value orientations affect children's outcomes by influencing their need to excel and their willingness to plan and work hard, they 'do not determine the areas in which such excellence takes place' (Rosen 1959: 57). Unless parents express high educational and occupational aspirations, Rosen proposed that the other family influences will not necessarily be associated with children's success in school.

In a further refinement of the classification of family influences, Bourdieu (1984, 1998) proposed a two-dimensional model of family social space. The overall volume of economic and cultural capital possessed by individuals or available to them defines the vertical dimension. In contrast, the horizontal dimension indicates the structure of individuals' capital and it is assessed by the relative amounts of economic and cultural capital within the total volume of their capital. While economic capital refers to financial resources and assets, cultural capital includes: (a) the habits and tastes acquired by individuals as they grow up in different family settings; (b) cultural objects such as paintings, antiques, and books accumulated by individuals or families; and (c) formal educational qualifications attained by individuals.

Bourdieu's theoretical orientation suggests that educational and social mobility are related to changes in the availability of capital resources and that, unless these changes occur, childhood social positions are translated into similar adult positions. Such restricted social trajectories are explained, in part, by the proposition that people in different social positions are conditioned by their access to capital resources. Individuals in the same sector of a family space are assumed to acquire similar sets of dispositions. They develop similar tastes, habits, preferences, and perceptions; they begin to construct a 'feel' for the meaning of the relations between their social positions and possible lifestyles; and given their cumulative exposure to certain social conditions, they begin to anticipate probable realistic educational and occupational outcomes. That is, their *habitus* begins to form and develop in response to the consistent or changing nature of their social conditions.

Between relatively remote family social and economic conditions and immediate family social and cultural capital, there are intermediate family influences that may be associated with children's school outcomes. Such influences include the sibling structure of families, whether children live in single-parent households, and general family disruption. There has been a long-standing fascination, for example, with exploring relations between sibling variables and children's outcomes.

One of the most significant theoretical models used to examine relationships between sibling variables and children's cognitive growth is the confluence model developed by Zajonc and Markus (1975). They proposed that the cognitive development of individuals in any period is determined by influences such as the number of siblings, the age spacing among siblings, and whether children are only or last-born children in families. The confluence model has generated vigorous controversy. Rodgers (2001: 71) observed, for example, 'The confluence model is creative, complex, and intriguing. It also has critical weaknesses, both theoretical and empirical. Its major theoretical weakness is that is was built to match apparent patterns that weren't really there.'

Another intermediate family influence that has attracted much attention is the effect on children's outcomes of growing up in a single-parent family (Guttmann 1987; Guttmann and Lazar 1998). Theoretical orientations have included the no-impact hypothesis, the social control proposition, and the instability, change, and stress perspective (Wu 1996). Because of the limitations of much family structure research, new theoretical orientations are beginning to: (a) discriminate among different types of single-parent families such as divorced, separated, widowed, or never married; (b) include various social-status measures as indicators of family background; (c) control for the possible effects of changes in family income as a background and mediating variable; (d) separate the effects of the social and ethnic/race backgrounds of families, and (e) differentiate between the effects on outcome of single-parent families headed by fathers or by mothers. In addition, Pong (1998) suggested that the challenge is not only to investigate whether family type has an impact on an individual student's outcomes, but if a 'school's concentration of students from single-parent families affects the social context of learning for *all* students, regardless of an individual student's family type' (Pong 1998: 24).

From such theoretical orientations, Marjoribanks (2002) proposed a family model that might be adopted when examining relationships between family influences and children's outcomes. In the model, family background is defined by economic and human capital, parents' aspirations, and cultural context (the family's ethnic/race group membership). In contrast, more immediate or proximal family settings are characterised by measures of social capital, such as parental practices and parenting style, and by cultural capital, which indicates the availability of cultural resources. Marjoribanks suggested that the combination of social and cultural capital be defined as family educational capital. Strong family educational capital indicates that parents or other family members provide supportive interactive environments that allow children to gain access to those cultural resources associated with school success. In addition, strong family educational capital provides children with access to parents' aspirations and to the economic and human capital resources available in families, as well as access to the resources of cultural contexts, schools, and other institutions.

Lareau and Horvat (1999) suggested there is a need to distinguish between the possession and activation of family capital: '[P]eople who have social and cultural capital may choose to activate it or not, and they vary in the skill with which they activate it' (Lareau and Horvat 1999: 38). Family educational capital can be considered to reflect the extent to which cultural capital has been activated or accessed through the development of supportive adult-child networks in families. In addition, Marjoribanks' family model proposes that between children's family background and educational capital there are intermediate family structures that provide opportunities for or barriers to children's successful participation in schooling. As indicated earlier, such intermediate structural characteristics include the sibling structure of families, family type, and general family disruption.

It is often proposed that parent–child interactions in families are more powerful predictors of children's school outcomes than are measures of more remote influences. The family model suggests that for a more complete understanding of family influences it is necessary to consider that associations between family educational capital and school outcomes are embedded in relationships involving children's family background and family structural characteristics. That is, the model supports a claim made over 30 years ago by Halsey (1975) that children's membership of certain social and cultural contexts should not be 'trivialised to the point where differences of parental attitude are conceived of as separate factors rather than as an integral part of the work and community situation of children' (Halsey 1975: 17).

In the following section, investigations are considered that have examined relationships between family influences and children's school-related outcomes.

Empirical investigations

Much of the impetus for examining relationships between families and children's school outcomes was provided by the findings of the landmark Coleman *et al.* (1966) and Plowden (1967) surveys. From a controversial study of some 570,000 children and 60,000 teachers from 4,000 US schools, Coleman *et al.* (1966: 316) concluded:

> Differences in school facilities and curriculum which are the major variables by which attempts are made to improve schools, are so little related to differences in achievement levels of students that, with few exceptions, their effects fail to appear in a survey of this magnitude.

Instead, the study revealed that family influences were much more important than school characteristics in explaining differences in children's academic achievement (also see Al-Nhar 1999).

The findings of the Coleman investigation had a major impact on policies related to compensatory education and to racial discrimination in schooling. In England, the Plowden report had a similar influence on policies for elementary school children. It was a particularly refined large-scale survey of the environmental correlates of the school outcomes of three cohorts of children aged 7, 8, and 11 years. As in the Coleman study, the Plowden report indicated strong associations between family influences and measures of children's school performance.

Studies that have used parent interviews to assess family capital tend to show that the family variables have medium to large associations with children's cognitive outcomes whereas family influences are related more modestly to affective characteristics. From such investigations, Kellaghan *et al.* (1993) identified five family measures that may be considered to be significant in making a difference to children's learning. They were designated as the work habits of the family (i.e. preference for educational activities over other activities); academic guidance and support (parents' guidance on school matters and the provision of facilities in the home for school learning); stimulation to explore and discuss ideas and events (opportunities in the home to explore ideas, events, and the wider social context, and the use of games, hobbies, and other imagination-provoking activities); the language environment of homes, and parents' academic aspirations.

Much of the early family environment research assessed the alpha press of families. Grolnick and Slowiaczek (1994) observed, however, that in family investigations, phenomenological experiences need to be examined 'as the child must experience the resources for them to have their influence. Such a viewpoint represents the child as an active processor of information rather than a passive recipient of inputs' (Grolnick and Slowiaczek 1994: 248). Similarly, Wentzel (1994: 264) concluded that children's school outcomes 'may be more highly related to their own perceptions of parenting than to what parents think they are doing in the home.' Plomin (1995: 62) suggested:

> [E]xtant environmental measures are much more passive than active despite the shift from passive to active models of environmental influence. Progress in the field depends on developing measures of the environment that reflect children's active role in constructing and reconstructing experience.

In a set of penetrating studies that have used ethnographic methods, Lareau (1987, 1989), Lareau and Shumar (1996), and Lareau and Horvat (1999) examined the involvement in schooling of parents from different social classes. Lareau (1987) concluded, for example, that working- and middle-class parents share an expectation for their children's success, but family background leads them to develop different pathways as they attempt to realise their hopes. It is suggested that for working-class families, relations with schools 'are characterized by separation. Because these parents believe that teachers are responsible for education, they seek little information about either the curriculum or the educational process, and their criticisms of the school center almost entirely on non-academic matters' (Lareau 1989: 8). In contrast, upper-middle-class parents were found 'to forge relationships characterized by scrutiny and interconnectedness between family life and school life. These parents believe that education is a shared responsibility between teachers and parents' (Lareau 1989: 8; also see McNaughton *et al.* 1992).

In an investigation involving 18-year-old African students in South Africa, Marjoribanks and Mboya (2001) examined relationships among family background, perceptions of family social capital, goal orientations, and the adolescents' self-concept. Family background was defined conjointly by family human capital and perceptions of parenting style. The findings indicated that family background and social capital measures combined to form large associations with social self-concept and medium associations with presentation self-concept scores. In particular, the investigation suggested that future research which examines relations between family context and students' school outcomes might move beyond traditional background measures such as social status.

Marjoribanks (2002) used alpha and beta press measures in a longitudinal analysis involving Australian youth. Family background was defined conjointly by family social status and parents' aspirations, and by family ethnicity. Immediate family influences were assessed using data gathered from parents and children. The findings indicated, for example, that adolescents from different social and cultural contexts were more likely to stay on at school if they had high academic achievement, strong academic self-concept, and positive concrete attitudes towards schooling at the beginning of secondary school; strong perceived parent and teacher support during secondary school; and high personal aspirations (see also Marjoribanks 2004; Livaditis *et al.* 2003). Rumberger and Thomas (2000) emphasised the importance of identifying such predictors, as 'research has demonstrated conclusively that students who drop out of school suffer from a host of negative consequences, ranging from high unemployment and low earnings to poor health and increased criminal activity' (Rumberger and Thomas 2000: 40).

In general, family environment research suggests that an academically oriented family for elementary school children tends to be one where parents have high aspirations for their children, provide stimulating reading and other learning experiences, have an understanding of the importance of schooling, and have knowledge of their children's schoolwork. High school students benefit when parents provide, or are assisted in providing, a family setting in which they encourage their children to stay on at school, talk about the importance of schooling, praise children for schoolwork and homework, show interest in what their children are doing at school, and have high aspirations for their children.

Sonuga-Barke *et al.* (1995) offer a caution, however, when relationships between family influences and children's outcomes are being interpreted. In an investigation into relations between parents' expectations and children's school performance, they concluded that early parental expectations may be affected by child characteristics. They proposed: 'While correlated with school performance, expectations might make no independent contribution to predictions of attainment' (Sonuga-Barke *et al.* 1991, 147). This caution indicates the need for longitudinal research that examines the interactions between family and individual measures and children's outcomes. In the following section, some directions for family learning environment research are discussed.

Future directions for family environment research

Typically, family environment research has concentrated on measuring within-family educational capital. Such within-family capital refers to the opportunities, encouragement, and support provided by family members in education-related activities. Hao and Bonstead-Bruns (1998) indicated that when examining differences in school outcome for children from different social and cultural groups, investigations should also examine between-family educational capital. Such capital is generated from relationships that develop among families, schools, the church, and other institutions. Hao and Bonstead-Bruns suggested that for immigrant groups, for example, between-family educational capital is reflected in the premium that some groups place on education, ambition, and persistence. Another form of such capital relates to trustworthiness and solidarity, which allows some communities to share economic and educational resources to support children's education. Future family research would be enhanced by including measures of within- and between-family educational capital.

Family environment research has indicated that children from certain cultural and social contexts receive fewer school rewards for changes in family educational capital than do children from dominant social groups. School organisational and academic structures can create constraints on the educational opportunities of children from different family backgrounds. The placement of children into certain schools or in ability groups within schools, for example, may relate as much to family background considerations as to children's academic potential and educational capital. When differences in children's school outcomes are examined, investigations need to assess the within- and between-family educational capital available to children, and examine the opportunities and constraints provided in school settings for children from different family backgrounds.

Riding and Wheldall (1981:7) stated: 'The great need of educational psychology is to understand how children effectively learn, within the school setting, skills and information relevant to everyday life'. The purpose of this chapter has been to suggest that such an understanding will be enriched by examining the intricate nature of the interrelationships among family settings, school settings, individual characteristics, and outcomes for children from different family social and cultural contexts.

References

Al-Nhar, T. (1999). Determinants of grade 8 achievement in Jordan: A multilevel analysis approach. *Educational Psychology, 19*: 37–53.

Bloom, B. S. (1964). *Stability and change in human characteristics.* New York: Wiley.

Bourdieu, P. (1984). *Distinction: A social critique of the judgement of taste.* London: Routledge & Kegan Paul.

Bourdieu, P. (1998). *Practical reason: On the theory of action.* Cambridge, UK: Polity Press.

Bronfenbrenner, U. and Ceci, S. J. (1994). Nature–nurture reconceptualization in development perspective: A bioecological model. *Psychological Review, 101*: 568–86.

Ceci, S. J., Rosenblum, T., de Bruyn, E. and Lee, D.Y. (1997). A bio-ecological model of human development. In R. J. Sternberg and E. L. Grigorenko (eds), *Intelligence, heredity, and environment.* Cambridge, UK: Cambridge University Press, 303–22.

Coleman, J. S. (1988). Social capital in the creation of human capital. *American Journal of Sociology, 94*: 95–120.

Coleman, J. S. (1990). *Foundations of social theory.* Cambridge, MA: Harvard University Press.

Coleman, J. S. (1993). The rational reconstruction of society. *American Sociological Review, 58*: 1–15.

Coleman, J. S. (1997). Family, school, and social capital. In L. J. Saha (ed.). *International encyclopedia of the sociology of education.* Oxford, UK: Pergamon, 623–5.

Coleman, J. S., Campbell, E., Hobson, C., McPartland, J., Mood, A., Weinfield, F. and York, R. (1966). *Equality of educational opportunity.* Washington, DC: US Government Printing Office.

Grolnick, W. S. and Slowiaczek, M. L. (1994). Parents' involvement in children's learning: A multidimensional conceptualization and motivational model. *Child Development, 65*: 237–52.

Guttmann, J. (1987). Test anxiety and performance of adolescent children of divorced parents. *Educational Psychology, 7*: 225–9.

Guttmann, J. and Lazar, A. (1998). Mother's or father's custody: Does it matter for social adjustment? *Educational Psychology, 18*: 225–35.

Halsey, A. H. (1975). Sociology and the equality debate. *Oxford Review of Education, 1*: 9–23.

Hao, L. and Bonstead-Bruns, M. (1998). Parent-child differences in educational expectations and the academic achievement of immigrant and native students. *Sociology of Education, 71*: 175–98.

Kellaghan, T., Sloane, K., Alvarez, B. and Bloom, B. S. (1993). *The home environment and school learning: Promoting parental involvement in the education of children.* San Francisco, CA: Jossey-Bass.

Lareau, A. (1987). Social class differences in family-school relationships: The importance of cultural capital. *Sociology of Education, 60*: 73–85.

Lareau, A. (1989). *Home advantage: Social class and parental intervention in elementary education.* London: Falmer Press.

Lareau, A. and Shumar, W. (1996). The problem of individualism in family-school policies. *Sociology of Education, 69*: 24–39.

Lareau, A. and Horvat, E. M. (1999). Moments of social inclusion and exclusion: Race, class, and cultural capital in family-school relationships. *Sociology of Education, 72*: 37–53.

Livaditis, M., Zaphiriadis, K., Samakouri, M., Tellidou, C., Tzavaras, N. and Xenitidis, K. (2003). Gender differences, family and psychological factors affecting school performance in Greek secondary school students. *Educational Psychology, 23*: 223–31.

Marjoribanks, K. (2002). *Family and school capital: Towards a context theory of students' school outcomes.* Dordrecht, Netherlands: Kluwer Academic.

Marjoribanks, K. (2004). Environmental and individual influences on Australian young adults' likelihood of attending university: A follow-up study. *The Journal of Genetic Psychology, 165*: 134–47.

Marjoribanks, K. and Mboya, M. (2001). Family capital, goal orientations and South African adolescents' self-concept: A moderation-mediation model. *Educational Psychology, 21*: 333–50.

McNaughton, S., Parr, J., Timperley, H. and Robinson, V. (1992). Beginning reading and sending books home to read: A case for some fine tuning. *Educational Psychology, 12*: 239–47.

Murray, H. (1938). *Explorations in personality.* Oxford, UK: Oxford University Press.

Plomin, R. (1995). Genetics and children's experiences in the family. *Journal of Child Psychology and Psychiatry, 36*: 33–68.

Plowden, B. (1967). *Children and their primary schools.* London: HMSO.

Pong, S. (1998). The school compositional effect of single parenthood on 10th-grade achievement. *Sociology of Education, 71*: 24–43.

Riding, R. J. and Wheldall, K. (1981). Effective educational research. *Educational Psychology, 1*: 5–11.

Rodgers, J. L. (2001). The confluence model: An academic 'Tragedy of the Commons'. In E. L. Grigorenko and R. J. Sternberg (eds), *Family environment and intellectual functioning.* Mahwah, NJ: Lawrence Erlbaum, 71–95.

Rosen, B. C. (1956). The academic syndrome: A psychocultural dimension of stratification. *American Sociological Review, 21*: 203–11.

Rosen, B. C. (1959). Race, ethnicity, and achievement syndrome. *American Sociological Review, 24*: 47–60.

Rosen, B. C. (1973). Social change, migration and family interaction in Brazil. *American Sociological Review, 38*: 198–212.

Rumberger, R. W. and Thomas, S. L. (2000). The distribution of dropout and turnover rates among urban and suburban high schools. *Sociology of Education, 73*: 39–67.

Sonuga-Barke, E. J. S., Stevenson, J., Thompson, M., Lamparelli, M. and Goldfoot, M. (1995). The impact of pre-school children's intelligence and adjustment on their parents' long-term educational expectations. *Educational Psychology, 15*: 141–59.

Wentzel, K. R. (1994). Family functioning and academic achievement in middle school: A social-emotional perspective. *Journal of Early Adolescence, 14*: 268–91.

Wu, L. L. (1996). Effects of family instability, income and income stability on the risk of premarital birth. *American Sociological Review, 61*: 386–406.

Zajonc, R. B. and Markus, G. B. (1975). Birth order and intellectual development. *Psychological Review, 82*: 74–88.

Chapter 6

Individual differences and educational performance

Richard Riding

In education, if account were taken of individual differences in student characteristics, then learning performance should be improved in comparison with an approach that takes no account of individual difference. However, while some progress has been made over the last 20–30 years, individual difference research still makes relatively little positive contribution to educational practice. That pupils differ in educational performance is self-evident. However, the identification of precisely why this is so in a particular individual is more problematic than might initially appear. Teachers acknowledge that some pupils are 'bright' and readily able to learn while others are less successful at learning, but the underlying reasons for these differences are not clear to them.

Challenges

There are a number of challenges to an implementation of a workable individualised approach to instruction: identification of the variables, the effect of variables on performance, the vagueness of educational objectives, and the practical management of variables in the learning situation. These are summarised below.

Identification of the variables:

- There are many variables that may contribute to performance.
- The definition and operational assessment of these variables is often difficult.
- The variables frequently affect one another making it difficult to identify basic variables.

The effect of variables on performance:

- There are different types of variable and the nature of their interactive relationship with performance is complex.
- The effect of a variable at a particular time will depend on the nature and difficulty of the task for the individual.

The vagueness of educational objectives:

- Educational systems are often vague about their objectives.
- The content and emphasis of an educational system often changes frequently.

The practical management of variables in the learning situation:

- There is a need to identify the critical state – the critical variables for the individual on a particular task.
- The management of an individualised approach is difficult within a group-teaching situation using traditional teaching methods.

The purpose of this chapter is to examine these requirements and to highlight progress over the last quarter of a century, and to consider research areas requiring attention if individual differences are to be effectively accommodated.

Variables

A first step is to identify the variables that are likely to have a practical effect on performance and then to refine methods of assessing them. Over the past 25 years progress has been made in the identification and assessment of specific dimensions of individual difference. Gender has become more prominent as a variable (e.g. Halpern (1992); Skaalvik and Rankin 1994); personality dimensions have been further identified (e.g. Eysenck (1998); McCrae and John 1992); information processing and working memory are better understood (e.g. Baddeley 2000); notions of intelligence have been refined (e.g. Mackintosh 1998), and cognitive style research has advanced (e.g. Riding and Rayner 1998). Advances have also been made in identifying aspects of the home background that affect performance (e.g. Darling and Steinberg 1993). This work has laid the foundation for a further push forward to reconcile outstanding uncertainties.

Range of variables

There will be differences within the individual, between schools/colleges, within schools/colleges from teacher to teacher, and in the home background, which will each contribute to differences in performance. These could include the following.

Variables particular to the individual student

There are variables within the individual and within the individual's environment. Within the individual, the variables include present knowledge, intelligence (reasoning), working memory efficiency, anxiety-stability, gender, wholist-analytic style, verbal–imagery style, and introversion–extraversion. This is in approximate order of their likely effect on performance. In considering within-pupil differences, an initial task is to define the individual difference constructs operationally. The basic problem is that most of the above constructs are inferred from behaviour, but not from directly observable origins. This probably also applies to some extent to gender, which may be more of a continuum than a dichotomy.

Within the student's home background, variables include emotional support and stability, genetic and nurture components of intelligence, and the educational and material resources available. Often these differences will theoretically be open to direct inspection, although in practice this will be difficult because of the need to respect privacy, the unwillingness of parents to provide information, and, in the case of older students, the home situation may change with time.

Variables particular to the educational system and the institution

There will be characteristics of both the educational system and the educational institution. Within the educational system, curriculum content and its perceived relevance to the pupil should be considered. There is also the problem of defining what education is and its purpose in terms of fitness for life and relevance for employment. A particular educational system will reflect the society and value system it is in and hence systems may differ greatly from society to society, even within the same country. A system will also change with time. For instance, education within the UK has changed considerably over the last 100 years in its emphases and values. In objective terms these changes are not necessarily improvements, they are just different, and often reflect political changes and shifts in value systems in a crude manner rather than reflecting the range of abilities of individuals and the actual needs of society.

Within the school/college/university/learning system, the following characteristics are important: the ethos of the institution, the quality of teaching and the availability of resources, teaching style, characteristics of the task and its relative difficulty, and peer values. These differences will theoretically be open to direct inspection. However, there is the difficulty of defining what they represent. The term 'learning system' has been included here since an educational system at any stage could make use of a system of education that is radically different in method from the traditional school-college-university model. Such a system could make more use of technology-based learning via computer packages, the internet, digital radio, and television. At the secondary stage of education, such a system could be used in conjunction with vocational apprenticeships that combine practical experience with theoretical underpinnings.

Definition and assessment of variables

The identification and definition of individual difference constructs

Some variables are open to direct observation, such as the home, while others, such as intelligence or anxiety-stability, are not, and have to be inferred from behaviour. In this second case, a distinction is necessary between the actual variable and its construct. A construct is what is inferred from behaviour but the underlying mechanisms are assumed. This is so in cases where the variable is not directly observable but has to be inferred from behaviour. A variable is likely to be different from its construct. Any difference between a variable and its construct will be because of the difficulty of, and inaccuracies in, assessment. In this sense a construct is in reality what the test of it measures!

Psychological constructs usually have their origin in casual observation. For instance, one pupil appears to be more outgoing and lively than another who is reserved and more withdrawn. This observation leads to the labelling of the behaviour according to a pupil's position on a dimension labelled 'introversion-extraversion'. The next step is that a test is devised to assess the degree of introversion-extraversion. This is where a major problem arises. There is the possibility that the observed construct is not the same as the actual variable – the 'construct-variable difference'.

In the design and development of a test, there can be a focus largely on reliability and factors, and insufficient concern about the test's psychological validity. For instance, with a questionnaire comprising 20 items of four types in groups of five, the fact that the types load on four factors is not in itself evidence of validity or that the test measures anything that is practically useful. It may be internally consistent and may be reliable, but may not measure anything of psychological consequence.

The problems of construct assessment

The assessment of constructs provides many challenges. The methods include performance, self-report questionnaire, peer rating, and external rating. Each of these methods has limitations and difficulties. Further, all these methods cannot be applied to all the individual difference variables. Consequently, comparisons are not always like with like. Table 6.1 shows some available assessment methods for variables. For instance, for gender and self-report, a question might be, 'Are you male or female?'

Some examples of assessment difficulties include the following. With perform-ance, in the case of style, there is the need to not measure ability. With self-report, there are several possible problems: an individual may not be honest and may answer in a way that they think is socially desirable, they may not be serious about completing the questionnaire, and also may not actually know how they behave. Peer rating may suffer from bias either through envy or other motives,

Table 6.1 Possible methods of assessment of individual difference variables

| Variable | Performance | **Possible method of assessment** | | |
		Self-report questionnaire	Peer rating	External rating
Present knowledge	Yes	Perhaps	No	Perhaps
Intelligence (reasoning)	Yes	No	Perhaps	Yes
Working memory efficiency	Yes	No	No	Perhaps
Anxiety-stability	Perhaps	Yes	Yes	Yes
Introversion-extraversion	Perhaps	Yes	Yes	Yes
Gender	Perhaps	Yes	Yes	Perhaps
Wholist-analytic style	Yes	Yes	No	No
Verbal-imagery style	Yes	Yes	No	No

or if the rater does not know the person sufficiently well. External rating of behaviour by an observer could be laborious. It may take a long time to observe all the possible behaviours, and these behaviours can be difficult to interpret.

Physiological correlates of behaviours or constructs may ultimately be the way forward as new and more detailed measures of brain function become available.

The variables will often influence one another

Over the past two and a half decades there has been a growing awareness that a variable should not be considered in isolation, but that other variables will affect its nature and degree (e.g. Furnham 2001).

'Trait' versus 'state' variables and the underlying nature of variables

A distinction may be made between the underlying characteristic and the level of the characteristic at a particular time. Identifying the 'trait' variable rather than the 'state' variable can be difficult. With anxiety, the observed level will depend on the level of stress the individual is currently under. While it is true that individuals with a high trait level of anxiety will have a high level of state anxiety, this will only apply between individuals if the level of stress is the same for both. In other words, the trait level is like the 'resting' level. Blood pressure appears to present a similar case: if two individuals are compared where one has been resting for a while and the other has been physically energetic, their observed pressures will be different, even if their resting levels are the same.

Several variables will have an effect on individual states – home stability will affect anxiety, peer pressure will affect anxiety, home background will affect intelligence, the quality of teaching and intelligence will affect present knowledge, etc. Some of the dimensions are either the same as others or are dependent on them to some degree and so there will be overlap between them. For instance:

- Extraversion–introversion may derive from the same underlying mechanism as verbal-imagery style. The former dimension will be the social and the latter the cognitive manifestations of the same mechanism.
- The degree of harmony in the home will affect the state level of anxiety-stability, which in turn will affect working memory efficiency.
- The intellectual level in the home and the facilities available for intellectual stimulation will affect crystallised intelligence.

These examples show the extent of the interdependence of variables. If state anxiety is considered, then it is likely to be affected by trait anxiety, but the school and the home environment will also influence it. Further, it may be affected by cognitive style. In addition, state anxiety will affect the effective working memory capacity, which in turn will affect the level of cognitive confusion, which will then have an adverse effect on the level of state anxiety. It is evident that the interplay between variables is very complex and fluid; changes in one variable's state are likely to affect others.

The distinction between primary and secondary constructs

In the individual differences literature there are many names of variables listed (e.g. Jonassen and Grabowski 1993). In the area of cognitive styles alone there are probably in excess of 50 different labels. In individual differences as a whole the number probably exceeds 100. If there were in fact this number of individual difference variables, then it would be futile to try to incorporate individual differences into educational presentations.

Part of the reason behind this large number of different labels is that workers in a particular area name a variable on which they are working without reference to other researchers and theorists. Consequently, many terms are simply synonyms for one another. With respect to the cognitive style labels mentioned above, these could probably be reduced to two dimensions. Researchers need to be disciplined in their approach and ensure that their work fits into what has been done by others.

Another reason behind the number of labels is that some constructs are fundamental and basic and not derived from other constructs. By contrast, others are secondary, in the sense that they are the result of two or more fundamental constructs. What is required is an identification of the primary constructs, secondary constructs, tertiary constructs, etc. In a discipline such as physics there are some fundamental primary concepts such as mass (force), length, and time, which in combination give at the secondary level, for instance, speed (length/time) and area (length × length), and at the tertiary level, for instance, acceleration (speed/time) and pressure (force/area), and so on.

In psychology there is still not clear agreement about primary individual difference constructs, as evidenced by the controversy over whether in personality there are the great three (extraversion, stability, and psychoticism) or the big five (extraversion, stability, agreeableness, conscientiousness, and openness). In addition, and perhaps not surprisingly, there is lack of clarity about the relationship of the fundamental variables to what are probably secondary ones such as emotional intelligence and self-esteem.

Further, the construct of intelligence, as assessed within the educational context, is probably a secondary rather than a primary variable, since it reflects crystallised rather than fluid intelligence. That is, it represents both intelligence and previous learning of both facts and strategies. Since there is often a large amount of the latter in the measurement, it is not surprising that it frequently correlates highly with school performance. An additional secondary variable will be motivation. This is likely to be derived from a number of primary variables, including prior knowledge, peer values, and home background.

Effects of variables on performance

In studying the effects of variables on performance, several points need to be taken into account. These include the variables, their interrelationships, and critical states.

Variables and relationships

Over the last 25 years there has been a growing awareness of the need to take a broader view of research. Eysenck (1997), amongst others, has argued for a more inclusive, integrated, and experimental approach that pays attention to both individual difference variables and experimental rigour. The general point can be made that this work is not important just to those engaged in individual difference research, but also to those who would seek to adopt a more experimental approach. The effect of an experimental intervention may well interact with one or more individual difference characteristics of the students. Consequently, in a group situation, individual variation is going to add to the error term and obscure the true effects of the intervention. For this reason, individual difference research also has an importance and relevance for experimentalists. Experimental

Table 6.2 Unipolar and bipolar variables

Unipolar	Bipolar
Present knowledge	Male-female gender
Intelligence (reasoning)	Wholist-analytic style
Working memory efficiency	Verbal-imagery style
Anxiety-stability	Introversion-extraversion

studies need to include, either as variables or as controls, individual difference dimensions that may be relevant.

Distinctions and limitations of studies

Unipolar versus bipolar variables

Some variables will be unipolar, in the sense that high is always good and low is always bad. Others are bipolar, whereby in some tasks or situations one end of the dimension will be best while in others the other end of the continuum will be advantageous. These are shown in Table 6.2.

Unipolar dimensions are abilities and will sum to an overall ability, while the bipolar ones are more in the nature of styles.

Linear versus curvilinear relationships

Correlation is frequently used in investigating relationships. However, the limitation of simple correlation is that it assumes a rectilinear relationship, while in practice curvilinear relationships are likely to be common. Obviously a curvilinear relationship between variables, when investigated with linear correlation, could suggest no relationship where there is actually one.

The variables in interaction

In situations where there are several variables that may affect performance, it is frequently found that some of these variables will interact in their influence on behaviour. A variable by itself may well appear to have no or little main effect. However, when analysed with other variables present there is often an interaction of their effects on performance.

Study size

Applying an individual approach to education has the problem that there are many individual difference variables to be controlled for in a teaching situation, even if only the core fundamental variables are considered. One effect of this is that studying the effects of individual differences will require the use of very large samples sizes ($n > 1000$). Small samples will limit the research to either the consideration of only a few variables, or have cell sizes that are too small to permit reliable conclusions.

Institutional characteristics

A further problem arises here since, taking schools as an example, the number of pupils of a given age in a single school will not really be large enough to support a proper study. However, when several schools are used, differences between the schools (in terms of ethos, quality of teaching, and characteristics of the catchment areas) will also be a variable.

Critical states

The past 25 years or so have seen a growing awareness of the importance of critical states (e.g. Riding 2003). There is the problem of deciding which variables matter and which have little effect. Studies of individual differences often find that individual difference variables have little or no effect, and there are simple reasons for this.

When the task is very easy or very difficult then there will be no individual difference effects. Consider, for example, the effect of coaching in high-jump performance on a group of fit 18-year-olds. A control group receives no coaching while a treatment group has 10 sessions of instruction in jumping techniques. If the final assessment is too easy, say with a bar height of one metre, then this will probably be cleared by all and show no effect of the coaching. Similarly, if the bar is set at three metres, then this will be impossible for all, and again no effect will be observed. An intermediate range of heights will need to be used to detect whether there is any effect. In general, the major individual effects will be at the intermediate level of task difficulty. There will be an inverted U-shaped relationship between the degree of effect and the relative difficulty of the task for the individual.

A similar effect will be apparent for individual characteristics and educational performance. The effect of a particular individual difference variable will be dependent on the level of other variables. For instance, if intelligence, parental support, and school factors are very high or very low, then style and gender will have little effect. However, when they are moderate, then style is worth considering as a variable that may have an effect.

Figure 6.1 shows that two or three variables can negate the rest and these will vary from person to person. For instance, very low intelligence can mean that other variables are of little relevance. However, in those with moderate ability the style dimension has a relatively greater effect.

In deciding when it is appropriate to take an individual approach in education,

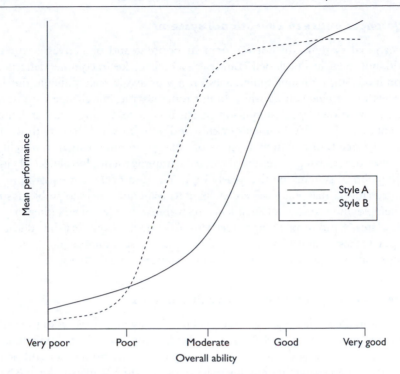

Figure 6.1 Probable performance for a style dimension and overall ability.

account needs to be taken of the relative levels of the individual difference variables.

Educational objectives

Over the last quarter of a century there have been changes in educational systems. These will be considered in general terms since practices will have varied considerably from country to country.

The nature of educational systems

While education is generally considered to be of value, there is often little clarity regarding exactly what it is to achieve. Little prominence is given to philosophies of education. The general feeling is that education is a good thing and that it equips people for life. However, exactly how it is to do this is not clearly stated. By default, the objectives are reduced to being able to perform well in public examinations. There is also the feeling that 'academic' subjects are of more value than 'vocational' ones. However, many teachers consider that they teach more widely than this and that education should be more inclusive (e.g. Topping and Maloney 2005).

Differences between educational systems

Educational systems are not uniform in content and objectives across the world, not even in developed countries, which makes recommendations for accommodating individual differences on a worldwide scale difficult. Further, even within a single country they do not remain static, but change with developments in knowledge, fashion, and political climate. Changes in curriculum content that reflect developments in knowledge are reasonable, as are those that reflect the needs of a society in terms of changes in employment possibilities. However, other changes are not necessarily improvements, but reflect changes in the political system; the five-yearly or so election cycle that exists in many countries means that politicians are inclined to want quick fixes to problems such as unemployment or school attendance to impress the electorate rather than to achieve steady, monitored longer-term improvement. Given that the education of a pupil takes around 11 years of basic compulsory schooling, rapid short-term changes often make any real progress in education difficult to assess.

Differences in perceptions between students

Richardson (2005) has highlighted researchers' growing awareness of the variation between students' practical views of learning objectives. Since some students will see the purpose and outcome of learning differently from others, the actual information processing they employ will not be the same. While on the one hand some will pursue a 'deep' approach aimed at a real understanding of the topic, others will use a 'surface' strategy such as rote memorisation. Teachers, similarly, may emphasise an 'understanding' approach or a 'cramming' method. The effect of these different approaches by both students and teachers can blur the results of studies of learning unless the assessments used are capable of distinguishing between the different types of learning.

Thus, individualising instruction is even more difficult, because the goals are not clear, are constantly changing, and are perceived differently by individual students.

The management of individualised instruction

Recognising the main/critical variables for the individual

In Table 6.3, the sum of the four unipolar abilities may probably be considered to be an indication of overall ability. If together they are just sufficient for the task, then performance will be affected by the bipolar styles. If they are not, or if they are more than sufficient for the task, then the bipolar styles will have little effect. Verbal–imagery style may be the cognitive result of the same underlying mechanism as introversion-extraversion (although this has still to be demonstrated). This approach makes management more possible since it reduces the effective total number of different individual difference variables. The level of relative difficulty of a learning task for an individual will be related to overall ability.

Student and teacher self-awareness

While individuals are in some aspects of their work introspectively aware of what is difficult and what is not, in others they are not. This arises because many aspects of the information processing system are automatic and not open to introspection. Since people only experience themselves, they are unaware of what it is like to be good at something at which they themselves are not. Similarly, if they find a subject easy, they take this for granted and assume that all find it similarly easy. An emotional response will also be assumed to be common to all, so that an anxious student will assume that all feel the same. Consequently, students often will not be good at realising what they personally find easy or difficult with respect to their peers. Teachers will tend to think that the way in which they find it easy to understand will be the way in which their students best learn. Raising student and staff awareness of individual differences opens them up to the view that, in many learning situations, there are several different ways of achieving learning. Teachers could usefully broaden their teaching style to encompass a variety of approaches.

Practical aspects of management

There has been a developing interest in the practical treatment of individual difference (e.g. Hayes and Allinson 1996).

Accommodating versus coping strategies

When taking account of individual differences, two basic approaches are possible in instruction. One is to accommodate the material and the mode of teaching to the individual characteristics of the student. Accommodation could, for instance, involve matching the material content, structure, and mode to the cognitive style of the student. Revision of a student's present knowledge may be necessary for the achievement of new learning, since learning is somewhat similar to building

Table 6.3 Abilities versus styles

General unipolar ability	Bipolar styles
Present knowledge	Male-female gender
Intelligence (reasoning)	Wholist-analytic style
Working memory efficiency	Verbal-imagery style
Anxiety-stability	Introversion-extraversion

a wall where, to be successful, each course must have one beneath it already in place. The presentation rate of material could be adjusted to maximise working memory efficiency. Reducing the stress of the learning environment could relieve pressure on the anxious student.

The other approach would be to teach coping strategies (e.g. Carver *et al.* 1989) to enable students to process material that they naturally find difficult. With respect to cognitive style and mode of presentation, this could involve teaching students how to translate material into the mode of presentation that suits them. Pupils could be made aware of the need to review past related material before embarking on a new topic. Strategy development should increase success in learning and build confidence.

The difference between these two approaches lies with the locus of control – in the former it is with the teacher and in the latter with the student. A progressive shift from the former to the latter is desirable over time. The choice of method chosen may depend on the ability of the students.

Group versus individual instruction

Within a group teaching situation the management of individual variables is difficult. The traditional approach in education to addressing individual variation has been streaming or setting. However, this supposes that levels of performance are a reflection of levels of an individual variable, and this may not be the case. For example, poor performance in two pupils may be due to very different reasons. Truly individualised instruction is probably only possible using a computer-presented cafeteria approach.

A scheme for research

In order to build on progress in individual difference research of the past 25 years, an integrated approach that includes most dimensions in a single model is required. This would make it possible to take individual differences into account more realistically in education in a manner that improves performance. There are four major challenges facing the application of individual differences to practical educational situations:

* The fundamental individual difference dimensions need to be further clarified, and a model of their relationship to the secondary constructs produced. Simple, valid, and reliable ways of assessing these variables are also required.
* An identification of the factors affecting the educational situation is needed, as are decisions about which variables affect performances that are critical for a particular situation.
* Educational objectives need to be clarified and made operational.
* Methods of accommodating individual differences need to be developed.

Identification of individual difference dimensions

It is very unlikely that a single individual difference variable will be found that has a large main effect on performance. Intelligence, which usually has the largest effect, is usually of the crystallised form, which in reality is likely to include a reflection of environmental influences and previous learning. However, the observation that current measures of most individual difference variables are fairly crude, but they still appear to detect something, suggests that better measures, and particularly physiological ones, might show more substantial effects.

The future lies in identifying the range of variables affecting educational performance. A hindrance to progress has been the indiscipline of researchers – on the one hand not integrating their work into that of other investigators, and on the other tending to be simplistic in expecting one or two variables to account for large differences in performance.

Identifying the interactive effects of variables

In view of the complexity of the possible individual effects, large-scale studies are needed which include substantial sample sizes and a wide range of variables. These studies need to allow for interactions and non-linear effects. From a practical viewpoint, it would be useful to explore the notion of critical state and methods of identifying the most important variables for an individual in a particular type of learning situation.

Clarification of educational objectives

While those studying the psychology of education are not likely to be curriculum planners or politicians, they can contribute to the process of refining curriculum content by identifying what the practical learning outcomes of particular curricula may be. These outcomes may well not be those intended by the planners. This difference needs to be highlighted and could be a useful step towards having a curriculum that actually achieves what is intended.

Determining methods of accommodating individual differences

Here, four areas requiring investigation include: (a) identifying the most critical individual difference variables; (b) studying the role of self-awareness in performance and considering ways of raising it; (c) exploring accommodating presentation to match an individual's style versus developing methods of improving coping strategies, and (d) developing methods of individualising instruction, particularly utilising the new technologies.

If these challenges are met then individual difference research in the future is likely to make a very significant contribution to educational research and practice.

References

Baddeley, A. D. (2000). Short-term and working memory. In E. Tulving and F. I. M. Craik (eds), *The Oxford handbook of memory*. New York: Oxford University Press, 75–92.

Carver, C., Scheier, M. and Weintrab, J. (1989). Assessing coping strategies: A theoretically based approach. *Journal of Personality and Social Psychology, 56*: 267–83.

Darling, N. and Steinberg, L. (1993). Parenting style as context: An integrated model. *Psychological Bulletin, 113*: 487–96.

Eysenck, H. J. (1997). Personality and experimental psychology: The unification of psychology and the possibility of a paradigm. *Journal of Personality and Social Psychology, 73*: 1224–37.

Eysenck, H. J. (1998). *Dimensions of personality*. New Brunswick, NJ: Transaction.

Furnham, A. (2001). Test-taking style, personality traits and psychometric validity. In M. J. Collis and S. Messick (eds), *Intelligence and personality: Bridging the gap in theory and measurement*. Mahwah, NJ: Lawrence Erlbaum.

Halpern, D. E. (1992). *Sex differences in cognitive abilities*, 2nd ed. Hillsdale, NJ: Lawrence Erlbaum.

Hayes, J. and Allinson, C. W. (1996). The implications of learning styles for training and development: A discussion of the matching hypothesis. *British Journal of Management, 7*: 63–73.

Jonassen, D. H. and Grabowski, B. L. (1993). *Handbook of individual differences, learning and instruction*. Hillsdale, NJ: Lawrence Erlbaum.

Mackintosh, N. J. (1998). *IQ and human intelligence*. Oxford, UK: Oxford University Press.

McCrae, R. R. and John, O. P. (1992). An introduction to the five-factor model and its applications. *Journal of Personality, 60*: 175–215.

Richardson, J. T. E. (2005). Students' approaches to learning and teachers' approaches to teaching in higher education. *Educational Psychology, 25*(6): 673–80.

Riding, R. J. (2003). Cognitive style and school performance in adolescents. In F. Pajares and T. Urdan (eds), *International perspectives on adolescence*. Greenwich, CT: Information Age, 45–69.

Riding, R. J. and Rayner, S. G. (1998). *Cognitive styles and learning strategies*. London: David Fulton.

Skaalvik, E. M. and Rankin, R. J. (1994). Gender differences in mathematics and verbal achievement, self-perception and motivation. *British Journal of Educational Psychology, 64*: 419–28.

Topping, K. and Maloney, S. (2005). *The RoutledgeFalmer reader in inclusive education*. London: RoutledgeFalmer.

Chapter 7

Progress in communication intervention for individuals with developmental disabilities

Jeff Sigafoos

It may seem strange to include a paper on communication intervention in this collection of perspectives on educational psychology. Communication intervention is, after all, usually associated with speech-language pathologists, not with educational psychologists. However, educational and behavioural psychologists – often working in collaboration with speech-language pathologists – have made major contributions to the field.

In this chapter, I will review some of the major psychologically oriented works that have shaped the field of communication intervention for individuals with developmental disabilities over the past 25 years. The specific focus is on the development of symbol-based or graphic-mode alternatives to speech and the application of these alternative communication systems in training programmes for individuals with developmental and physical disabilities.

The advances made over the past 25 years in this specific area have been dramatic and have enabled many non-speaking individuals with developmental and physical disabilities to communicate effectively in community settings (Schlosser 2003). One of the major findings is that the mere provision of a communication device is usually not sufficient to ensure functional use of the device. There is more to communication intervention than merely assessing the individual and then prescribing a communication mode or device. What is needed, in addition to selecting an appropriate mode of communication, is systematic implementation of empirically validated training procedures. It is in the development of empirically validated training procedures that psychologists have made major contributions to the field.

The aim of my brief foray into history is not to provide an encyclopaedic review, but rather a more personal perspective on developments in the area of symbol-based or graphic-mode communication systems for individuals with developmental and physical disabilities. My plan is to relate how I came into personal contact with what I consider to be some of the seminal works and significant contributors from educational and behavioural psychology, considering in particular how these works and contributors have advanced the science and practice of communication intervention for individuals with developmental disabilities. In doing so, I will reflect on how these works affected me at the time, and how they kindled my interest in communication intervention and shaped my behaviour as an applied researcher.

David Premack and ape-language research

As an undergraduate at the University of Minnesota during the early 1980s, I decided to major in psychology because of David Premack's work on teaching language to chimpanzees. I did not know it at the time, but his use of plastic shapes as a mode of communication was to have a profound impact on me and on the field of communication intervention, ushering in an era of rapid development in augmentative and alternative systems of communication (AAC). The defining moment came on a fine spring day in 1981. I took the lift up to the fifth floor of Elliot Hall to check my exam grade for a class. In the lift, two distinguished – or at least greying – professors were talking about Premack's ape-language research and vaguely about the possibility of his prized chimp escaping from the lab. I imagined people fleeing from the wandering primate while fretful lab assistants searched in vain for their missing charge. At the time, I had been weighing up both sociology and psychology as possible majors, but this chance bit of eavesdropping tipped the balance for psychology. Forget Ward and Sumner. Forget symbolic interaction and conflict theory. Psychology had talking apes running down the halls! Psychological research sounded as exciting as it was outlandish. Imagine some guy trying to teach language to a chimp! This Premack fellow, I thought, must be some kind of wonderful eccentric, a real live Dr Dolittle. I felt relieved to have made the decision. I would major in psychology.

Later, I was disappointed to learn in an email from David Premack (personal communication, 9 March 2005) that the loose chimp incident never occurred and that he never actually worked at the University of Minnesota. The concerns expressed by my elevator mates probably arose from the fact that when Premack was initially planning to undertake a fellowship at Minnesota, there was apparently some discussion amongst the psychology professoriate about a 'brute swaggering mutinously through the hall, even perhaps commandeering the faculty washroom' (Premack 1976: xi). When this fellowship was delayed, he went to work at Missouri, where he conducted his famous reinforcement experiments that led to the now widely applied Premack Principle (Premack 1959). His ape-language research started later at the University of California-Santa Barbara (about 1966–76) and then moved to the University of Pennsylvania (about 1977–88).

Still, hearing about this work in the elevator prompted me to find out more about this Premack guy and his monkey business. I remember going to the library to search for articles by David Premack shortly after hearing the mythical tale in the elevator. The first article that I found was 'A Functional Analysis of Language' (Premack 1970). In it, Premack made two important points that underlie many contemporary communication intervention programmes for individuals with developmental disabilities. First, he emphasised the need to define language from a functional perspective, rather than focusing on the structure of language, which is of course the domain of the linguist. Second, he outlined the types of question that one would need to ask (and answer) in order to determine whether or not an organism (chimpanzees in this case) had 'language' (e.g. 'When is a response a word?').

The paper taught me three important lessons that I have tried to remember and pass on to my students. First, the function of behaviour, including communicative behaviour, is often more important than its form. Second, an important part of research, indeed perhaps the most important part, is coming up with good questions. And third, if you are ever going to use the word organism in a lecture, pause and think very carefully before you say it.

I also found and quickly read Premack's 1976 classic book *Intelligence in Ape and Man*. Here Premack showed that with the right training and with a suitable response mode (those little plastic forms that looked like weirdly shaped refrigerator magnets), chimpanzees could acquire communicative behaviours that had all the characteristics of a proper language. While many were impressed by the final performances of the chimps, I was more impressed by the detailed and carefully structured training procedures that lead to this high level of 'linguistic' competence in the lowly primate. To this day, one would be hard pressed to find any better description of how to teach language, be it to chimp or child.

At the time, I was not yet thinking in applied terms and had not grasped the clinical implications of his work. Instead of thinking about how this work might be adapted to individuals with disabilities, I delved deeper into the ape-language literature. As an idealistic student, I was eager for anything that confirmed my emerging behavioural perspective that there was nothing all that special about human behaviour – or, put another way, that there was nothing un-special about the behaviour of other (non-human) organisms.

In addition to Premack's landmark book on the topic, two other works were particularly memorable from the ape-language genre. First, Herb Terrace – the man behind errorless learning – had a marvellously readable book out on teaching sign language to his whimsically named subject Nim Chimpsky (Terrace 1979). From Terrace's (1979) work, I became temporarily motivated to try to learn a few signs, but never became fluent. (As an aside, my lack of proficiency with signs is partly why I later turned my research interests to picture-boards and voice-output communication devices.)

Second, Savage-Rumbaugh published a paper in the *Journal of the Experimental Analysis of Behavior* (1984) that nicely delineated a paradigm for teaching chimps to make requests and name objects by pointing to illuminated abstract symbols on a fancy electronic display. It was just the sort of simplicity that I needed to help me understand the 'function' of language. The Savage-Rumbaugh paper was perhaps the first to strike a chord with my applied side. I was not only moved to acquaint myself with Skinner's (1957) verbal operants, but it also inspired some of my first applied intervention studies (Sigafoos *et al.* 1989; Sigafoos *et al.* 1990).

Although I did not know it at the time, others had already recognised the applied relevance of Premack's ape-language research, even going so far as to adopt his tangible symbol system as a mode of communication for individuals with developmental disabilities. Evans and Spittle (1981), for example, published an account of using Premack symbols to improve the communication skills of two children with severe disabilities. Unfortunately, I did not come across this paper until many years later.

Reichle and graphic-mode AAC

Fortunately, I was not to remain ignorant of the applied relevance of the ape-language research for long. As my undergraduate days ended, I bumbled into graduate school and happily fell under the mentorship of Professor Joe Reichle. Joe Reichle was a pioneer in the field of communication intervention and remains a major contributor to the science and practice of augmentative and alternative communication for individuals with severe disabilities (e.g. Reichle et al. 2002). His graduate seminar introduced me to the key papers in the field and taught me how to 'read' the literature. He was also a master clinician who could effortlessly translate basic principles into effective techniques for application. While many a student wants to learn a bunch of instructional techniques, I am grateful that Professor Reichle focused less on the technique and more on the basic principles that underlie effective instruction. Each day I become even more convinced that the best preparation for both applied researcher and clinician is a firm command of the basic operant and respondent learning principles that underlie effective interventions. His classes were demanding, but I survived and also had a lot of fun. In addition to critiquing the literature, he also got us doing hands-on practical work, such as building micro-switches and creating communication symbol books.

He brought me into his research programme, which at the time focused on the nitty-gritty of procedures for teaching individuals with severe disabilities to use graphic-mode communication systems. At the time, Reichle was busy developing and empirically evaluating operantly based training procedures for teaching children how to communicate requests, comments, and even protest. The communicative forms he was teaching included pictures and line drawings that were affixed to communication boards and wallets. I was amazed at how quickly one could teach the children to use these graphic-mode alternatives to speech. This operant conditioning stuff really worked! It seemed so easy, but that was only because I had learned from an expert who only made it look easy. I was soon to learn that it's not always so easy and that some children just won't do what the textbook says they should.

Bondy, Frost, and PECS

One day I remember trying to teach a student with autism to request food and drink by pointing to corresponding line drawings on a communication board. The teaching paradigm was just as Savage-Rumbaugh had outlined in her 1984 paper, so I was now beginning to make use of all that reading I had done about apes. The procedure was very simple. I would offer the child some food or drink and then physically prompt him to point to the corresponding symbol on his communication board. However, this child kept peeling the velcro-backed line drawings off the communication board and handing them to me. Stupidly, I viewed this as a problem and kept insisting that he point with this index finger. I recall having coffee later that day with a peer and venting my annoyance at this child who just wouldn't point! 'How hard can it be to point?' I asked in frustration.

A few years later, I read a paper in *The Behavior Analyst* (Bondy and Frost 1993) describing the Picture Exchange Communication System (PECS) and realised that this child was trying to teach me about picture exchange, but I was too dumb to catch on. In the PECS system, students are taught to pick up line drawings or symbol cards and hand them over to an adult. The exchange of the picture constitutes a communicative act that requires social interaction, which is of course highly sought after when working with students with autism and related developmental disabilities. Since this early description in 1993, PECS has caught on like wildfire and numerous studies have shown it to be a highly effective approach to communication intervention for individuals with autism and related developmental disabilities. I had certainly missed the boat on this one, but it did teach me never again to ignore the cardinal rule of applied behaviour analysis, which is to take what the learner gives you. In this case, I should have heeded the rule both literally and figuratively. As it turns out, Bondy and Frost were more responsive to the ongoing behaviour of their students, which is how they came up with the idea for PECS in the first place. It seems that they were working with one child who also just wouldn't point. In a recent email, Andrew Bondy described how he and Lori Frost came up with the procedure. His description is worth quoting at length:

> Lori Frost was working as an SLP while I was the director of a statewide program for students with autism. We had worked on developing speech, sign, and picture-point modes of communication. Some very young children were not yet skilled at matching-to-sample; others were sloppy pointers – they slapped several pictures at once; still others liked to tap on things so when they touched a picture it was not meant as communication. Lori asked me to help with one young boy who did all three. We decided to isolate the single picture of the item he liked [in order] to avoid discrimination errors. I sat behind him while Lori silently offered the item. As he reached for the item, I guided his hand to the picture and helped him pick it up and put it

into Lori's other hand. She immediately gave him the item while naming the item. I then relatively quickly eliminated my physical prompts and he continued to pick up the picture and give it to Lori.

(Andrew Bondy, personal communication, 28 March 2005)

This is a great example of troubleshooting an intervention by taking what the learner gives you and running with it. It is the mark of the good clinician. Bondy and Frost (1993) knew they had something interesting here and they went on to develop a brilliant new approach to communication intervention.

Back to the future with voice-output communication aids (VOCAs)

After missing the PECS boat, I looked for some other niche in which to specialise. Unexplored territory was difficult to find, even in the rather specialised field of AAC for individuals with developmental and physical disabilities. The answer came when I visited a school one day and saw a bunch of voice-output communication devices sitting up on the shelf. 'Why aren't these things being used?' I asked, and the teacher replied, 'Oh those things. We tried them, but none of the kids know how to use them.' Thinking that they did not know how to use the devices because no one had ever taught them how, I offered to give it a shot. 'Be my guest,' was her reply, and that is how I came to devote so much of my attention to issues surrounding the use of voice-output devices in communication intervention programmes for individuals with developmental disabilities.

Conclusion

Skinner (1956) advised that when you find something interesting, drop everything else and study it. The trick, of course, is to know when you have found something interesting. Because there is so much that I continue to find interesting in communication intervention, it has not been a problem whatsoever to drop other things (such as my administrative duties) and study it. And over the past 25 years, so much of what made it interesting has come from the labs of educational and behavioural psychologists.

References

Bondy, A. S. and Frost, L. A. (1993). Mands across the water: A report on the application of the Picture-Exchange Communication System in Peru. *The Behavior Analyst*, 16: 123–8.

Evans, P. L. C. and Spittle, J. A. (1981). The development and use of a Premack symbol system in improving the communication skills of two children with severe learning difficulties. *Educational Psychology*, 1: 87–99.

Premack, D. (1959). Toward empirical behavior laws: I. Positive reinforcement. *Psychological Review, 66*: 219–33.

Premack, D. (1970). A functional analysis of language. *Journal of the Experimental Analysis of Behavior, 14*: 107–25.

Premack, D. (1976). *Intelligence in ape and man*. Hillsdale, NJ: Lawrence Erlbaum.

Reichle, J., Beukelman, D. R. and Light, J. C. (2002). *Exemplary practices for beginning communicators: Implications for AAC*. Baltimore: Paul H. Brookes.

Savage-Rumbaugh, E. S. (1984). Verbal behavior at a procedural level in the chimpanzee. *Journal of the Experimental Analysis of Behavior, 41*: 223–50.

Schlosser, R. W. (2003). *The efficacy of augmentative and alternative communication: Toward evidence-based practice*. Boston: Academic Press.

Sigafoos, J., Doss, S. and Reichle, J. (1989). Developing mand and tact repertoires in persons with severe developmental disabilities using graphic symbols. *Research in Developmental Disabilities, 10*: 183–200.

Sigafoos, J., Reichle, J., Doss, S., Hall, K. and Pettitt, L. (1990). 'Spontaneous' transfer of stimulus control from tact to mand contingencies. *Research in Developmental Disabilities, 11*: 165–76.

Skinner, B. F. (1956). A case history in scientific method. *American Psychologist, 11*: 221–33.

Skinner, B. F. (1957). *Verbal behavior*. Englewood Cliffs, NJ: Prentice-Hall.

Terrace, H. S. (1979). *Nim*. New York: Knopf.

Chapter 8

Students' approaches to learning and teachers' approaches to teaching in higher education

John T. E. Richardson

The last 30 years have seen considerable developments in our understanding of how students set about learning in higher education. Nowadays, the larger part of my professional work is concerned with exploring and evaluating the student experience (albeit within the distinctive context of distance education), and thus I had little hesitation in identifying this as an area that deserved to be recognised. Moreover, the last 20 years have seen similar developments in our understanding of how teachers set about teaching in higher education. In this chapter, I shall briefly trace the parallel evolution of these two distinctive areas of research.

Approaches to studying in higher education

Interview-based research carried out in Britain and Sweden during the 1970s had identified three predominant approaches to studying in higher education: a deep approach, based upon understanding the meaning of course materials; a surface approach, based upon memorising the course materials for the purposes of assessment; and a strategic approach, based upon obtaining the highest grades. Even so, the same student could exhibit different approaches to studying in different situations. In general, the choice of one approach to studying rather than another appeared to depend upon the content, the context, and the demands of particular tasks (Laurillard 1979; Marton 1976; Ramsden 1979; for a review, see Richardson 2000).

Various questionnaires were developed to measure approaches to studying in larger numbers of students, including the Approaches to Studying Inventory (Entwistle and Ramsden 1983) and the Study Process Questionnaire (Biggs 1987). Investigations using instruments of this sort confirmed that the same students may adopt different approaches, depending upon the demands of different course units (Eley 1992), the quality of the teaching (Vermetten et al. 1999), and the nature of the assessment (Scouller 1998). All these results suggest that one could bring about desirable approaches to studying by appropriate course design, appropriate teaching methods, or appropriate forms of assessment.

This has been confirmed in research studies comparing problem-based learning and traditional, subject-based curricula: students following problem-based curricula are more likely to adopt a deep approach to studying and are less likely to adopt a surface approach to studying (Newble and Clarke 1986; Sadlo and Richardson 2003). In other research, however, interventions aimed at inducing desirable approaches to studying have proved to be largely ineffective (Gibbs 1992; Hambleton *et al.* 1998; Kember *et al.* 1997). Eley (1992) found considerable variation in how different students perceived the requirements of the same courses. One possibility is that the effects of contextual factors are mediated by students' perceptions of their academic environment, and therefore educational interventions will not be effective in changing students' approaches to studying unless they also serve to bring about changes in the students' perceptions.

To measure variations in students' perceptions, Ramsden (1991) devised the Course Experience Questionnaire (CEQ). This contains 30 items in five scales relating to different aspects of effective instruction: good teaching; clear goals and standards; appropriate workload; appropriate assessment; and emphasis on independence. Subsequent research has shown that the CEQ provides a reliable and valid way of monitoring the perceptions of both students and graduates across a variety of disciplines and in several different countries. It has also shown that there is an intimate relationship between students' perceptions of the quality of their courses and the approaches to studying that they adopt on those courses (Richardson 2005).

Conceptions of learning in higher education

Nevertheless, students still vary significantly in their approaches to studying, even when variations in their perceptions of their courses have been taken into account (Sadlo and Richardson 2003). Why should students with the same perceptions of the same course adopt different approaches to studying? One possibility is that students may adopt one approach rather than another, depending on their conceptions of learning and their conceptions of themselves as learners.

To explain why different students adopted different approaches on the same course, Marton (1976) argued that students who adopt a deep approach take an active role and see learning as something that they themselves do, whereas those who adopt a surface approach take a passive role and see learning as something that just happens to them. Nevertheless, conceptions of learning show more variety than this. Säljö (1979) asked 90 people aged between 15 and 73 at institutions of further and higher education in Sweden what 'learning' meant to them. He found five different conceptions (Säljö 1979: 19):

1 Learning as the increase of knowledge
2 Learning as memorising
3 Learning as the acquisition of facts or procedures
4 Learning as the abstraction of meaning
5 Learning as an interpretative process aimed at the understanding of reality.

Van Rossum and Schenk (1984) carried out a study with 69 psychology students at a university in the Netherlands. They asked them to read a short text and then asked them to say how they had approached the task of reading the text and how they approached their studies in general. Van Rossum and Schenk were able to classify the students into Säljö's five conceptions of learning. Most of the students who showed Conceptions 1–3 had used a surface approach to read the text, but most of the students who showed Conceptions 4 and 5 had used a deep approach to read the text. Thus, the approaches to studying that students adopt in particular learning tasks are linked to their conceptions of learning. This provides another reason why educational interventions may be of limited effectiveness: students who hold a reproductive conception of learning through exposure to a subject-based curriculum may simply find it hard to adapt to a more student-centred curriculum (e.g. Newman 2004).

Van Rossum and Taylor (1987) interviewed 91 arts students at a university in the Netherlands. They confirmed the existence of Säljö's five conceptions of learning, but they found a sixth conception that they (Van Rossum and Taylor 1987: 19) characterised as:

6 A conscious process, fuelled by personal interests and directed at obtaining harmony and happiness or changing society.

Van Rossum and Taylor found that men and women were equally likely to hold these various conceptions of learning, but that older students were more likely than younger students to hold the more sophisticated conceptions (Conceptions 4–6).

Morgan et al. (1981) also confirmed the existence of Säljö's five conceptions of learning in 29 students who were taking courses via distance education with the Open University in the United Kingdom. Marton et al. (1993) followed 10 of these students through their studies with the Open University over a period

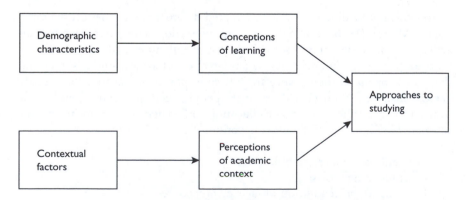

Figure 8.1 An integrated model of students' approaches to studying, conceptions of learning, and perceptions of their academic context.

of six years. In their later years of studying, some showed the sixth conception of learning found by Van Rossum and Taylor, which Marton *et al.* (1993) called 'Changing as a person'. Marton *et al.* (1993) argued that the six conceptions constituted a hierarchy through which students proceeded during the course of their studies in higher education (see also Beaty *et al.* 1997).

Figure 8.1 represents my attempt to integrate what we know about the relationships between students' approaches to studying, their conceptions of learning, and their perceptions of their academic context as a result of the last 25 years' research.

Approaches to teaching in higher education

Research into teachers' approaches to teaching in higher education was directly modelled on the concepts, methods, and findings of research into students' approaches to studying. Trigwell and Prosser (1993) interviewed 24 staff teaching first-year courses in chemistry and physics. They identified five different approaches to teaching among these teachers that were differentiated in terms of their intentions and their teaching strategies: some approaches were teacher-focused and were aimed at the transmission of information to the students; others were student-focused and were aimed at bringing about conceptual change in the students.

Prosser and Trigwell (1993) then developed the Approaches to Teaching Inventory (ATI) to measure approaches to teaching in large numbers of teachers. Trigwell *et al.* (1999) showed that students whose teachers adopted a student-focused approach according to their scores on the ATI were more likely to adopt a deep approach to learning and less likely to adopt a surface approach to learning than students whose teachers adopted a teacher-focused approach. In other words, a student-focused approach to teaching engenders more desirable approaches to studying in the students than does a teacher-focused approach.

Prosser and Trigwell (1997) devised the Perceptions of the Teaching Environment Inventory to measure various aspects of the perceived teaching context. They found a close relationship between teachers' perceptions of their teaching context and their approaches to teaching according to their scores on the ATI. In particular, teachers who adopted a student-focused approach were more likely than teachers who adopted a teacher-focused approach to report that their departments valued teaching, that their class sizes were not too large, and that they had control over what was taught and how it was taught.

Conceptions of teaching in higher education

Even so, when they are confronted with the same teaching context, different teachers still adopt different approaches to teaching. Some researchers have ascribed this to constitutional attributes of the teachers themselves: to different styles of lecturing, styles of thinking, or personality characteristics. However, others have argued that different approaches to teaching reflect different underlying conceptions of teaching. Indeed, interview-based investigations have identified a number of different conceptions of teaching. Kember (1997) reviewed these investigations and suggested that most of them converged on five different conceptions:

1 Teaching as imparting information
2 Teaching as transmitting structured knowledge
3 Teaching as an interaction between the teacher and the student
4 Teaching as facilitating understanding on the part of the student
5 Teaching as bringing about conceptual change and intellectual development in the student.

Many researchers assume that teachers' conceptions of teaching in higher education change with experience, usually from being more teacher-centred and content-orientated to being more student-centred and learning-orientated, and that this will inevitably have benign consequences for the teachers' performance in the classroom. There is, in fact, little evidence that teachers' conceptions of teaching really do develop with increasing teaching experience (Norton *et al.* 2005). There is also little evidence that conceptions of teaching change as a result of formal training, although Ho (2000) found some promising results from a teaching development programme that was specifically aimed at bringing about conceptual change.

Surveys of university teachers in the United States have found that beliefs about teaching vary markedly across different disciplines, and that these variations are related to the teachers' beliefs about the nature of the discipline that they are teaching. In a questionnaire-based study, Norton *et al.* (2005) found that conceptions of teaching varied across different disciplines, but that teachers teaching the same disciplines at different institutions had relatively similar conceptions of teaching.

Trigwell and Prosser (1996) compared approaches to teaching and conceptions of teaching in their 24 teachers of courses in first-year chemistry and physics. They found that teachers who held a particular conception of teaching tended to adopt a commensurate approach to teaching. Thus, teachers who hold a student-centred and learning-orientated conception of teaching are more likely to adopt a student-focused approach to teaching. So, if institutions of higher education want their teachers to adopt a more student-focused approach to teaching, they need to ensure that their teachers hold a commensurate conception of teaching – and a brief training course will not be sufficient to achieve this.

However, in Trigwell and Prosser's (1996) study, more than half of the teachers described approaches to teaching that were less learner-focused and more teacher-focused than would have been expected from their reported conceptions of teaching. This drift towards teacher-focused approaches to teaching and away from learner-focused approaches to teaching was confirmed in the

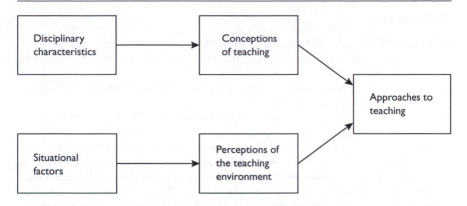

Figure 8.2 An integrated model of teachers' approaches to teaching, conceptions of teaching, and perceptions of the teaching environment.

study by Norton *et al.* (2005). It suggests that contextual factors tend to frustrate teachers' intended approaches to teaching (e.g. Gibbs 1992). Senior staff who hold traditional, teacher-focused conceptions of teaching may raise issues about standards and coverage of the curriculum (Estes 1999), or else the students themselves may conspire to induce the teachers to adopt a more didactic approach (Newman 2004).

Figure 8.2 represents my attempt to integrate what we know about the relationships between teachers' approaches to teaching, their conceptions of teaching, and their perceptions of their teaching environment as a result of the last 15 years' research.

Conclusion

Research into learning and teaching in higher education over the last 25 years has provided a variety of concepts, methods, and findings that are of both theoretical interest and practical relevance. For instance, it has provided a range of tools that can be exploited for developing our understanding of learning and teaching in particular contexts as well as for assessing and enhancing the student experience on particular courses and programmes. Of course, the teachers constitute an important part of the learning context for the students, and the students in turn constitute an important part of the teaching environment for the teachers. Regardless of the changes that may impact on higher education across the world during the next 25 years, future research needs to aim at illuminating the interplay between the view of student learning shown in Figure 8.1 and the view of teaching shown in Figure 8.2.

References

Beaty, E., Dall'Alba, G. and Marton, F. (1997). The personal experience of learning in higher education: Changing views and enduring perspectives. In P. Sutherland (ed.), *Adult learning: A reader.* London: Kogan Page, 150–65.

Biggs, J. B. (1987). *Student approaches to learning and studying.* Melbourne: Australian Council for Educational Research.

Eley, M. G. (1992). Differential adoption of study approaches within individual students. *Higher Education, 23*: 231–54.

Entwistle, N. J. and Ramsden, P. (1983). *Understanding student learning.* London: Croom Helm.

Estes, D. M. (1999, August). 'Issues in problem-based learning'. Paper presented at the annual meeting of the National Council of Professors of Educational Administration, Jackson Hole, WY.

Gibbs, G. (1992). *Improving the quality of student learning.* Bristol, UK: Technical and Educational Services.

Hambleton, I. R., Foster, W. H. and Richardson, J. T. E. (1998). Improving student learning using the personalised system of instruction. *Higher Education, 35*: 187–203.

Ho, A. S. P. (2000). A conceptual change approach to staff development: A model for programme design. *International Journal for Academic Development, 5*: 30–41.

Kember, D. (1997). A reconceptualisation of the research into university academics' conceptions of teaching. *Learning and Instruction, 7*: 255–75.

Kember, D., Charlesworth, M., Davies, H., McKay, J. and Stott, V. (1997). Evaluating the effectiveness of educational innovations: Using the Study Process Questionnaire to show that meaningful learning occurs. *Studies in Educational Evaluation, 23*: 141–57.

Laurillard, D. (1979). The processes of student learning. *Higher Education, 8*: 395–409.

Marton, F. (1976). What does it take to learn? Some implications of an alternative view of learning. In N. Entwistle (ed.), *Strategies for research and development in higher education.* Amsterdam: Swets and Zeitlinger, 32–42.

Marton, F., Dall'Alba, G. and Beaty, E. (1993). Conceptions of learning. *International Journal of Educational Research, 19*: 277–300.

Morgan, A., Gibbs, G. and Taylor, E. (1981). *What do Open University students initially understand about learning?* Milton Keynes, UK: The Open University, Institute of Educational Technology.

Newble, D. J. and Clarke, R. M. (1986). The approaches to studying of students in a traditional and in an innovative problem-based medical school. *Medical Education, 20*: 267–73.

Newman, M. (2004). *Problem-based learning: An exploration of the method and evaluation of its effectiveness in a continuing nursing education programme.* London: Middlesex University.

Norton, L., Richardson, J. T. E., Hartley, J., Newstead, S. and Mayes, J. (2005). Teachers' beliefs and intentions concerning teaching in higher education. *Higher Education, 50*: 537–71.

Prosser, M. and Trigwell, K. (1993). Development of an Approaches to Teaching question-naire. *Research and Development in Higher Education, 15*: 468–73.

Prosser, M. and Trigwell, K. (1997). Relations between perceptions of the teaching environment and approaches to teaching. *British Journal of Educational Psychology, 67*: 25–35.

Ramsden, P. (1979). Student learning and perceptions of the academic environment. *Higher Education, 8*: 411–27.

Ramsden, P. (1991). A performance indicator of teaching quality in higher education: The Course Experience Questionnaire. *Studies in Higher Education, 16*: 129–50.

Richardson, J. T. E. (2000). *Researching student learning: Approaches to studying in campus-based and distance education*. Buckingham, UK: SRHE and Open University Press.

Richardson, J. T. E. (2005). Students' perceptions of academic quality and approaches to studying in distance education. *British Educational Research Journal, 31*: 7–27.

Sadlo, G. and Richardson, J. T. E. (2003). Approaches to studying and perceptions of the academic environment in students following problem-based and subject-based curricula. *Higher Education Research and Development, 22*: 253–74.

Säljö, R. (1979). *Learning in the learner's perspective: I. Some common-sense assumptions* (Report no. 76). Göteborg: University of Göteborg, Institute of Education.

Scouller, K. (1998). The influence of assessment method on students' learning approaches: Multiple choice question examination versus assignment essay. *Higher Education, 35*: 453–72.

Trigwell, K. and Prosser, M. (1993). Approaches adopted by teachers of first year university science courses. *Research and Development in Higher Education, 14*: 223–8.

Trigwell, K. and Prosser, M. (1996). Changing approaches to teaching: A relational perspective. *Studies in Higher Education, 21*: 275–84.

Trigwell, K., Prosser, M. and Waterhouse, F. (1999). Relations between teachers' approaches to teaching and students' approaches to learning. *Higher Education, 37*: 57–70.

Van Rossum, E. J. and Schenk, S. M. (1984). The relationship between learning conception, study strategy and learning outcome. *British Journal of Educational Psychology, 54*: 73–83.

Van Rossum, E. and Taylor, I. P. (1987, April). 'The relationship between conceptions of learning and good teaching: A scheme of cognitive development'. Paper presented at the annual meeting of the American Educational Research Association, Washington, DC.

Vermetten, Y. J., Lodewijks, H. G. and Vermunt, J. D. (1999). Consistency and variability of learning strategies in different university courses. *Higher Education, 37*: 1–21.

Chapter 9

Reflections on the database of educational psychology and effective teaching research

Gregory C. R. Yates

'These research findings are just obvious,' glares the critic. On the receiving end of such criticism, the seminar presenter feels a mixture of anguish and momentary worthlessness. Can it be the case that educational researchers, especially those whose base draws upon the discipline of scientific psychology, spend years striving to advance propositions already known to all thinking people? Were such notions known already to the intelligent person in the street even at the time our great-grandparents were alive? If what we do is validate truisms, then are we not wasting our energies? Houston (1983: 208) stated this cogently: 'A great many of psychology's principles are self-evident. One gets the uneasy feeling that we have been dealing with the obvious but did not know it.'

The present writer can recall several such moments of unease. For example, there was a seminar based on data from my initial degree programme. In a simple experimental design, young children had been asked to make choices between small immediate prizes and larger rewards available after a week (Yates 1974). Modelling and persuasion constituted the independent variables. Brief videotaped teacher modelling (i.e. behavioural delay choices) and verbal persuasion (teacher figure providing good reasons to delay) had equal effects on the children's subsequent choice patterns, shifting responding from around 50 per cent to 70 per cent delay preferences. But when the teacher both modelled and provided good reasons, the level shifted to about 90 per cent, indicating additive effects. At the seminar, various critics noted the findings as (a) obvious, and (b) in conflict with Piagetian theory. A strange thing for a young graduate's findings to be seen simultaneously as obvious and at variance with one of the field's major statements.

Another time, I was dismantling test equipment, talking with a parent of a child who had participated in a project into young children's delay ability (Yates *et al.* 1981). The parent quizzed me intelligently about the central hypothesis. Against my better judgement, I disclosed that we were wanting to establish that 'thinking happy thoughts' would be a mental strategy young children could use to help them to wait in a boring room, in order to maximise the number of available prizes. The experimental procedure had been developed earlier by Walter Mischel, and would later be cited as the marshmallow experiment in the best-selling *Emotional Intelligence* (Goleman 1995). The parent told me this was so obvious. Of course happy thoughts will enable people to wait. She could have told us this without having to do an experiment. Such a silly thing, to conduct research into the obvious. Oddly enough, we may have even validated this parent's perspective several years later, when investigating young children's metacognitive awareness of delay of gratification strategies (Yates *et al.* 1987). We administered a mock test to 4-, 6-, and 8-year-olds. The percentage of children who were able to tell us, relatively unprompted, of mental strategies that would enable them to defer gratification increased across age levels, from 12 per cent, to 18 per cent, to 47 per cent. And when we asked a direct yes/ no prompt, 'Would happy thoughts enable you to wait longer?' then levels rose from 66 per cent in 4-year-olds, to 90 per cent in 6-year-olds, to 93 per cent for the 8-year-old children.

One first-line defence, open to all researchers, is to note that even when laypeople appear to be aware that variables will relate to each other, it still takes research to expose the magnitude of relationships, or to map the complexities and interactions that exist. For example, although TV viewing is unhealthy in terms of child development indices, viewing of less than an hour a day may not appear to produce negative effects. Such knowledge can come only from research into putatively obvious relationships.

Returning to the personal level, however, the obviousness critique is one that has accompanied me many times when I have been speaking about the field of teacher effectiveness and its major findings. It is disquieting to present clear and informative research findings and then be informed that you have articulated what teachers all knew anyway. Before discussing this aspect further, however, it is important to examine some of these specific findings.

The research base of effective teaching

If we define effective teaching in terms of the relationship between teacher behaviour and student learning, then a strong proposition stands out: the dynamics of effective teaching are well documented within scientific reports. A large body of data provides a coherent picture of how classroom teachers help students acquire knowledge and skills. Stated simply, there are documented link-ages between aspects of teacher behaviour and how students later perform upon measures that indicate successful learning has taken place. There is considerable debate about how teachers might use research findings, and about what type of research addresses classroom agendas (Nuthall 2004), but the existence of a scientific database is not in doubt.

Since the body of data is extensive, it can be difficult for reviewers to group findings into coherent orderings. Groupings made by different reviewers will alter slightly, in accord with parsing practices. The present writer tends to group findings in terms of natural skill acquisition being the fundamental outcome goal. Skill development, through accumulating high levels of task-related success, is seen as the final common path of the instructional process. A synthesis of major findings is shown in Table 9.1, which is based chiefly upon a number of reviews (Berliner 1984; Brophy and Good 1986; Gage 1985; Rosenshine and Stevens 1986; Stallings and Kaskowitz 1974; Wang et al. 1993; Yates and Yates 1990).

Table 9.1 Synthesis from process-product studies: fundamental traits of highly effective classrooms

1 Management structures	• A positive and proactive teaching style; use of authoritative statements, i.e. rules are specified, and expected procedures are both numerous and genuinely taught; the system is known to all parties. • Response consequences are overt, predictable, and fair. • Stimulus controls are established and defended; teachers negotiate with the class as to the meaning of certain subtle body-language cues.
2 Opportunities to learn and respond (input and output factors)	• Genuine curriculum coverage, allowed by generous time allocations. • High level of teacher input, and use of resources, books, etc. • High level of expected output, with opportunities to respond actively and frequently over time; practice is distributed over time.
3 Academic expectations	• Goals expressed directly in academic terms; teacher talks about and enthuses over these goals with abundant use of the 'can-do' rhetoric. • Expectations conveyed that every child will do well on overt indices such as tests, projects, and portfolios. • Teacher is a clear academic model in traits such as reading, thinking, love of knowledge, inquisitiveness, and enjoyment of learning.
4 Instructional scaffolding	• Use of the user-friendly direct instruction teaching cycle to teach both content and process (i.e. what and how to think). • Active monitoring of student responses allows both regular assessment and knowledge of when to reduce teacher input; high frequency of questions used along with aspects such as wait-time. • Teaching strategies which allow for remediation, reteaching, or individualisation, as normal and natural classroom routines.
5 Skill development via accumulating academic learning time	• Initial learning is seen as fragile and inflexible, so repetition is programmed to develop skill, and allow the skill to become accessible. • Skill acquisition requires high levels of engagement on curriculum materials, accumulated over time. • Engagement translates into responding at a high level of success under relatively independent practice conditions. • Academic learning time (ALT) presages individual achievement gains and self-efficacy (i.e. task-specific confidence) on future indices.

Effective teaching research has drawn on several experimental designs; a key one has been the process–product paradigm, in the form as used in the decade following 1974. Arguably, the process–product work managed by Jane Stallings was amongst the most spectacular, large-scale, well-run, and important pieces of classroom-based research ever conducted. Her work gave rise to the central focus on engagement time and opportunity to learn as key factors underlying skill development within classrooms. By the mid-1980s the large-scale, highly expensive, process–product design had run its course, and different designs emerged from the basic functional model (see Berliner (2004a) on this specific point). But the basic research findings remain as strong statements describing natural relationships between teacher behaviour and student development. The literature review contributed by Brophy and Good in the 1986 *Handbook of Research on Teaching* stands as both a historical document and a statement of the remarkable scientific productivity associated with the process–product research at that time.

From around the mid-1980s, teacher effectiveness research used designs which were cheaper and easier to handle. One highly productive design was the expert–novice contrast, as borrowed directly from the discipline of psychology. Over the past 20 years a remarkable portrait of the expert teacher has emerged, depicted, by way of synthesis, in Table 9.2. Substantially, this information is based upon a number of research and literature reviews (Berliner 1986, 1994, 2004b; Borko and Livingston 1989; Hogan *et al.* 2003; Leinhardt and Greeno 1986; Sternberg and Horvath 1995). There is considerable overlap between the content of Tables 9.1 and 9.2. This convergence is especially interesting since the level of analysis changed dramatically between research designs.

The information portrayed in Table 9.1 stems from measures of behaviour, typically expressed as statistical correlations between teacher actions and student learning gains (i.e. test–retest differences) aggregated across many classrooms. The power of this approach lies in the analysis of trends, whereby individual patterns are submerged and the unit of analysis is the action, rather than the person. This type of research identifies effective behaviours, rather than effective practition-ers. In fact, one common misconception was that the process–product model identified effective teachers, which of course it did not.

The information in Table 9.2 stems from comparisons of groups of individuals, often based on case studies, with the assumption that the differences obtained are worthy of note. The power of this type of research stems from the fact that it maps a few carefully selected participants. Expert–novice research generally will use qualitative methods rather than statistical aggregates.

Given these divergent methods, the convergence in findings across experimental designs is remarkable. It becomes possible to suggest that an individual's expertise (having localised, situated, and bounded qualities) builds directly upon some of the more generic teacher attributes that were identified through statistical means in the earlier process–product era.

A sensible picture emerges. Substantial support is given to David Berliner's

Table 9.2 Findings from teacher expertise research: qualities experts possess

1 Curriculum knowledge	• Extensive pedagogical knowledge (e.g. multiple ways to teach the same content).
	• Planning appears cursory and brief, but actually involves chunking many tasks, activities, and draws upon a rich improvisational repertoire.
	• Continually communicating goals, and using highly focused, task-related, goal-driven feedback.
2 Experts have complex stimulus control methods	• Scores of routines actively taught; classes are remarkably constant and predictable; the management system is strongly defended.
	• There is a subtle but complex system of cuing going on using the face, eyes, hands, voice, and body; automaticity means these teachers are often unaware of such gestures, but their students learn to 'read' the cues and respond quickly and appropriately.
3 Ability to explain	• Clarity in speech coupled with excellent use of mental modelling principles.
	• Remarkably complete explanations executed quickly, then students move into active practice under strong guidance.
	• Acute use of student feedback to gauge information flow; the experts have characteristic patterns of eye gaze with which they actively sample for certain types of information.
4 Advanced information processing skills	• Laboratory studies disclose experts' superior skills in the areas of memory and encoding of classroom events that are relevant to instruction, but poorer memory of irrelevant factors (such as students' clothing); attention is thus highly selective.
	• Experts have developed schemata enabling them to read classroom life visually in great depth.

(1987) contention that a 'simple theory' of classroom instruction based around notions of engagement time and academic learning time (ALT) holds 'great heuristic value' (Berliner 1987: 93) as a descriptive model of how teachers are implicated in facilitating students' classroom learning. One version of such a simple descriptive theory is given in Figure 9.1, as based upon a teacher education model.

Learning to teach: what the research can tell you

In learning to function as a classroom teacher you will acquire two sets of skills: (a) managerial skills that enable you to control students' behavioural and attentional patterns; and (b) instructional skills which enable you to convey the information that students will require. Your students need this information since

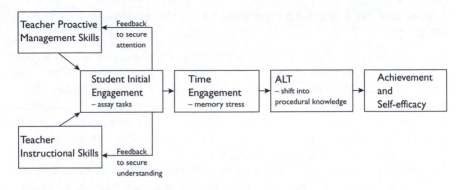

Figure 9.1 Sequence of effects in effective teaching.

there are 'school-type' tasks to be performed. These academic tasks are different from the things that students perform outside the classroom. You need to use high levels of instruction, encouragement, reassurance, and confidence building to ensure engagement. Initial engagements are contrived and will not result in enduring learning unless the students themselves assume responsibility for entering the academic game. They must envisage the desired outcomes, which will often take the form of products they will leave behind for evaluation. Thus, students' attention is drawn to identifying immediate outcomes, and assaying the types of knowledge they need to accomplish the necessary goals.

One crucial determinant in the process is their memory capability. Students must assay task demands and rely on their recall of what took place during instructional phases. Recalled information enables a student to engage with curriculum materials and begin the shift from declarative knowledge acquisition to procedural and conditional knowledge (i.e. the knowing how and when aspects). Some of the information needed to perform will come from other students, but a large percentage of the necessary information stems directly from the students' recall of teacher-supplied information.

Although initial task engagement involves somewhat tentative cognitive efforts, the provision of scaffolds, reinforcement feedback, and observable products serves to enhance students' levels of self-efficacy. One key factor underlying the process is described as engagement time. This can be defined more precisely as academic learning time, once success levels are considered. Through accumulating high levels of academic learning time on tasks aligned well with curriculum goals, students become skilful, resourceful, and confident. A process that begins with what the teacher does is then completed with a high level of student autonomy and self-regulation.

Good and bad ways to use teacher effectiveness findings

When discussing this body of work, it is crucial to differentiate the notion of the 'effective teacher' (indexed by student learning criteria) from that of the 'good teacher' (indexed by professional respect and humanistic criteria). Teacher effectiveness research has given rise to a well-replicated body of evidence highlighting the importance of a set of functional variables within classroom practice. But it would be a mistake to hold that such specifications translate into quick rating scales or checklists of 'important things'. We must not lose sight of the fact that the process-product design itself used low-inference measures that are, most definitively, not amenable to quick visual inspection or other superficial instant judgements. One is not entitled to walk into a teacher's classroom and match what can be seen readily against an artificial checklist based upon someone's interpretation of teacher effectiveness research.

There can be indicators in some classrooms signalling that enduring learning is unlikely (e.g. blatant lack of stimulus controls in management). But the clearest indicator is actual student ALT itself. This suggests an interesting twist: teacher effectiveness research itself implies that the primary indicator of effective teaching is located at the level of the student, rather than of the teacher. This is one of the implications stemming from the skills acquisition model. Indicators of effective teaching stem not from overt measures of teaching, but from more indirect measures based on student engagement, now seen as the final common path which presages achievement gain.

It is possible to envisage situations in which, initially, a teacher appears to be displaying many positive aspects, for example using strong levels of directive teaching, but, in fact, strong learning gains are not taking place due to the failure of students engaging with curriculum materials with high levels of ALT accumulated under relatively independent practice conditions. Indeed, many of the case studies of expert teachers comment upon the necessary orchestration of practices. Such orchestration of multiple practices hinges upon knowing multiple ways to promote key goals.

In the Vygotskian sense, teaching skill implies knowing both how to erect scaffolds to support student learning and, equally importantly, how to remove scaffolds gently. In behavioural theory, instruction ought to be clear, directive, and user-friendly, but then it must be faded and gently abolished as responsibility is shifted to the student. Knowing how to achieve this demands a very high level of professional skill. It should come as no surprise to discover that the research basis of psychology indicates that expertise hinges upon between 5 and 10 years of successful experience, and this specification is believed to apply also to classroom teaching (Berliner 1986, 2004b).

The body of teacher effectiveness research does not define a template against which individual teachers can be evaluated and, to my knowledge, no researcher within this area has made such a claim (see Brophy (1988) on this issue).

Inevitably, teacher evaluation hinges on many aspects of performance involving personal and moral criteria, whereas teacher effectiveness studies specifically target student achievement gain. The issues involved in teacher evaluation are complex and multifaceted. They are described cogently in a significant paper by Dunkin (1997). Similarly, Darling-Hammond and Sclan (1992) provide a balanced discussion of the dangers of attempting to translate teacher effectiveness findings directly into supervisory practices. More recently, Berliner (2005: 205) has commented upon the 'near impossibility of testing for teacher quality'.

At best, teacher effectiveness research provides some insight into how certain teachers have been successful in the past in achieving a narrow range of achievement goals, given constraints placed upon them by the nature of the employment context. But an idealised template is not possible, and any attempt to reduce the complexity of classroom interaction to a box-ticking exercise will not work. The value of the research lies in its use as a basis for serious personal reflection, for recognising the importance of key variables, and for the rethinking of pedagogical goals.

Besides personal development applications, teacher effectiveness research can be respected for its value in staff development and in teacher education. Brophy (1988), for example, has promoted the notion that teacher effects data help to define a viable 'starter set' of knowledge of considerable value to teachers in training. Of especial note are the skills of classroom management researched and described, using process-product designs, by Carolyn Evertson (Evertson 1987; Good and Brophy 2002). Instructional skills have been thoroughly described by Barak Rosenshine (Rosenshine and Stevens 1986; Good and Brophy 2002). Such analyses provide important and fundamental knowledge for the beginning teacher. For example, novices' attention can be drawn to issues such as the need for clear speech, the need for the careful fading of instructions, or the use of wait-time within interactions as factors to work on during training experiences.

Responses from teacher workshops

A remarkably diverse range of views and criticisms, both positive and negative, is associated with talking openly about the teacher effectiveness research base. From personal experience, some of the negative responses have included: (a) it is all obvious; (b) this is wrong since it conflicts with constructionism; (c) this is simply a technical or behaviouristic description of how low-level objectives might be attained through rote; (d) it is too positivistic; and similarly, (e) it provides a picture too simplistic to reflect complexities of classrooms (e.g. different students respond differently, hence attempts to define effective practices must be misguided).

At times, it is possible to identify some almost comic reactions, such as the following. A local teachers' journal published a statement from an apparent postmodernist saying that my work was 'serving to fashion instruments for the subjugation of teachers and students'. Several years ago I spoke to a teachers' group and was approached by three people from one location who told me that teacher effectiveness research would not apply to their school since they were 'not into test scores'. Would such people send their relatives to a hospital that did not believe in curing disease? Would they feel it appropriate for rich people to tell poor people that money is irrelevant? Shanahan (2002) noted a similar incident when communicating findings from the reading research literature and being told by one teacher, 'I disagree with that' (Shanahan 2002: 15), as if research findings invite personal choice, the issue being to locate one that you like.

Several times I have been told that the teacher effectiveness findings were at variance with what was taught at most Australian teacher training institutes. One teacher confided that she had developed into a highly directive teacher but had kept this 'a secret'. Another wrote to me saying that if she had known about this teacher effectiveness research at her training college, she would not have spent the initial five years of her career 'messing around'.

Another teacher informed me that the goal at his school was to raise self-esteem rather than academic achievement. I replied that this was a very strange goal for an educational institute, since self-esteem is not a quality most students lack. And worse, high levels of self-esteem are linked with many negative character traits such as narcissism, aggressiveness, overly inflated self-assessments, and risk taking, and with adolescent experimentation with drugs and sexual behaviour (Baumeister *et al.* 2003; Emler 2001). High self-esteem is associated with the ingroup bias effect (i.e. favouritism for 'my side', and prejudice against others seen as different) in a manner surely conflicting with wider humanistic goals (Aberson *et al.* 2000).

Further, it is known that self-esteem reflects a person's assessment of capability within life domains that are important and valued (Harter 1993). Should a teacher convince low-achieving students that school achievement is largely irrelevant in life (i.e. this domain does not matter), then he would be able to help them raise their self-esteem relatively more easily. Such a strategy could strongly assist self-esteem, at least within the immediate short term. But the cost could be that of deskilling and demotivating the student body and rendering them difficult to employ within a modern society. I inquired of this person if he thought that helping students believe that school achievement was unimportant might make for a viable study into self-esteem enhancement. But no reply was forthcoming.

'But this is all so obvious'

It is easy to undermine and dismiss the apparent criticisms of teacher effectiveness as listed in the above section. A valuable article debunking the fallacies behind such criticisms was contributed by Gage and Needels (1989). But from a personal view, the more disarming of the various criticisms come in the form, 'This is all so obvious.' This specific comment is disquieting, as the critic appears to be agreeing with and accepting of the research-derived information.

Of course, students learn more when their teachers teach them skills directly. Of course, students learn more when paying attention to relevant tasks and when they can remember the given instructions. Of course, knowledge is acquired slowly. Of course, learning is advantaged through spending more time on tasks. But did we not know this already?

One reply to such critics is to agree with them, in part, but then add that not all professionals share such a view. A consensual view of the variables underlying effective teaching methods has never emerged in the past. For example, in her final book Jean Chall (2000) described the history of tension between traditional and progressive education within the American context over the past century. It is possible that anyone who asserts that teacher effectiveness findings are obvious is exhibiting the mental error described within cognitive psychology as the false consensus effect (Gilovich 1991; Pronin *et al.* 2002). This reflects one type of egocentric belief: the belief that others construe the world in more or less the same way as oneself. Tom Gilovich and others have documented how this bias, as a natural mental default, can be quickly activated and leads people to make a host of faulty assessments and decisions.

It is notable that data from two empirical surveys directly challenge the notion that research into teaching has produced obvious findings. In separate studies, Townsend (1995) and Wong (1995) presented statements derived from process–product studies to teachers and student teachers, and requested them to rate how obvious the statements were. But in both studies there was a twist. The item statements were presented in either of two ways, specifically either with the correct finding, or with its opposite. For example, Wong's ninth item was expressed in two ways: students were found to get better scores on achievement tests in classes with either (a) more teacher control and less student freedom to select learning experiences, or (b) less teacher control and more student freedom to select learning experiences. In both studies, the overall finding was that participants rated the stated propositions (both the correct and incorrect versions) as equally obvious. In fact, for Wong's item above, the correct form (a) was rated as less obvious that the incorrect form (b).

Overall, statements that findings in the social sciences are obvious ones need to be treated with a healthy scepticism (Gage 1985, 1991). Information presented clearly and sensibly, and which is consistent with well-established principles, inevitably will appear obvious in hindsight. Such perception represents a normal and natural perceptual defence (i.e. a private assimilative thought). But an individual's private response does not constitute an evaluation of scientific worth. Further, in some contexts we can interpret such responses as instances of two known effects: the hindsight bias effect (Gilovich 1991), and the knowledge projection hypothesis (Stanovich 2003).

Obviousness as ego defence

Your existing knowledge base enables you to make rough predictions, or projections, about what is the most likely outcome of a set of contingencies. When a researcher produces a set of data that inherently makes sense, then the data set embodies 'truth'. Obviousness is a hindsight perception or the confirmation that you really knew the truth all along. Incoming data might just possess a threat, especially in the case of data stemming from a source claiming a level of authority. But this threat fails to materialise. The new data can be seen to fit rather well. The fit then serves two functions: confirming the self's command of knowledge, wisdom, and intelligence, and establishing how facile it was of another person or agency, using the cover of research, to try to upset the self's worldview. Labelling the new input as obvious neatly serves two essential self-functions with the same stroke.

For the most part, this private perception of obviousness is natural, facile, and reinforcing. But it can be made at the expense of intellectual honesty. When one is asked about the likelihood of known events, given a set of known conditions, people typically overestimate the extent to which the known outcome was predictable. This effect, referred to as hindsight bias, is well known to researchers who study mental errors (Gilovich 1991). Hindsight bias is the tendency for people with outcome knowledge to believe that they would have predicted the outcome. After learning of the occurrence of an event, people exaggerate the extent to which they had, or could have, foreseen the likelihood of its occurrence.

There are several explanations for the occurrence of hindsight bias. The position outlined so far is consistent with the notion of egotism or ego-protection. Another viable theory resides in the process of automatic memory updating. As information is assimilated, it may update the knowledge store remarkably quickly. People are generally unaware of how their information got there, and so presume automatically that it was known all along (Hoffrage *et al.* 2000).

Within modern cognitive psychology, both theories, defensive egotism and automatic memory updating, are supported by the available data. There is also a very rich set of studies demonstrating that people overestimate their knowledge or competencies most acutely when they are lacking in the relevant knowledge or competencies (Kruger and Dunning 1999). Indeed, hindsight bias effects have been found to be relatively stronger in less competent individuals, or novices, and to be attenuated somewhat in experts (Hertwig *et al.* 2003). Hence, whenever anyone declares, 'But, such findings are obvious,' one possible, albeit inadvisable, reply would be:

> This feeling that it is obvious stems from your elevated ego. You may be so naturally egocentric you believe others share your views. Believing such things are obvious is one way to protect your ego, but it also suggests a level of faulty memory processing. Furthermore, such perceptions on your

part could relate to the possibility that you presume to know far more than you actually do.

The role of prior knowledge

Categorising new information as obvious indicates quick and shallow (as distinct from slow and deep) mental processing. Such perception reflects the mind's use of a knowledge projection process. Knowledge projection is a normal and natural process in which prior knowledge is accessed and used as the basis of decision making in a manner that is fast, automatic, and unconscious (Bargh and Chartrand 1999). For the most part, one's prior knowledge is the basis of sensible and adaptive responding. Prior knowledge is the basis of understanding and becomes the point from which comprehension is launched (Yates and Chandler 1991). Prior knowledge is secure, both cognitively and emotionally. But security is purchased with cost.

The knowledge projection process brings with it cognitive liabilities. Stanovich (2003) refers to the collection of such liabilities as the fundamental computational bias. This bias is accounted for by the failure to disengage prior knowledge within a context wherein it leads to poor decision making. The specific liabilities identified by Stanovich are: (a) the tendency to contextualise a problem when the problem calls for abstract and context-free rule applications; (b) the tendency to socialise a problem when it ought not implicate interpersonal or social cues; (c) the tendency to see deliberative patterns within random events; and (d) the tendency to use narrative modes of thought (such as idiosyncratic stories) rather than abstract paradigms or statistical information.

Within the field of cognitive psychology, there exists a wealth of data indicating that human judgements are subject to a wide range of natural errors and biases (Gilovich 1991; Gilovich *et al.* 2002; Kahneman *et al.* 1982; Stanovich 2003). But Stanovich, in particular, draws attention to the biases that stem from one's prior knowledge and familiarity within an area. It is these in particular that make it difficult for educators to relate to the scientific database of effective teaching. How can one relate to scientifically advanced statistical statements if one has 20 years of personal data that also bear upon similar matters? The cognitive biases literature suggests that there are possible dangers in responding to such 'familiar' material too quickly.

What if the teacher effectiveness findings are not obvious?

In common with much social science research, teacher effectiveness findings stem from variations within the natural world. But if such findings are obvious, why should such variance exist (Gage 1985)? If it is obvious that students learn from accumulating time on task, following on from clear instruction, then why do all teachers not apply such knowledge equally well? How can such variations occur given such a level of consensus? Well, there is another view that can be articulated as follows: the teacher effectiveness findings as shown in Tables 9.1 and 9.2 represent phenomena which cannot be mapped by an individual observer. As such, it becomes logically nonsensical to describe them as obvious.

At my home institute, end-of-semester examinations are held routinely for teacher education students. The following question is embedded in one such paper: 'What are the traits of highly effective teachers?' In 2004 I sampled responses on this item from 100 students, all university graduates from a range of disciplines, undergoing training to become teachers. The discrepancy between what was written by these well-qualified candidates and the content of Tables 9.1 and 9.2 was striking. Not one of the 100 papers sampled was allocated full marks on that item. Not a single student cited the effective teacher's ability to articulate clearly, or to get students to maintain time engagement. The majority of responses described the more humanistic side of teaching, articulating the belief that effective teachers are warm, friendly, positive human beings. But such traits can be considered basic for all teachers, rather than traits associated specifically with achievement effectiveness criteria.

Similarly, we have asked small groups of teachers in professional development workshops to identify traits associated with effective teaching and expertise. In general, the experienced teachers do far better than our students. But in general, their responses still do not cover the content of Tables 9.1 and 9.2. However, when these tables are then presented, there is immediate recognition and wide agreement. Is it the case that the information in the tables is so obvious that teachers and trainee teachers simply did not believe it worth stating? Is this an example of the base-rate neglect phenomenon? As a cognitive bias, such neglect reflects the fact that people often fail to take into account important cues, such as frequency or probability, because attention is focused on less relevant aspects of the problem space, such as topicality or availability (Gilovich 1991).

Such general failure to articulate, unprompted, some of the key aspects of effective teaching almost certainly reflects base-rate neglect, another of the well-documented biases described within the cognitive psychology literature (e.g. Kahneman et al., 1982). We can advance this idea since teachers do appear to recognise the viability of Tables 9.1 and 9.2 once these have been sighted. But there is another, perhaps stronger, factor operating. It is impossible for any one unaided human observer to assay functional relationships that exist over time within complex environments. Necessarily, individual perceptions are limited. Our worldview is narrow, and not a universal one. It is virtually axiomatic within modern psychology to note that we perceive patterns because we believe they are there, rather than because they exist. There are many demonstrations within the psychological literature of illusory correlations and other occasions when human observers deduce patterns automatically from chaotic data inputs (Gilovich 1991). Arguably, the mind is set up to perceive meaningful, but frequently incorrect, patterns. Such patterns will be found in a manner that is, in part, independent of a sensory database, with many theorists arguing that such human tendencies represent the operation of fundamental evolutionary mechanisms.

Hence, we can speculate that people deduce beliefs about the characteristics of effective teachers as a result of knowledge projective tendencies. However, it is questionable what type of data might be available to an individual to help them make such an assessment. Individuals do not have access to formally collected data. One can observe that students engage with their studies, but how much observed engagement would be deemed sufficient before an individual mind would be entitled to deduce the existence of a correlative pattern? And exactly what perceivable variable would qualify as a correlate? What cue indicates what effect? As suggested earlier, walking into any one classroom will not provide the outside observer with a sufficient set of data upon which to advance presumptions about teacher effectiveness indicators.

In essence, it becomes gratuitous to label statistical findings as obvious when the individual does not have access to a database upon which a given relationship could be based, and does not possess a mental process that would allow such a relationship to be expressed within appropriately descriptive language. If there is a correlation between school achievement and time engagement, then no one can claim to have 'seen' this relationship within any perceivable datum.

Such considerations suggest that it is not within the purview of any one individual to deduce such correlational patterns with any genuine level of certainty. One might project that certain trends ought to exist. And it is reassuring to find prior assumptions and beliefs apparently consistent with a body of recognised research (i.e. expensive and laboriously collected observations followed by hundreds of hours devoted to analyses). But to attest such analyses redundant since the same information 'was already known' places such a critic in the position of claiming to be a superhuman data aggregation machine possessing sensitivity to factors beyond the observational span of any individual.

The misconception that knowledge discovered is superior to knowledge transmitted

Another of my professional encounters with the notion of obviousness took place at a local seminar on science teaching. A presenter was advocating an inquiry-based approach. I value inquiry-based teaching methods as a sensible means to generate motivation. But it was galling to hear the presenter go on to propound that it is obvious that children learn better when they create and test their own hypotheses. Apparently such 'discovered' knowledge is more meaningful than knowledge transmitted by a teacher. At one point it was suggested that knowledge cannot be transmitted, since it has to be constructed within the mind of each individual student. We were informed that a teacher is not a transmission source, but a facilitator of student learning. Sitting in the audience, it was painful to hear the term 'cognitive psychology' being associated so incorrectly with this message. But I can hardly blame the presenter. He may have read the article in which the distinguished Howard Gardner (2002: 49) noted:

> As a cognitive psychologist, I know that children must construct knowledge for themselves; they cannot simply be 'given' understanding of any important issue. This insight – shared by thousands of cognitive researchers all over the world – does not prevent legislators from calling time and again for 'direct instruction' or drill-and-kill regimens.

As a student of cognitive psychology for over 30 years, I have great difficulty with such notions and am ignorant of whatever database Gardner is invoking. The idea of a teacher as a knowledge facilitator is flawed, since it invokes false dichotomies and confuses motivational goals with instructional methodology. Put simply, the goal of direct instruction is to promote understanding, and there is no conflict between constructing knowledge and listening to a superb teacher explain complex processes (Chinn and Malhotra 2002; Good and Brophy 2002). In fact, one of the initial findings from the process–product era was that it becomes nonsensical to distinguish indirect from direct teachers (i.e. a false dichotomy) as the process indices representing both such attributes were found to correlate positively (see Brophy and Good (1986: 333–6) on this specific issue).

Simplistic notions of constructivism understate the natural human ability to learn efficiently through inherently social and verbal means. When people use words within social interactions, they do so in the expectation that others will be able to understand their intended meanings. One fundamental assumption is that we possess the ability to communicate and transmit effectively to other members of the species (i.e. Gricean principles). Indeed, the species has evolved remarkably effective means of communication and knowledge transmission, involving the correlation of three distinct modes: verbally articulated words, visually modelled actions, and calibrated feedback. The ability to calibrate feedback with goal-driven sensitivity towards its effects can be referred to as the reinforcement process.

In learning to teach others, instructors learn how to (a) articulate using words with an appreciation of the rules of clear speech; (b) demonstrate with an appreciation of the principles of observational learning; (c) present information with an appreciation of cognitive load principles; and (d) apply feedback with an appreciation of the principles of reinforcement. Being able to adjust and adapt one's teaching in a manner thoroughly consistent with these four principles requires a massive personal investment involving years of expertise development.

In recent years teachers in Australia have been exhorted to move away from a pedagogy that stresses the development of their teacher skills, toward a pedagogy that emphasises the nature of student learning. But the model of student learning often articulated is that of constructivism, a metaphorical term that does not have clear focus. Often, it is used in a manner attempting to redefine the goals and purposes of general education. In a related vein, Stanovich (1993) noted a level of frustration with certain agendas within the field of reading research: 'But future historians will find it difficult to explain how the political goal of restructuring educational resources got tied up with the issue of whether teachers should say s makes the /s/ sound' (Stanovich 1993: 286). Within the same text, he referred pointedly to constructivism as a 'mélange' (ibid.: 288), often adopted by people advancing agendas divergent from that of mainstream science.

It is beyond the scope of this essay to develop this perspective further. However, it is suggested that a preferable metaphor for student learning is found within the construct of knowledge building, such as that advanced by Chan *et al.* (1997). Within such a model, the student is assumed to use all available resources, and especially social resources, in the attempt to understand the relationship between current understandings and complex incoming data. The assumption is made that data are handled within the mind in accordance with well-established principles of cognitive load, schemata fitting, and gradual conceptual refinement as subtle discriminations are made and built upon. A high level of social comparison is especially valuable. The present writer holds that, as a model of student learning, the social knowledge building metaphor holds greater promise than many of the current notions of constructivism which appear to be advanced in the absence of (and sometimes denial of) a psychology of learning. Meandering, quasi-philosophical abstractions cannot replace a scientifically validated model of knowledge acquisition.

One issue often tends to surface. Is there any difference between knowledge acquired through 'constructivistic' teaching approaches and knowledge acquired from more intentionally 'instructivistic' sources? No, since it is a similar learning process that has to occur. At times, some of the constructivist writers endorse notions remarkably close to non-directive or discovery learning, possibly unaware that the construct of discovery learning, as promoted over the past 40 years, lacks scientifically acceptable data (Chall 1999). All too often, discovery learning is associated with relatively poor learning outcomes. Relevant studies were reviewed by Richard Mayer (2004) in his keenly entitled article, 'Should There Be a Three-Strikes Rule Against Pure Discovery Learning?'

It is valuable to review the work of David Klahr of Carnegie Mellon University as an example of a relevant research programme. As a productive cognitive psychologist, Klahr has focused an extensive research programme into the development of the control of variables strategy (CVS) in young children's thinking. The CVS is a key curriculum objective and a component essential to attainment of scientific thinking. If students can uncover the strategy without being taught directly its underlying dimensions, this represents an impressive mental achievement which augers well for non-directive, constructionist teaching approaches.

Will nine-year-old children be able to master the principles underpinning the CVS strategy through discovery-learning lessons on this topic? Klahr and Nigam (2004) found that 25 per cent of them could. When they exposed a comparable group to brief direct instruction training, it was found that 80 per cent of the students now achieved mastery. In the second part of this study, it was found that similar levels of knowledge generalisation were apparent in all students who had acquired the skill, irrespective of how their initial knowledge was acquired. Thus, levels of acquisition and generalisation were (three times) higher in the instruction group than in the discovery group. Such findings are consistent with Klahr's other work in the child development area – that conceptual understanding produces generalisation, and that children who have the advantage of clear instructional cues will achieve understanding more readily than children expected to acquire knowledge via less directive teaching methods.

The following misconception is noted: knowledge is acquired superficially through direct instruction, but acquired more meaningfully though personal discovery. Besides findings from Klahr's programme, this idea did not find support in the myriad experiments conducted using Piagetian tasks (Brainerd 2003; Mayer 2004). Instead, the added burden of attempting to discover or 'problem-solve' new knowledge actively can increase cognitive load in such a way as to interfere with learning in novices (Tuovinen and Sweller 1999).

Inevitably, new knowledge is fragile and requires consolidation, repetition, and reinstatements. Such reinstatements should occur ideally within a two-day window, as was shown by Nuthall (2000, 2004) in studies tracking how individual students build their knowledge from classroom experiences. The proposition that knowledge is automatically stronger when you discover it for yourself lacks scientific support, appears fundamentally incorrect, and should be identified as a misconception concerning human learning.

In a manner contrary to some constructionist agendas, it is possible to suggest that information communicated via direct social and verbal transmission can be more durable, more available, and more resilient than knowledge uncovered and constructed through an individual's onerous inductive processing. Socially transmitted information may arrive efficiently organised, with sequences and terminology well defined. Critical variables are emphasised, subtle discriminations and conditional elements are identified, and the appropriate vocabulary (i.e. schema) is activated. The underlying elements are articulated even when they remain relatively invisible, as in the case with high-level abstract qualities. Attention is drawn to aspects that are well beyond immediate purview.

Indeed, should you try to navigate your way through a new software package, you discover just how unsatisfactory and frustrating an experience of individual discovery can become. Compare this experience with spending a brief period in the company of someone who can teach, using clear pedagogical skills, what the software can do, what features it possesses, and exactly how it can be used in the service of your own goals. Suddenly, the notion of personal discovery is seen as a gauche vehicle for your own goal-directed development. On the other hand, you can solve new problems, and use your skills creatively, once having experienced, through clear instruction, the opportunity to learn.

A further factor can be brought in here: emotional learning. In a study conducted with high school students, Lepper et al. (1986) found that students who were unsuccessful in solving matrix problems because they received incomplete instructions learned to rate themselves as poor in this skill area. Similar students who were given the full set of direct instructions for the same tasks went on to a higher success level on the test and then rated themselves as high in ability for this type of task.

As implied earlier, one notable misconception is that direct instruction produces superficial or rote learning, whereas discovery produces meaningful learning. On the other hand, available data suggest that when procedures are complex, when learning is difficult, and when learners are novices or unable to proceed on their own, then clear explanations and direct instructional methods are used to help them achieve deep and meaningful cognitive learning outcomes (Anderson *et al.* 1995; Chinn and Malhotra, 2002; Klahr and Nigram, 2004; Mayer, 2004).

Coda

A popular bumper sticker for one's car once declared, 'If you can read this, then thank your teachers'. Teachers play an inevitable role as active transmitters of essential bodies of knowledge and skill. Modern cognitive theory stresses that thinking skills and intellectual work are driven by the availability of content knowledge to the individual mind (Yates and Chandler 1991). Recognising the importance of knowledge acquisition processes and the teaching functions linked with knowledge building allows teachers to attain a clear role definition. Naturally, teachers work within complex worlds and strive to achieve many outcomes – sometimes conflicting ones. But knowledge goals are highly important and have the advantages of visibility and of being readily understood in the general public arena.

Some assurance can be taken from the findings of a recent survey stemming from this writer's department. We asked primary school teachers if they believed that direct instructional methods were viable methods to use in pursuit of their professional goals. A remarkable 81 per cent of these teachers responded in the positive direction on our attitude survey measure, with degree of positivity correlating with years of teaching experience (Demant and Yates 2003). We find such data reassuring.

Finally, just how does the present writer deal with the issue of obviousness whenever it surfaces after seminars on effective teaching? The response verbatim takes this form:

> OK, but there is a parallel between obviousness and common sense. And what did Voltaire note about common sense? The problem with common sense, he said, is that it is not so common.

References

Aberson, C. L., Healey, M. and Romero, V. (2000). Ingroup bias and self-esteem: A meta-analysis. *Personality and Social Psychology Review*, 4: 157–73.

Anderson, J. R., Corbett, A. T., Koedinger, K. and Pelletier, R. (1995). Cognitive tutors: Lessons learned. *Journal of the Learning Sciences*, 4: 167–207.

Bargh, J. A. and Chartrand, T. L. (1999). The unbearable automaticity of being. *American Psychologist*, 54: 462–79.

Baumeister, R. F., Campbell, J. D., Krueger, J. I. and Vohs, K. D. (2003). Does high self-esteem cause better performance, interpersonal success, happiness or healthier lifestyles? *Psychological Science in the Public Interest*, 4: 1–44.

Berliner, D. C. (1984). The half-full glass. A review of research on teaching. In P. Hosford (ed.), *Using what we know about teaching*. Alexandria, VA: Association for Supervision and Curriculum Development, 51–77.

Berliner, D. C. (1986). In pursuit of the expert pedagogue. *Educational Researcher*, 15(7): 5–13.

Berliner, D. C. (1987). Simple views of effective teaching and a simple theory of classroom instruction. In D. C. Berliner and B. V. Rosenshine (eds), *Talks to teachers: A festschrift for N. L. Gage*. New York: Random House, 93–110.

Berliner, D. C. (1994). Expertise: The wonders of exemplary performance. In J. N. Mangieri and C. Collins Block (eds), *Creating powerful thinking in teachers and students*. Fort Worth, TX: Holt, Rinehart and Winston, 161–86. Available online at http://courses.ed.asu. edu/berliner/readings/expertise.htm

Berliner, D. C. (2004a). Toiling in Pasteur's quadrant: The contributions of N. L. Gage to educational psychology. *Teaching and Teacher Education*, 2: 329–40.

Berliner, D. C. (2004b). Describing the behavior and documenting the accomplishments of expert teachers. *Bulletin of Science, Technology and Society*, 24: 200–12.

Berliner, D. C. (2005). The near impossibility of testing for teacher quality. *Journal of Teacher Education*, 56: 205–13.

Borko, H. and Livingston, C. (1989). Cognition and improvisation: Differences in mathematics instruction by expert and novice teachers. *American Educational Research Journal*, 26: 473–98.

Brainerd, C. J. (2003). Jean Piaget, learning research, and American education. In B. J. Zimmerman (ed.), *Educational psychology: A century of contributions*. Mahwah, NJ: Lawrence Erlbaum, 251–87.

Brophy, J. E. (1988). Research on teacher effects: Uses and abuses. *Elementary School Journal*, 89: 3–21.

Brophy, J. E. and Good, T. L. (1986). Teacher behaviour and student achievement. In M. C. Wittrock (ed.), *Handbook of research on teaching*, 3rd ed. New York: Macmillan, 328–75.

Chall, J. S. (2000). *The achievement challenge: What really works in the classroom*. New York: Guilford Press.

Chan, C., Burtis, J. and Bereiter, C. (1997). Knowledge building as a mediator of conflict in cognitive change. *Cognition and Instruction*, 15: 1–40.

Chinn, C. A. and Malhotra, B. A. (2002). Children's responses to anomalous scientific data: How is conceptual change impeded? *Journal of Educational Psychology*, 94: 327–43.

Darling-Hammond, L. and Sclan, E. (1992). Policy and supervision. In C. D. Glickman (ed.), *Supervision in transition*. Alexandria, VA: Association for Supervision and Curriculum Development, 7–29.

Demant, M. S. and Yates, G. C. R. (2003). Primary teachers' attitudes toward the direct instruction construct. *Educational Psychology, 23*: 483–9.

Dunkin, M. J. (1997). Assessing teachers' effectiveness. *Issues in Educational Research, 7*: 37–51.

Emler, N. (2001). *Self-esteem: The costs and consequences of low self-worth.* York, UK: York Publishing.

Evertson, C. M. (1987). Managing classrooms: A framework for teachers. In D. C. Berliner and B. V. Rosenshine (eds), *Talks to teachers: A festschrift for N. L. Gage.* New York: Random House, 54–74.

Gage, N. L. (1985). *Hard gains in the soft sciences.* Bloomington, IN: Phi Delta Kappa.

Gage, N. L. (1991). The obviousness of social and educational research results. *Educational Researcher, 20*(1): 10–16.

Gage, N. L. and Needels, M. C. (1989). Process-product research on teaching: A review of the criticisms. *Elementary School Journal, 89*: 253–300.

Gardner, H. (2002, September 4). The quality and qualities of educational research. *Education Week, 22*: 49.

Gilovich, T. (1991). *How we know what isn't so: The fallibility of human judgment in everyday life.* New York: Free Press.

Gilovich, T., Griffin, D. and Kahneman, D. (eds). (2002). *Heuristics and biases: The psychology of intuitive judgment.* Cambridge, UK: Cambridge University Press.

Goleman, D. (1995). *Emotional intelligence.* New York: Bantam Books.

Good, T. L. and Brophy, J. E. (2002). *Looking in classrooms,* 9th ed. Boston: Allyn and Bacon.

Harter, S. (1993). Causes and consequences of low self-esteem in children and adolescents. In R. F. Baumeister (ed.), *Self-esteem: The puzzle of low self-regard.* New York: Plenum Press, 87–116.

Hertwig, R., Fanselow, C. and Hoffrage, U. (2003). Hindsight bias: How knowledge and heuristics affect our reconstruction of the past. *Memory, 11*: 357–77.

Hogan, T., Rabinowitz, M. and Craven, J. A. (2003). Representation in teaching: Inferences from research of experts and novice teachers. *Educational Psychologist, 38*: 235–47.

Hoffrage, U., Hertwig, R. and Gigerenzer, G. (2000). Hindsight bias: A by-product of knowledge updating. *Journal of Experimental Psychology: Learning, Memory and Cognition, 26*: 566–81.

Houston, J. P. (1983). Psychology: A closed system of self-evident information. *Psychological Reports, 52*: 203–8.

Kahneman, D., Slovic, P. and Tversky, A. (1982). *Judgement under uncertainty: Heuristics and biases.* Cambridge, UK: Cambridge University Press.

Klahr, D. and Nigam, M. (2004). The equivalence of learning paths in early science instruction: Effects of direct instruction and discovery learning. *Psychological Science, 15*: 661–7.

Kruger, J. M. and Dunning, D. (1999). Unskilled and unaware of it: How difficulties in recognizing one's own incompetence lead to inflated self-assessments. *Journal of Personality and Social Psychology, 77*: 1121–34.

Leinhardt, G. and Greeno, J. G. (1986). The cognitive skill of teaching. *Journal of Educational Psychology, 78*: 75–95.

Lepper, M. R., Ross, L. and Lau, R. R. (1986). Persistence of inaccurate beliefs about the self: Effects in the classroom. *Journal of Personality and Social Psychology, 50*, 482–91.

Mayer, R. E. (2004). Should there be a three-strikes rule against pure discovery learning? The case for guided methods of instruction. *American Psychologist, 59*: 14–19.

Nuthall, G. (2000). The role of memory in the acquisition and retention of knowledge in science and social study units. *Cognition and Instruction, 18*: 83–139.

Nuthall, G. (2004). Relating classroom teaching to student learning: A critical analysis of why research has failed to bridge the theory-practice gap. *Harvard Education Review, 74*: 273–306.

Pronin, E., Puccio, C. and Ross, L. (2002). Understanding misunderstanding: Social psychological perspectives. In T. Gilovich, D. Griffin, D. and D. Kahneman (eds), *Heuristics and biases: The psychology of intuitive judgment*. Cambridge, UK: Cambridge University Press, 636–5.

Rosenshine, B. and Stevens, R. (1986). Teaching functions. In M. C. Wittrock (ed.), *Handbook of research on teaching*, 3rd ed. New York: Macmillan, p. 376.

Shanahan, T. (2002). What reading research says: The promises and limitations of applying reading research to education. In A. E. Farstrup and S. J. Samuels (eds), *What reading research has to say about reading instruction*. Newark, Delaware: International Reading Association, 8–24.

Stallings, J. and Kaskowitz, D. (1974). *Follow through classroom observation evaluation*. Menlo Park, CA: SRI International.

Stanovich, K. E. (1993). Distinguished educator series: Romance and reality. *The Reading Teacher, 47*: 280–91. Available online at http://tortoise.oise.utoronto.ca/kstanovich/pdfs/reading/rdtch93.pdf

Stanovich, K. E. (2003). The fundamental computational biases of human cognition: Heuristics that (sometimes) impair decision making and problem solving. In J. E. Davidson and R. J. Sternberg (eds), *The psychology of problem solving*. New York: Cambridge University Press, 291–342.

Sternberg, R. J. and Horvath, J. A. (1995). A prototype view of expert teaching. *Educational Researcher, 24*(6): 9–17.

Townsend, M. A. R. (1995). Effects of accuracy and plausibility in predicting results of research on teaching. *British Journal of Educational Psychology, 65*, 359–65.

Tuovinen, J. E. and Sweller, J. (1999). A comparison of cognitive load associated with discovery learning and worked examples. *Journal of Educational Psychology, 91*: 334–41.

Wang, M. C., Haertel, G. D. and Walberg, H. J. (1993). Toward a knowledge base for school learning. *Review of Educational Research, 63*: 249–94.

Wong, L. Y. (1995). Research on teaching: Process-product findings and the feeling of obviousness. *Journal of Educational Psychology, 87*: 504–11.

Yates, G. C. R. (1974). Influence of televised modelling and verbalization on children's delay of gratification. *Journal of Experimental Child Psychology, 18*: 333–9.

Yates, G. C. R. and Yates, S. M. (1990). Teacher effectiveness research: Towards describing user-friendly classroom instruction. *Educational Psychology, 10*: 225–38.

Yates, G. C. R. and Chandler, M. (1991). Cognitive psychology of knowledge: Basic findings and educational implications. *Australian Journal of Education, 35*: 131–53.

Yates, G. C. R., Lippett, R. M. K. and Yates, S. M. (1981). The effects of age, positive affect induction, and instructions on children's delay of gratification. *Journal of Experimental Child Psychology, 32*: 169–80.

Yates, G. C. R., Yates, S. M. and Beasley, C. J. (1987). Young children's knowledge of strategies in delay of gratification. *Merrill-Palmer Quarterly Journal of Developmental Psychology, 33*: 159–69.

Chapter 10

Evidence-based practice for education?

Reg Marsh

It is over 50 years since I began study at university. Since then there have been developments in knowledge and practice that were unimaginable at that time. It was still a year, for example, before Tijo and Levan could show us pictures of human chromosomes (this would happen in 1956) and a further three years before Lejune, Turpin, and Gautier demonstrated clearly the chromosomal defect that caused Down syndrome. Now we have the human genome. That's how far genetics has gone in 50 years, but how have we done in psychology?

In education and psychology, Freudian and post-Freudian concepts were embedded in our thinking by that time, and Piaget was beginning to be ascendant. Now, while we acknowledge Freud's discovery of unconscious motives in determining behaviour, we are more concerned with correcting the overt circumstances and behaviours associated with behaviour problems than with tracing the possible unconscious sources of such behaviour. And most of us now accept that Piaget's descriptions of what he thought were latent traits are not much more than manifestations of surface factors arising from the characteristics of the particular situation. So while we have changed in our appreciation of theorists current at that time, little has changed in the way we check new ideas before we put them into practice.

Recently in education, we have seen a change in the application of what was conventional wisdom, acquired and shaped by trial and error over perhaps a couple of hundred years, that related to the ways we raised and provided for children in our society, and in the administrative and organisational structures we used through schools to do this. These practices vary from how we set up and run our schools to the kinds of courses we teach and how we examine them. The changes have been forced on us not so much by changes in knowledge about education and society, or by finding what works and what does not work, but a particular economic outlook and its corollaries. It is naturally quite different from the ideas of the liberal thinkers of the eighteenth and nineteenth centuries, particularly Rousseau, Bentham, J. S. Mill, and T. H. Green, which were concerned about the well-being of mankind and out of which our values for education grew. The current approach, which has been widely adopted to different degrees within more developed English-speaking countries, looks at education as a commodity that is to be evaluated in terms of cost and benefit using monetary units, where benefit is defined in narrow economic terms. In all this consideration the idea of society, its direction and purpose, and the well-being of individuals has been set aside.

As a result, schools in some countries which may have up to 3,000 pupils are staffed by teachers who have short-term contracts, no superannuation, and a peer–assessment system unstandardised and without independent review. There are national systems of examinations where there are no calibration systems to allow for the variation between markers, schools, and occasions (i.e. unreliability is not a consideration and validity is only of the face kind at best). Head teachers' (now called chief executives) most time-consuming role is balancing a one-line budget for the school, for which they are not trained, leaving them much less time to do the things that a school requires of a head if it is to run optimally. And now in this country (New Zealand) we have, at the end of school, a system of pupil evaluation that is inefficient, inaccurate, cumbersome, and costly. We also have schools recruiting children as young as five from foreign cultures. They come and live with basically unselected families from the local culture to provide further income for the local schools, which are being marginally funded and often badly managed. There are also schools where teachers are being pathologically bullied by both pupils and head teachers. Alongside this there are greater amounts and kinds of behaviour problems in youth even though the unemployment rate is dropping. At the tertiary level, the fees are so high that they are discouraging men particularly from entering teaching and related professions which have relatively poor salaries, and we are seeing advertisements for lecturers for bachelors courses asking that applicants only be doing masters degrees.

This is a clear lesson that when one has an education system based on a loose combination of theory and fact, no proper standards for trials before changes are made in the system, then the system is wide open to intrusion from trendy theories of all kinds in all areas. That has happened in the present case with appalling effect on the system, the people who work within it, the children who are subjected to it, and ultimately to society. What has happened to our knowledge, experience, common sense, and humanity?

It was signs of the introduction of the exclusive monetary yardstick that made me turn with despair from education to work in other countries and in a different professional area. Is there something we can do about it? I believe there is.

About 20 years ago Archie Cochrane, an epidemiologist in the UK, frustrated with a level of practice in medicine that was often based on little more than habit and myth, decided something had to be done about it. He carried out analyses of the degree, within medical specialties, to which practices were based on verifiable trials and rated specialties accordingly. While some appeared relatively sound, others were clearly faulty. The worst four he awarded dunce's caps (they included psychiatry – a discipline that shares a lot of common knowledge with psychology); the wooden spoon went to obstetrics. His efforts had an effect. An organisation, the Cochrane Collaboration, was established to achieve evidence-based medicine (see http://www.cochrane.org/). In 12 years it has grown to have a membership of more than 10,000 based around 16 centres spread internationally – each relating to a different area of medical interest. There is even one on health economics.

Evidence-based practice in this case is more than just a good-sounding phrase. Its core is a system of reviews. Highly detailed methods have been worked out for evaluating and combining the results of research into individual topics; a meta-analysis underlies the reviews (health workers got the idea from Gene Glass – although their methods are different and they work on the raw data from all contributing studies). The investigator follows procedures outlined in a 250-page manual of how to do the reviews properly. The results are checked and reviewed by expert panels and their conclusions are then published as a Cochrane report. The authors have a responsibility to try to update these every two years so that they constantly reflect the state of the art otherwise their validity lapses.

Something similar for education was set up in the US a couple of years ago – the What Works Clearinghouse (WWC) (see http://www.w-w-c.org/). It is, however, different in a number of key ways. First, it does assess published experimental studies in education, but only by evaluating their experimental design and methods of analysis and checking for obvious incongruities in the characteristics of groups being compared. It seems to do this fairly rigorously, but does not take the further step, as in Cochrane, of then combining the raw data from the methodologically acceptable studies to perform a meta-analysis.

Furthermore, it is the product of just one institutional organisation – and a government one at that – and governments have vested interests in education that may not be the same as those of significant other portions of society. Also, a government department, even in the USA, would not have the human resources that are available to an international organisation in terms of either range or numbers. A particular strength of the Cochrane organisation is that it is not the product of one institution. It is a collaboration of individuals; there is no hierarchy in the organisation and anyone who has the technical skills and is prepared to abide by its conventions can undertake a review and submit it. There is a greater chance of the review being totally independent, and it does come up with a data-based verdict on the topic, which WWC does not do.

How does this relate to current concerns in education? Historically, educational innovation or change has been based on a mixture of theory and some empirical studies, but it has been a haphazard affair. Many innovations in psychology and education have been made on the basis of no more than, 'It seems a good idea.' Freud, Piaget, De Bono (1986) and properties wrongly attributed to left and right brain differences, etc., were all launched into educational practice with often not much more than anecdotal support. Moreover, and worse, established and verified knowledge is allowed to be overthrown because someone who doesn't refer to the existing literature has a different idea – like Gardiner's (1985) seven different types of intelligence, which ignores the many hundreds of studies showing the contrary. And we have masters degrees in psychoanalytic psychology being offered – so much for the scientist–practitioner model.

We must not have a convention whereby there can be a massive overthrow of existing educational practice on the basis of a little evidence or no evidence at all, or even a lot of evidence to the contrary. As we have seen, the education system is totally exposed to the kind of encroachment by carpet-bagging theorists from other disciplines that we have seen in the last two decades. I have been told, in surprise, by the head of a national educational research organisation that they 'thought statistical analysis was out now'! This clearly comes from that group of people teaching research methods who present qualitative and quantitative methods as equal alternative approaches to research. They are not alternatives, but complementary; qualitative approaches allow us to generate and investigate hypotheses while quantitative methods allow us to verify the hypotheses. I ask: what have we created and what have we allowed?

To reduce the chances of such a takeover ever happening again, and to eliminate the results of the present one, we need to take an entirely new initiative. We must have a basis of rigorously derived evidence for all our practice in education. The days of haphazard research and its more haphazard application must go if we are to be professionally and socially responsible. The way in which major educational changes have happened, particularly in the last 20 years, must be made unacceptable. Rigorous trials must be insisted upon before major changes are made. Our teachers and teacher trainers must be taught that this is the only acceptable way. Policy makers would then have an independent benchmark against which to assess proposals. And they should be made to understand that they could be ignored only at their professional or electoral peril. The evidential basis alone would not make the change, but also the difference in ethos one expects it to produce.

My message is this – and it is a challenge to our profession and those others associated with education – let us set a standard for practices and developments in teaching and all its related activities, from its administration to its economics, that in concept is similar to that of the Cochrane collaboration. The different nature of most of the material in health and education fields means that in detail it must be different, but the concept of an accepted and rigorous evidential basis for innovation and change would be the same.

References

De Bono, E. (1986). *De Bono's thinking course.* New York: Facts on File.
Gardiner, H. (1985). *Frames of mind.* New York: Basic Books.

Chapter 11

Recent research on troublesome classroom behaviour

Robyn Beaman, Kevin Wheldall and Coral Kemp

Effective classroom behaviour management is probably even more crucial today than in the past given contemporary commitment to educating students with a diverse range of special educational needs within the least restrictive environment. The inclusion of students with disabilities within regular classrooms requires teachers to have high-level classroom management skills, as well as the necessary skills to programme effectively for all students in the class. Teachers engaged in such a complex instructional mission need highly effective behaviour-management techniques in order to meet the needs of all the students in their classrooms.

Moreover, while students with severe behaviour and/or emotional disorders are relatively easily identified (and, as a consequence, typically receive special education provision and placement), a substantial proportion of children who experience serious behavioural and emotional difficulties attend regular schools (Harris *et al.* 1993; Swinson *et al.* 2003). Chazan (1994) argued that the vast majority of children with emotional and behavioural difficulties are educated in their usual classes in mainstream schools, and 'the question of removing them does not arise' (Chazan, 1994: 261). These students, as well as typically developing students with more commonplace disruptive behaviours, may well present management challenges to their teachers.

Conway (2005) has pointed out that one of the most pressing concerns of teachers when students with 'additional needs' (Conway, 2005: 213) are included in their classrooms is the emotional and behavioural needs of these students. But he also successfully argues that behavioural issues are not restricted to students with special educational needs, but are 'common across both students with additional needs and their regular class peers' (ibid.: 214). Clearly, some behavioural problems are likely to be a feature of nearly every classroom. It is not surprising then that problems of classroom order and discipline frequently stimulate public interest and debate. The role of the media in building and shaping public perception must be continually assessed. In the Australian context, Jacob (2005: 6) has argued that 'well publicised violent events in recent years have exaggerated the public's perception of the level of disruptive behaviour in schools, and created the impression that misbehaviour is more pervasive than is the case'. Inaccurate perceptions about what occurs in classrooms can seriously damage education systems, demoralise staff and students, and make the teaching profession an unattractive option for a future workforce. Researchers have an important role to play in informing with data the debate about matters such as school and classroom discipline. This is particularly the case when topics attract such media and public interest. Researchers can provide the evidence whereby widely held perceptions can be challenged or confirmed.

Interest in behaviour in classrooms is not limited to public debate. Given the impact of inappropriate or disruptive classroom behaviour on the effective use of instructional time in classrooms, it is not surprising that the study of troublesome classroom behaviour has long been evident in the educational research literature, as noted by Beaman and Wheldall (1997) in their review of the literature relating to troublesome classroom behaviour. It is the purpose of the present review to update the findings of Beaman and Wheldall in the light of more recent research completed over the past decade or so.

Beaman and Wheldall (1997) focused on three major themes: the prevalence of troublesome classroom behaviour, gender differences in troublesome classroom behaviour, and the types of classroom behaviour teachers found to be the most troublesome and the most frequent. They found that prevalent rates of troublesome classroom behaviour from studies around the world were somewhat equivocal; that there were clear gender differences in relation to the most troublesome students in the class, with boys being consistently nominated as the most troublesome students; and that the classroom misbehaviours that teachers found most troublesome were relatively innocuous but occurred so frequently as to be a recurrent cause for concern. Beaman and Wheldall also emphasised that reports of classroom violence had been overstated and that the most persistent and irritating classroom misbehaviours that concerned teachers appeared to be *talking out of turn* and *hindering other students*.

At the outset, it may be useful to reiterate what is meant by the terms troublesome, inappropriate, or disruptive classroom behaviour. Merrett and Wheldall (1984) defined disruptive classroom behaviour as activity that interferes significantly with a student's own learning, interferes with another student's learning or responses, interferes with the teacher's ability to operate effectively, or any combination of these. This definition remains appropriate for the purposes of this review.

The focus of this review is not on diagnosed emotional disturbance and behaviour disorder per se, as the vast majority of students nominated by teachers as being problematic could not be considered as having a diagnosed or diagnosable condition. Problematic behaviours are, however, on a continuum and inevitably some of what occurs to distress teachers in classrooms will be the result of some students who manifest behaviours that are consonant with emotional disturbance and behaviour disorder.

Context has always been an important consideration when it comes to defining or describing troublesome or disruptive behaviour. When troublesome classroom behaviour from the perspective of teachers is the focus, it would appear that teachers are most concerned with those behaviours that affect them in the course of their teaching, more so than the behaviour problems that cause difficulties for the students they teach. Mertin and Wasyluk (1994) have gone so far as to say that teachers perceive different problems than are perceived by others involved in the care of children, observing that much depends on the nature of the problem and who defines it. They argue that teachers' determination of a problem is based more on the practical issues such as classroom management and the more obvious and evident indicators of behavioural and emotional disturbance, with teachers more likely to define as a problem a behaviour directly related to the classroom or playground environments (Mertin and Wasyluk, 1994). It is classroom behaviour that is the focus of the present review.

In order to allow comparison with Beaman and Wheldall (1997), this review is similarly structured, considering, in turn, the prevalence of behaviourally troublesome students; time spent managing troublesome behaviour; gender differences; and types of classroom (mis)behaviour, their severity and their frequency. Table 11.1 comprises a summary of recent studies relevant to this review, including details of the samples involved.

Prevalence of behaviourally troublesome students

Beaman and Wheldall (1997) concluded that, while findings were equivocal as to estimated prevalence rates of behaviourally troublesome students in classes, 'the average classroom teacher could typically expect to find from two to nine students with some level of behaviour problem in his/her class of thirty students at any one time' (Beaman and Wheldall 1997: 50). Mertin and Wasyluk (1994) reported that the number of children with emotional and/or behavioural problems in the general population is generally regarded to be in the order of 10 per cent. Those with more severe forms of problematic behaviour – for example, conduct disorder – are estimated to represent between approximately 2 per cent and 6 per cent of the population when considering children aged 4–18 years (Kazdin 1995).

Similarly, Jenson et al. (2004) estimated that students with externalising disorders (such as non-compliance, aggression, impulsivity, arguing, and rule breaking) make up 3–5 per cent of the students in public school classrooms, and 'are some of the most difficult students to manage in an educational setting' (Jenson et al. 2004: 67). When less serious forms of disruptive behaviour are also considered, the proportion of students who have the potential for disruptive behaviour in the classroom is much higher. In a large study of elementary school students in the USA (see Table 11.1 for details), Kamphaus et al. (1997) found that 20 per cent of the sample was classified within two of seven clusters they identified, namely, *Disruptive Behavior Disorder*, which accounted for 8 per cent of the sample, and a sub-clinical form of disruptive behaviour problems which the researchers labelled *Mildly Disruptive*, which accounted for a further 12 per cent, amounting to a total

of 20 per cent of the sample for these two clusters. (The other clusters identified were *Well Adapted* and *Average* [together accounting for 53 per cent of the
sample], *Learning Disorder* [17 per cent], *Physical Complaints/Worry* [6 per cent],
and *Severe Psychopathology* [4 per cent] (Kamphaus *et al.* 1997).) While significant
behavioural disorders occur relatively infrequently, when combined with the less
disruptive behaviours, it is clear that a significant minority of a class may present
as behaviourally troublesome to classroom teachers.

Behaviour management challenges are evident from the early years of
schooling. Stephenson *et al.* (2000) explored the behaviours of concern to
teachers in the early years of school in an Australian study involving teachers of
Kindergarten to Year 2 students (see Table 11.1 for more details). They found
that additional management strategies were considered necessary for 5 per cent
of male students and 2 per cent of female students. In another Australian study,
Herrera and Little (2005) found that 9 per cent of Kindergarten teachers
reported behaviour problems in their students (see Table 11.1). These trends
continue in the primary school years and beyond. Little *et al.* (2000) reported
that about 10 per cent of teachers in their study of Australian primary to early
secondary school students (see Table 11.1) also experienced difficulties dealing
with student behaviour.

As detailed in Table 11.1, in Hong Kong, Leung and Ho (2001) have found
that 15 per cent of the class are behaviourally troublesome to primary teachers.
In a parallel study involving Hong Kong secondary school teachers, Ho and
Leung (2002) again found 15 per cent of the class to be behaviourally troublesome (see Table 11.1). While these Hong Kong data indicate a similar level of
disruptiveness at both the primary and the secondary school levels, other studies
show an increasing proportion of the class as being troublesome as students move
through the school system.

Oswald (1995) showed a progressive rise in the percentage of students who
were considered to have failed to respond to student discipline strategies in a
large Australian study dealing with the number of difficult primary children by
school year (see Table 11.1). Comprising 6 per cent of the sample at Reception
(or Kindergarten), the proportion of troublesome students rose appreciably and
steadily to 16 per cent in Year 7 (with the exception of Year 6 when a small
decline from the figures for Year 5 was evident). Consistent gender differences,
with boys being identified much more frequently as being difficult to manage,
were also evident in this study, an issue to be reconsidered later.

Arbuckle and Little (2004) similarly reported gender differences and increased incidence in behaviour management challenges as students progressed
from primary to secondary schooling in their Australian study. As detailed in
Table 11.1, about 18 per cent of male students and 7 per cent of female students
required additional management support for disruptive behaviour. Moreover,
the incidence of disruptive behaviour increased from primary school to lower
secondary school, particularly in the case of boys (Arbuckle and Little 2004). The
rise in the number of difficult-to-manage students with increasing age (and the

preponderance of boys being troublesome) demonstrated by Oswald (1995) and Arbuckle and Little (2004) supports the statement by Kazdin (1995: 10) that, 'In general, antisocial behaviors are of the externalising type and are much more evident in boys and adolescents'. A similar phenomenon had been observed in the UK in the earlier troublesome classroom behaviour studies where Wheldall and Merrett (1988) found 16 per cent of students in primary classes to be troublesome, rising to 20 per cent in the secondary school study (Houghton *et al.* 1988).

The emotive issue of the apparently increased prevalence and severity of behaviour problems over time has recently been addressed by Jacob (2005). Jacob has provided interesting detail of education department reports over a 20-year period. Jacob cited a 1984 Departmental Review entitled, 'The Incidence and Management of Alienated, Disturbed and/or Disruptive Students in High and District High Schools' as indicating that 'there had been a substantial increase in the number of difficult students that secondary schools were dealing with and that the situation was now bordering on a crisis' (Jacob 2005: 6). Figures in the 1984 report indicated that an average of 3.8 per cent of the secondary school population (with a variation of 1–12 per cent between schools) presented with difficult or challenging behaviours.

Nearly 20 years on, Jacob chaired a working group dealing with the policy statement on students with challenging behaviour in Tasmania, Australia. Again, teachers considered that the number of difficult students had 'increased substantially' (Jacob 2005: 6) in recent years. But in 2002, teachers estimated around the *same* proportion of students with extreme behaviour difficulties, around 2–4 per cent, with similar wide-ranging estimates from school to school as had been found in 1984 (Jacob 2005). As Jacob observed: 'In both cases, 20 years apart, teachers reported that there had been a significant increase, yet the estimated percentage of children with difficult behaviour was approximately the same' (ibid.: 6).

Notwithstanding the fact that the variation in prevalence rates reported in the various research studies probably reflects the variations in students' age, location, and behaviour problem identification techniques (as noted by McGee *et al.* 1984), it still holds that the average classroom teacher could typically expect to find at least two and perhaps up to nine students with some level of behaviour problem to be present in a class of 30 students at any one time (Beaman and Wheldall, 1997). Prevalence rates for disruptive behaviour may vary, but what is apparent from the research presented in this review is more evidence of a rising percentage of behavioural difficulties in classrooms as students move from the early years to adolescence. This suggests a pattern of increasing disruption as students move into the secondary school system.

Table 11.1 Summary of studies relating to troublesome classroom behaviour

Study	Date	Country	Participants	Relevant findings
Early years and primary studies (including lower secondary)				
Herrera and Little	2005	Australia	63 Kindergarten teachers	9% of teachers reported problems with student behaviour
Kamphaus, Huberty, Distefano and Petoskey	1997	USA	1,227 elementary school children (6–11 years)	20% of the sample classified within two of seven clusters, *Disruptive Behavior Disorder* (8%) or *Mildly Disruptive* (12%)
Leung and Ho	2001	Hong Kong	144 teachers from 10 primary schools	1 15% of the class is behaviourally troublesome 2 93% of teachers nominated a boy as the most troublesome student in the class 3 Only 24% of primary teachers use less than 10% of their time managing student behaviour
Little, Hudson and Wilks	2000	Victoria, Australia	189 5- to 14-year-olds	10.5% of teachers reported difficulties with student behaviour
Oswald	1995	South Australia	2,354 students in Reception (K)-7	1 Progressive rise in behaviour management challenges with increasing age – 6% in Reception to 16% in Year 7 2 Boys identified much more frequently as troublesome

Table 11.1 (continued)

Study	Date	Country	Participants	Relevant findings
Early years and primary studies (including lower secondary)				
Poulou and Norwich	2000	Greece	170 primary teachers	1 Work avoidance, depressive mood, and negativism as the top three most serious misbehaviours 2 Lack of concentration, talking without permission, and untidiness the top three most frequent misbehaviours
Stephenson, Linfoot and Martin	2000	Western Sydney, NSW, Australia	130 teachers K-2 teachers (5- to 8-year-olds)	1 5% of males and 2% of females require additional behaviour management strategies 2 Distractability/attention span/does not listen caused the most concern to teachers at the K-2 level.
Secondary school studies				
Borg	1998	Malta	605 teachers from 16 (single-sex) state secondary schools	Drug abuse, cruelty/bullying, and destroying top three most serious behaviours. Stealing also a problem.
Ho and Leung	2002	Hong Kong	187 teachers from 14 secondary schools	1 15% of the class is behaviourally troublesome 2 71% of teachers nominated a boy as the most troublesome student in the class

(continued)

Table 11.1 (continued)

Study	Date	Country	Participants	Relevant findings
Secondary school studies				
Little	2005	Victoria, Australia	148 secondary school teachers	1 68% of teachers thought they spent too much time on classroom behaviour problems 2 Found 5.3 troublesome students in an average class – 3.5 of these are boys (66%) 3 Talking out of turn nominated as the most troublesome (35%) and most frequent (37%) misbehaviour, followed by idleness
Infantino and Little	2005	Victoria, Australia	350 secondary school students	Talking out of turn was the only behaviour perceived by both students and teachers as being the most troublesome and most frequent classroom misbehaviour of concern
Haroun and O'Hanlon	1997	Jordan	28 male secondary school teachers	Talking out of turn, inattention and lack of motivation were the top three disruptive behaviours nominated by teachers
Stuart	1994	NSW, Australia	105 secondary teachers	Stealing, destroying school property and cruelty/bullying were the three most serious behaviours faced by teachers.

Table 11.1 (continued)

Study	Date	Country	Participants	Relevant findings
Other studies across primary and secondary school levels				
Arbuckle and Little	2004	Australia	96 primary to lower secondary students	1 Progressive rise in behaviour management problems from primary school to lower secondary 2 18.2% of male students and 7.25% of females required additional behaviour-management support.
Langdon	1997	USA	714 elementary and high school teachers	58% of respondents reported that lessons were regularly disrupted by student misbehaviour.
Hart, Wearing and Conn	1995	Victoria, Australia	Primary and secondary teachers	Teachers, on average, spent 24.5% of their time managing behaviour.

Time spent managing classroom behaviour

Research has consistently shown that around 50 per cent of teachers, at all levels, typically claim to spend more time on problems of order and control than they believe they should (reviewed by Beaman and Wheldall 1997). In a recent Australian secondary school study, Little (2005) also found a relatively high percentage of teachers (68 per cent) who considered that they spent too much time on order and control in the classroom (see Table 11.1). In line with the generally large amounts of time spent on classroom management in the UK and in Australia cited above, Langdon (1997) reported that, in a national survey of teachers in the USA, 58 per cent of respondents reported that their lessons were regularly disrupted by student misbehaviour.

The issue of how much time spent on order and control is too much time appears to be an arguable point. In a Victorian study in Australia, Hart et al. (1995) argued that classroom behaviour management was not a major source of stress for teachers given that teachers, on average, spent around 25 per cent of their time managing behaviour. Losing nearly a quarter of available time on classroom management, however, represents a very significant loss of instructional opportunities. In their Hong Kong studies, Leung and Ho (2001) and Ho and Leung (2002) found that only 24 per cent of primary teachers used less than 10 per cent of their time in class managing behaviour, leaving three-quarters of teachers spending more than 10 per cent of their time on classroom management. At the secondary level, teachers reported spending less time managing classroom behaviour than their primary teacher colleagues (with 46 per cent of secondary teachers spending less than 10 per cent of their time), a finding contrary to the secondary studies referred to above (in terms of perceptions of time spent at least). Suffice to say, and as Leung and Ho (2001: 230) pointed out:

> If we consider spending 20% or more time on classroom management had reached the level of concern, then 39.3% of the teachers we surveyed were confronted with discipline problems. If the criterion was lowered to 10% or more, then almost 76% of teachers could be considered spending excessive time on problems of order and control.

Gender differences

Boys have long been the focus of attention when it comes to troublesome or disruptive behaviours and research has consistently confirmed that boys appear to be perceived as more troublesome than girls, as Beaman and Wheldall (1997) made clear. The more recent classroom behaviour research literature also supports such a finding. As detailed in Table 11.1, Little (2005) found that of the 5.3 troublesome students in an average Australian secondary class, 3.5 of these students were boys (66 per cent) (see also Arbuckle and Little 2004). Moreover, in the Hong Kong studies of primary (Leung and Ho 2001) and secondary

(Ho and Leung 2002) teachers' perceptions of disruptive classroom behaviours, styled after the Wheldall and Merrett studies, boys were found to be the most troublesome students by 93 per cent of primary teachers and 71 per cent of secondary teachers.

Kann and Hanna (2000) have noted that there is a primary difference in the way boys and girls present symptoms of disruptive behaviour disorders and, as a consequence, are likely to come to the attention of the teacher. They summarised this as follows:

> Externally directed behaviours generally associated with boys are acts that are harmful to others or the environment, such as stealing, lying, fighting, and destructiveness. Behaviours that are internally focused are more common in girls and include anxiety, shyness, withdrawal, hypersensitivity and physical complaints. (Kann and Hanna 2000: 268)

The findings on this issue, then, are unequivocal: boys are consistently perceived as more behaviourally troublesome than girls at both primary and secondary levels. The more externalising nature of boys' behaviour identifies them more readily to teachers as being problematic in the classroom. Moreover, the range of behaviours boys typically engage in are more likely to have an impact on those around them, including the teacher.

Types of classroom behaviour, their severity, and their frequency

Turning to the types of classroom behaviour teachers find most problematic, the earlier research found a consensus of opinion among teachers that the most common and the most troublesome classroom behaviours were relatively trivial, a finding that was subsequently to be frequently (and almost universally) replicated (Beaman and Wheldall 1997). Rather than identifying serious and threatening behaviours, the earlier research consistently identified talking out of turn as the most troublesome, and the most frequent, misbehaviour in primary and high school classrooms. This was also true even for the most troublesome behaviours of the particularly troublesome individual children in the class.

Studies carried out over the course of the last decade or so have largely come to very similar conclusions. In Australia, Little (2005) explored teachers' perceptions of students' problem behaviour in secondary schools in Victoria (see Table 11.1). Seeking to replicate aspects of the UK secondary school study of Houghton *et al.* (1988) in an Australian context, Little surveyed 148 secondary teachers using a modified version of the questionnaire used in the UK study. Little found that talking out of turn was both the most troublesome (35 per cent of teacher responses) and the most frequent (37 per cent of teacher responses) troublesome behaviour selected by secondary teachers out of the 10 behaviours itemised on the questionnaire. *Idleness* followed talking out of turn as the most troublesome (22 per cent) and the most frequent (21 per cent) misbehaviour, followed by *hindering others* at 17 per cent and 13 per cent respectively for the most troublesome behaviour and most frequent troublesome behaviour. While *disobedience* (13 per cent) was another behaviour category that attracted more than 10 per cent of responses for the most troublesome behaviour, no other behaviour registered above 10 per cent for most frequent troublesome behaviour. *Aggression*, which arguably causes some considerable concern for teachers, attracted only 2 per cent of responses for most troublesome behaviour and less than 1 per cent for most frequent troublesome behaviour. Clearly, it is the relatively trivial but frequent misbehaviours that cause teachers the most concern in Australian schools, as well as in UK schools and elsewhere.

Little (2005) also asked teachers to consider the questions regarding the most troublesome and most frequent misbehaviours across years they taught. Analysed by year levels (Years 7 and 8; Years 9 and 10; and Years 11 and 12) some differences in the responses of teachers were apparent. While talking out of turn was the first choice of teachers of Years 7 and 8 (48 per cent) and Years 9 and 10 (33 per cent) students for the most troublesome behaviour, for teachers of Years 11 and 12 students the most troublesome behaviour was idleness (41 per cent), followed by talking out of turn (23 per cent). These data suggest that, in the senior years of secondary school, teachers were finding the lack of application on the part of their students more problematic than inappropriate classroom talk. Moreover, in a recent secondary school study by Infantino and Little (2005), talking out of turn behaviour (including talking back) was the only behaviour perceived by both students and teachers as being the most troublesome and most frequent classroom misbehaviour of concern (see Table 11.1).

Further evidence of the dominance of talking out of turn as the principal irritant for teachers was found in a study conducted in a single-sex Jordanian secondary school. Haroun and O'Hanlon (1997) elicited information about the kinds of student misbehaviour teachers had to deal with in the course of their classroom teaching (see Table 11.1). They were also asked which of the behaviours they nominated were the most frequently occurring and why they thought these behaviours occurred. Seeking the behaviours from the teachers themselves resulted in very similar types of behaviour to those found by earlier researchers, as noted by Haroun and O'Hanlon. Teachers identified eight misbehaviours with the following frequency (listed here from most frequent to least frequent): talking out of turn; inattention; lack of motivation; out of seat; inappropriate banter; non-verbal noise; asking to leave classroom; and bullying. Haroun and O'Hanlon drew attention to the fact that the first seven of these behaviours were similar in that they all 'interrupt the planned teaching and learning process in classrooms' (1997: 34). This phenomenon is similar to that found by Wickman (1928) in his early study, that teachers identify those things as problematic in the classroom that are active disturbances; that is, those things that stop them from getting on with what they think they should be doing. In other words, teachers are troubled by those behaviours that are a problem 'not so much related to learning outcomes as to teaching intentions' (Haroun and O'Hanlon 1997: 34).

More recent studies in Hong Kong building on the work of Wheldall and Merrett (1988) and Houghton *et al.* (1988) have been completed at the primary and secondary school levels (Ho and Leung 2002; Leung and Ho 2001). Using a modified version (using 15 behaviour categories rather than 10) of the questionnaire used in Wheldall and Merrett (1988), primary school teachers rated talking out of turn as the most disruptive (42 per cent of teacher responses) and most frequent (54 per cent), followed by *non-attentiveness* as the next most disruptive (14 per cent) and the next most frequent (13 per cent) behaviour. While *forgetfulness* attracted 10 per cent of teacher responses for both most disruptive and most frequent misbehaviour, no other behaviours scored above 10 per cent.

In the parallel secondary school study, Ho and Leung (2002) found that disruptive behaviours in secondary school were a continuation of those found at primary school level. Talking out of turn was again the most disruptive (30 per cent) and most frequent misbehaviour (39 per cent), followed by non-attentiveness for the next most disruptive and next most frequent (both at 19 per cent). As can been seen by the relative percentages, however, the problem with non-attentiveness did increase in the secondary years (if not overtaking talking out of turn) as a problematic behaviour, a similar finding to that of Little (2005) in Australia. Forgetfulness was also quite common, with 15 per cent of teacher responses indicating that it was a frequent problem (as well as being considered as most disruptive by 11 per cent of secondary teachers). Other more prominent behaviour problems at the secondary level were idleness/slowness, again similar to recent Australian research (Little 2005) (scoring nearly 10 per cent for both most disruptive and most frequent), and *verbal abuse*, which also scored nearly 10 per cent for the most disruptive behaviour in secondary classes, with secondary teachers reporting a wider variety of behaviours than their primary school colleagues.

In the Hong Kong studies talking out of turn was perceived as the most disruptive and the most frequent behaviour by the majority of teachers at both primary and secondary school levels. As others had found, disruptiveness and the likelihood of occurrence of the behaviour (frequency) were 'very much related' (Ho and Leung 2002: 225). These findings add further weight to the considerable and accumulating evidence from around the world that behaviours that cause the most problems for teachers are of a mild, but constant, nature.

In summary, talking out of turn has been shown to be the consistent first choice of teachers in terms of what causes most disruption in the classroom. Irrespective of geographic location or level of schooling, talking out of turn is clearly the behaviour at the core of classroom disorder. This has been reported in the research literature for over 20 years.

Other perspectives

Some researchers have chosen to focus on the seriousness of student misbehaviour, rather than its troublesomeness or frequency in investigations of what causes difficulties for teachers.

Poulou and Norwich (2000) reported that Greek primary school teachers (see Table 11.1) rated as most serious "'work avoidance", "depressive mood", "negativism", "school phobia" and "lack of concentration"' (Poulou and Norwich 2000: 184). While these more internalising behaviours caused the most concern to teachers, it was, however, "'lack of concentration", "talking without permission", "untidiness" and "fidgeting"' (ibid.: 181) that were the most frequent behaviour problems encountered by these teachers.

Following earlier studies by Borg and Falzon (1989, 1990), Borg (1998) investigated secondary school teachers' perceptions of the seriousness of students' undesirable behaviour. This large study, involving 605 randomly selected teachers (302 female teachers and 303 male teachers) from 16 state secondary schools (all secondary schools in Malta are single-sex schools), comprised roughly equal numbers of teachers drawn from girls' and boys' schools (47 per cent from girls' schools, 53 per cent from boys' schools). At the secondary level, Borg found *drug abuse, cruelty/bullying* (in common with the primary study) and *destroying* to be the top three ranked most serious behaviours. *Stealing*, which had ranked as the most serious behaviour problem in the primary school study, was again ranked highly (fourth out of 49 behaviours), thereby still considered to be a problem at the secondary level. (Stuart (1994) had similar findings in her Australian study, i.e. stealing, destroying school property, and cruelty and bullying being the three most serious or undesirable behaviours faced by teachers of New South Wales secondary teachers, to be discussed below.)

Borg (1998) also found significant grade-level differences in perceived seriousness of behaviour, as well as a number of significant pupil sex and teacher sex differences. He argued that certain teacher, pupil and school characteristics acted as 'moderators' of the perceived seriousness of problem behaviours, adding further evidence to the effect of certain variables on teacher perceptions of problematic behaviour found in the earlier primary school studies in Malta (Borg and Falzon 1989, 1990). In contrast to the findings of other researchers at both the primary and secondary levels (e.g. Conway *et al.* (1990); Houghton *et al.* (1988); Little (2005); Merrett and Wheldall (1984); Wheldall and Merrett 1988), *interrupting* and *talkative/tattling* (both of which could be considered as talking-out-of-turn behaviours) were *not* considered serious for these Maltese teachers and were ranked a long way down the list in terms of perceived seriousness, ranking 37/49 and 43/49 respectively in this secondary school study (Borg 1998).

Moreover, in an Australian study seeking to determine if the findings of Wickman's seminal study (1928) were stable over time and culture, Stuart (1994) surveyed teachers using the 50 items from Wickman's list (1928). Stuart asked teachers how serious or undesirable each of the behaviours was in any Year 8 boy or girl. She found stealing (ranked second on Wickman's list), destroying school property (ranked tenth on Wickman's list), and cruelty and bullying (ranked eighth on Wickman's list) to be the three most serious or undesirable behaviours faced by teachers.

These findings may appear to be somewhat at odds with the general pattern of findings from the UK, Australian, and other studies in the area. The framing of the question focusing on seriousness should be borne in mind here, however. It could be argued that the terminology used by researchers such as Wheldall, Merrett, and Houghton in terms of signifying the degree or severity of the problem behaviour (most troublesome) (as opposed to frequency – most frequent) may well be interpreted differently by teachers from a request to consider what is the most serious problem behaviour of the student or class. Interestingly, Stuart (1994) commented that teachers' responses were similar regardless of whether they were asked to rate the behaviour of a particular student or to consider student behaviours more generally, a finding consistent with those of Wheldall, Merrett, and Houghton in their studies where the troublesome behaviour of the most troublesome individual students was invariably the same as those nominated for the class as a whole (Houghton *et al.* 1988; Merrett and Wheldall 1984; Wheldall and Merrett 1988).

In Australia, Stephenson *et al.* (2000) surveyed K-2 teachers about which child behaviours concerned them, as well as their needs for support in dealing with such behaviours (see Table 11.1). They found that the cluster of behaviours described as *distractibility or attention span a problem/does not listen* caused the most concern. This was followed by, in equal proportions, the four behaviours described as *physically aggressive with others/bullies; excessive demands for teacher's attention/does not work independently; does not remain on-task for a reasonable time;* and *disrupts the activities of others*.

Stephenson *et al.* (2000) noted that their results might have reflected some high levels of concern about relatively infrequent behaviour. Again, the manner in which a research question is framed may influence the findings. For instance, if one asks a teacher what might be the *serious* classroom behaviours with which they have to deal, the more dramatic, even dangerous, behaviours might be provided. The frequency of these types of behaviour, however, may be extremely low. In terms of the everyday impact on the teacher with regard to them 'getting on with their job' it might be quite small. This is not to say that incidents of serious classroom behaviour are not a cause for concern; they clearly are. What is of concern here, however, is the behaviour that causes day-to-day disruption in the classroom.

Without seeking to diminish the impact of isolated and infrequent serious events in schools, it could be argued that it is the daily, high-frequency, trivial classroom behaviours that are wearying for teachers over time. It is likely that it is these troublesome, but not serious, behaviours that are responsible for the stress related to classroom teaching.

Conclusion

What is clear from the literature reviewed above is that, while the evidence concerning estimates of the prevalence rates of behaviourally troublesome students remains somewhat equivocal, there is further evidence that disruptive classroom behaviour appears to increase as students move from the early years into the secondary years of schooling. There is also further, consistent evidence to show that teachers continue to perceive boys as more behaviourally troublesome than girls. Similarly, there is also convincing and mounting evidence to suggest that the classroom misbehaviours that teachers find most troublesome are relatively innocuous but occur so frequently as to be a recurrent cause for concern. This does not mean, however, that such misbehaviour does not affect teachers and their ability to do their job.

The findings from the present review point to the need to redouble our efforts in imparting sound, behaviourally inspired management skills in the preparation programmes for new teachers and in professional development programmes for existing teachers. It is perplexing that so few advances have been made in the successful management of disruptive classroom behaviour over the period of this and the previous review. Equipping teachers with the knowledge and skills to deal more positively with the inevitable challenges of classroom teaching is an essential element in improving the educational environment for students and teachers alike.

It would be a travesty if, as quickly as students with intellectual, physical, and sensory impairments were being included in regular classrooms, increasing numbers of students with behaviour problems were being excluded from the mainstream and moved into segregated educational settings. The push, often politically motivated, to remove turbulent students from the educational mainstream arguably has potentially dangerous outcomes, not only for the students themselves, but also for the community as a whole. Devoid of good role models, these students may not be best served by being thrust together in an environment in which aberrant behaviour is the norm. Parallels with the prison system should not go unnoticed. It must surely be a priority for education systems that as many students as possible are educated in the least restrictive educational environment and we must collectively guard against students with disruptive or troublesome behaviour becoming 'the new excluded'.

References

Arbuckle, C. and Little, E. (2004). Teachers' perceptions and management of disruptive classroom behaviour during the middle years (years five to nine). *Australian Journal of Educational and Developmental Psychology*, 4: 59–70.

Beaman, R. and Wheldall, K. (1997). Teacher perceptions of troublesome classroom behaviour. *Special Education Perspectives*, 6(2): 49–53.

Borg, M. (1998). Secondary school teachers' perception of pupils' undesirable behaviours. *British Journal of Educational Psychology*, 68: 67–79.

Borg, M. and Falzon, J. (1989). Primary school teachers' perception of pupils' undesirable behaviours. *Education Studies, 15*: 251–60.

Borg, M. and Falzon, J. (1990). Primary school teachers' perceptions of pupils' undesirable behaviours: The effects of teaching experience, pupils' age, sex and ability stream. *British Journal of Educational Psychology, 60*: 220–6.

Chazan, M. (1994). The attitudes of mainstream teachers towards pupils with emotional and behavioural difficulties. *European Journal of Special Needs Education, 9*: 261–74.

Conway, R., Tierney, J. and Schofield, N. (1990). Coping with behaviour problems in NSW high schools. In S. Richardson and J. Tizard (eds), *Practical approaches to resolving behaviour problems*. Hawthorn, Australia: ACER.

Conway, R. (2005). Encouraging positive interactions. In P. Foreman (ed.), *Inclusion in action*, 3rd ed. Southbank, Vic., Australia: Thomson Learning, 209–58.

Haroun, R. and O'Hanlon, C. (1997). Teachers' perceptions of discipline problems in a Jordanian secondary school. *Pastoral Care, June*: 29–36.

Harris, J., Tyre, C. and Wilkinson, C. (1993). Using the Child Behaviour Checklist in ordinary primary schools. *British Journal of Educational Psychology, 63*: 245–60.

Hart, P., Wearing, A. and Conn, M. (1995). Conventional wisdom is a poor predictor of the relationship between discipline policy, student misbehaviour and teacher stress. *British Journal of Educational Psychology, 65*: 27–48.

Herrera, M. and Little, E. (2005). Behaviour problems across home and kindergarten in an Australian sample. *Australian Journal of Educational and Developmental Psychology, 5*: 77–90.

Ho, C. and Leung, J. (2002). Disruptive classroom behaviours of secondary and primary school students. *Educational Research Journal, 17*: 219–33.

Houghton, S., Wheldall, K. and Merrett, F. (1988). Classroom behaviour problems which secondary school teachers say they find most troublesome. *British Educational Research Journal, 14*: 297–312.

Infantino, J. and Little, E. (2005). Students' perceptions of classroom behaviour problems and the effectiveness of different disciplinary methods. *Educational Psychology, 25*: 491–508.

Jacob, A. (2005). Behaviour – whose choice? *Australasian Journal of Special Education, 29*(1): 4–20.

Jenson, W., Olympia, D., Farley, M. and Clark, E. (2004). Positive psychology and externalising students in a sea of negativity. *Psychology in the Schools, 41*(1): 67–79.

Kann, R. and Hanna, F. (2000). Disruptive behaviour disorders in children and adolescents: How do girls differ from boys? *Journal of Counselling and Development, 78*: 267–74.

Kamphaus, R., Huberty, C., Distefano, C. and Petoskey, M. (1997). A typology of teacher-rated child behavior for a national US sample. *Journal of Abnormal Child Psychology, 25*: 453–63.

Kazdin, A. (1995). *Conduct disorders in childhood and adolescence*, 2nd ed. Thousand Oaks, CA: Sage.

Langdon, C. (1997, November). The fourth Phi Delta Kappa poll of teachers' attitudes towards the public schools. *Phi Delta Kappan, 78*: 212–10.

Leung, J. and Ho, C. (2001). Disruptive behaviour perceived by Hong Kong primary school teachers. *Educational Research Journal, 16*: 223–37.

Little, E. (2005). Secondary school teachers' perceptions of students' problem behaviours. *Educational Psychology, 25*: 369–77.

Little, E., Hudson, A. and Wilks, R. (2000). Conduct problems across home and school. *Behaviour Change, 17*: 69–77.

McGee, R., Sylva, P. and Williams, S. (1984). Behaviour problems in a population of seven year old children: Prevalence, stability and types of disorder: a research report. *Journal of Child Psychiatry, 25*: 251–59.

Merrett, F. and Wheldall, K. (1984). Classroom behaviour problems which junior primary school teachers find most troublesome. *Educational Studies, 10*, 87–92.

Mertin, P. and Wasyluk, G. (1994). Behaviour problems in the school: Incidence and interpretation. *Australian Educational and Developmental Psychologist, 11*(2): 32–9.

Oswald, M. (1995). Difficult to manage students: A survey of children who fail to respond to student discipline strategies in government school. *Educational Studies, 21*: 265–76.

Poulou, M. and Norwich, B. (2000). Teachers' perceptions of students with emotional and behavioural difficulties: Severity and prevalence. *European Journal of Special Needs Education, 15*(2): 171–87.

Stephenson, J., Linfoot, K. and Martin, A. (2000). Behaviours of concern to teachers in the early years of school. *International Journal of Disability, Development and Education, 47*: 225–35.

Stuart, H. (1994). Teacher perceptions of student behaviours: A study of NSW secondary teachers' attitudes. *Educational Psychology, 14*: 217–30.

Swinson, J., Woof, C. and Melling, R. (2003). Including emotional and behavioural difficulties pupils in a mainstream comprehensive: A study of the behaviour of pupils and classes. *Educational Psychology in Practice, 19*(1): 65–75.

Wheldall, K. and Merrett, F. (1988). Which classroom behaviours do primary school teachers say they find most troublesome? *Educational Review, 40*: 13–27.

Wickman, E. K. (1928). Teachers' list of undesirable forms of behaviour. In P. Williams (ed.) (1974). *Behaviour problems in school*. London: University of London Press, 6–15. (Reprinted from *Children's behaviour and teachers' attitudes*, New York, Commonwealth Fund.).

Chapter 12

Teachers' use of approval and disapproval in the classroom

Robyn Beaman and Kevin Wheldall

Since the 1960s, researchers have been demonstrating the power of teacher behaviour on the behaviour of both individual students and whole classes. Behavioural research and demonstration studies, carried out over the past 30 years or so, have consistently shown that teacher behaviour may be a powerful influence on the behaviour of both individual students and whole classes (see, for example, the classic studies by Becker *et al.* (1967); Madsen *et al.* (1968), and Thomas *et al.* 1968). Although such research was initially pioneered by behaviour analysts working in special education contexts, it has subsequently been clearly and unequivocally demonstrated, in a variety of educational contexts and settings, that such key teacher behaviours as contingent approval and disapproval may be systematically employed by teachers so as to increase both academic and appropriate social behaviours and to decrease inappropriate behaviours. (See, for example, Merrett (1981), Merrett and Wheldall (1987a, 1990), Wheldall and Merrett (1984, 1989), and Wheldall and Glynn (1989), for reviews of such studies.)

Consequently, it has become somewhat of a truism to advise teachers experiencing troublesome or inappropriate classroom behaviour to employ contingent praise strategies in order to encourage more appropriate behaviour (Merrett and Wheldall 1990; Wheldall and Merrett 1989). Moreover, the adoption of the principles of reinforcement originally developed by behaviour analysts in special education settings into the 'canon of teaching' leads many teachers to assert, when instructed on effective deployment of teacher approval and disapproval, 'But we do that already'. But how far is this, in fact, the case? Do teachers really selectively employ contingent approval or praise in order to reinforce desired classroom social behaviours? Or, when praise is given, is it employed in a non-contingent, unsystematic way? Do teachers even use more praise than reprimand?

While demonstrated effectively in the context of *experimental* studies, the research literature relating to non-experimentally manipulated or 'naturalistic' rates (White 1975) has been a more neglected area. White, in her seminal work on teacher approval and disapproval, suggested that 'little has been reported on rates of teacher verbal reinforcement as they actually occur in the classroom, that is, on what might be called *naturalistic* or *existing* rates' (White 1975: 367). The observation that Schwieso and Hastings (1987) made about the relative paucity of purely descriptive, naturalistic studies on the ways in which teachers typically use approval/praise in the classroom still holds true today. For this reason, this chapter will review studies involving teachers – teaching kindergarten classes to upper secondary classes – in an attempt to canvass the full range of studies dealing with naturalistic rates of teacher approval and disapproval.

The role and prevalence of teacher feedback

Clearly one of the most powerful factors in classroom interactions is that of teacher behaviour and, in particular, use of teacher approval and disapproval (e.g. praise and reprimand). In an article assessing the effects of 32 variables related to schooling in 7,827 studies using meta-analysis, Hattie (1992: 9) reported that 'the most powerful single moderator that enhances student achievement is feedback'. The effect-size for *reinforcement* (1.13) was found to be the largest of *all* variables.

While Schwieso and Hastings (1987: 124) acknowledged that 'it is a little obvious' to say that teaching is an interactive process, they do make the very valid observation that it is a point often ignored in the research into the complexities of the classroom. They also emphasised the importance of the interactive relationship between teacher behaviour and student behaviour in their discussion of teachers' rates of approval and disapproval in the classroom. They explained that while teachers' approval and disapproval may have some effect on their students, teacher responses are in part the effects or consequences of students' actions. 'Teachers do not approve or disapprove in vacuo' (Schwieso and Hastings 1987: 124). Or as Brophy (1981: 5) put it, 'much teacher praise is reactive to and under the control of student behavior rather than vice versa'. A more balanced perspective may be that of Nafpaktitis *et al.* (1985) who stated that in the feedback system of the classroom, 'students continually influence teacher behavior and vice versa' (Nafpaktitis *et al.* 1985: 366).

The study of natural rates of approval and disapproval in the classroom

Brophy (1981) provided a functional analysis of teacher praise. He reported findings from six separate studies carried out in the 1970s in the context of more general investigations into teacher–student interactions in the United States of America, all using the Brophy-Good dyadic interactions coding system. This system allowed for the separate coding of teachers' responses to academic performance versus classroom conduct (Brophy 1981), an important distinction in observations of teacher responses to student behaviour.

The data indicated that teachers *approved* of students' behaviour more than they disapproved and were most likely to praise 'good answers' or 'good work' than to criticise 'poor answers or poor work'. On the other hand, teachers were much more likely to criticise 'poor conduct' than to respond to 'good conduct'; teachers rarely praised students for appropriate behaviour (Brophy 1981: 6, 10). In all the studies reported by Brophy, praise for good conduct was the *least frequent* teacher response. Brophy's own summary of the data from these studies was that 'the typical teacher seldom praises good answers or good work and rarely praises good conduct' (ibid.: 10). This perception of infrequent praise was confirmed by Rutter *et al.* (1979). While investigating which within-school factors determined better behaviour, they reported that absolute rates of praise were 'rather low, usually only three or four instances per lesson' (Rutter *et al.* (1979), as cited in Schwieso and Hastings 1987: 127).

Seeking to determine the natural rates of teacher verbal approval and disapproval in classrooms, White (1975) reported the findings of 16 separate studies ($N = 104$) in the United States. Although some of the work of Brophy (and his colleagues) may have predated that of White, White's work is generally considered as the first to have as its *primary* focus natural rates of teacher approval and disapproval. Teachers in White's study were from a variety of schools teaching students from Grades 1 to 12.

White (1975) and her colleagues utilised an observation schedule known as TAD, an acronym for Teacher Approval and Disapproval Observation Record, in 16 separate studies. Teacher approval was defined as 'a verbal praise or encouragement', and teacher disapproval as 'a verbal criticism, reproach, or a statement that the student's behaviour should change from what was unacceptable to acceptable to the teacher' (White 1975: 368). A distinction was made between *instructional* versus *managerial* teacher responses in this study. To use other terminology, teacher responses were categorised according to whether they were in response to students' *academic* behaviour (instructional) or to their *social* behaviour (managerial). Contrary to Brophy's (1981) finding that teachers showed more approval than disapproval, the findings of White's analysis were that, with the exception of those teaching children in Grade 1 and Grade 2, teachers gave more *disapproving* than approving comments to their students overall.

White (1975) reported the highest teacher approval rate as being 1.3 verbal approval responses per observed minute occurring in Grade 2 (she did not report a mean rate per minute across all grades), with relatively high rates also occurring in Grade 1 (ranging from 0.27 to 0.95 responses per minute). As indicated above, after Grade 2, the rate declined sharply, until, according to White, it stabilised at about one teacher approval every 5 or 10 minutes. 'This means that in a typical class of 40 minutes, the teacher emits four to eight approvals during the entire class period' (White 1975: 369). Similarly, the rate of teacher disapproval peaked early in the years of schooling (in Grade 1 where in one study the rate was 0.89 per minute) and remained relatively high in Grade 2 where disapproval occurred at the rate of 0.69 per minute, on average.

In terms of responses to instructional or *academic* behaviour of students, teacher approval in White's study (1975) was *higher* than teacher disapproval in every grade.

Conversely, for managerial or social behaviour, teacher disapproval exceeded approval, once again, in every grade. Moreover, White (1975: 370) points to 'the almost nonexistent rate of teacher approval for managerial behaviour', with four of the 16 studies reported having a zero rate of approval statements to managerial behaviour in a total of 2,520 minutes of observation time (or 42 hours) (ibid.: 369). Given the evidence for the efficacy of approval or praise in reinforcing appropriate classroom social behaviour (see, for example, Merrett and Wheldall (1987a, 1990); Wheldall and Merrett (1984, 1989)) this is a disturbing finding.

In summary, White (1975) reported that students received more total teacher disapproval in every grade (with the exception of Grade 1 and Grade 2); for instructional behaviour alone, the rate of teacher approval was higher than the rate of teacher disapproval (particularly marked in the primary grades); and for managerial behaviour alone, teacher disapproval far outweighed teacher approval, the latter being 'almost nonexistent' (White, 1975: 370). Similarly, Heller and White (1975) investigated the effect of the ability level of the class on teachers' rates of verbal approval and disapproval. Five social studies teachers and five mathematics teachers from an inner-city junior high school were observed teaching both higher- and lower-ability classes. The researchers found that teachers 'emitted more disapprovals in lower ability classes than in the higher ability classes' (Heller and White 1975: 796). Moreover, the higher rate of disapprovals directed at students in lower-ability classes were predominantly *managerial* in nature, addressing social (rather than academic) behaviours. Rates of approval, however, did not change across ability groupings, were almost exclusively directed toward academic behaviour, and exceeded the number of disapprovals of academic behaviour (Heller and White 1975).

In terms of the subject taught there were differences evident between mathematics and social studies teachers, with disproportionate amounts of disapproval being found in social studies classes. In mathematics classes, on the other hand, the numbers of disapprovals and approvals were roughly equal. Like White (1975), Heller and White (1975) also found that, in general, 'teachers almost never praised pupils for behaving well socially' (ibid.: 796). An interesting anecdotal finding in this study was that, of the 1,105 evaluative verbal responses (EVRs, the total of approving and disapproving statements) teachers made to students' behaviour, only one of these teacher responses was a managerial (or social) approval statement. On this one occasion, a teacher said 'Good' after a student indicated that he had brought a pen to class that day (ibid.: 799). Clearly, teachers in this study did not praise students for behaving appropriately or for following classroom procedures.

Thomas *et al.* (1978) sought to compare their findings with the natural rates of approval and disapproval reported by White (1975) for Grade 7 teachers. They investigated the natural rates of teacher verbal approval and disapproval in ten Grade 7 classrooms in New Zealand. Their study did not, however, use the (useful if not critical) distinction between managerial (social) and instructional (academic) teacher responses, as White had done in her work. Moreover, observers only recorded, as an approval response, teachers' verbal responses that were contingent on the on-task behaviour of the student being observed. Similarly, a disapproval response was recorded contingent on off-task behaviour being observed (Thomas *et al.* 1978). In other words, as a consequence of this method of classification, any non-contingent approval or disapproval received by students was not recorded. While one would consider it logically unlikely that students would be praised (or reprimanded) non-contingently, other research (reviewed later) has suggested that this can be the case.

Despite differences in observation techniques employed (in addition to cultural and other differences between the samples) the results of the study by Thomas *et al.* (1978) were broadly similar to those of White (1975). The majority of teachers displayed individual rates of disapproval that were higher than their individual approval rates. Moreover, seven of the ten teachers had disapproval rates at least three times greater than their approval rates. It is interesting to note that the rates of disapproval per observed minute for seventh-graders in each study were *exactly* the same at 0.58. Approval rates per minute of observation in the study conducted by Thomas *et al.* (1978) were slightly lower at 0.20 than White (1975) reported for Grade 7 teachers (0.34).

All of the studies discussed thus far limited the definition of teacher approval and disapproval to *verbal* responses. In Australia, Russell and Lin (1977) broadened positive teacher attention or response to include non-verbal responses. In their study, approval responses were deemed to include 'contact, praise, facial attention, and academic recognition' (Russell and Lin 1977: 151), with disapproval responses being defined as criticism, threats, facial attention, ignoring, holding the child, sending the child out of the room, and punishment. Selected students in one (only) Grade 7 class of 37 students were identified as belonging to the 'worst-behaved' group (WB) (*n* = 10) and the 'best-behaved' group (BB) (*n* = 10).

Results of the study indicated that the WB group received more teacher attention – of any kind – than did the BB group. The teacher responded pro-portionately more to the inappropriate behaviour of the WB group, responding approximately 15 per cent of the time to the inappropriate behaviour of this group, and only 2 per cent of the time to the inappropriate behaviour of the BB group. This finding was predicted on the basis of the notion that teacher attention serves to maintain high rates of inappropriate classroom behaviour (Russell and Lin 1977). An unexpected finding of the study, however, was that the teacher also responded proportionately more to the *appropriate* behaviour of the WB group, about 16 per cent of the time, than to the appropriate behaviour of the BB group (3 per cent). On the basis of this finding, the authors suggested that the high levels of appropriate behaviour of the BB group were not being maintained by teacher attention to this behaviour, and could have been main-tained by factors other than teacher factors; some possibilities being intrinsic interest in work or satisfaction in achievement and mastery (Russell and Lin 1977). Caution should be exercised, however, in placing too much credence on explanations offered as a result of this study. Russell and Lin were relying, after all, on a sample of one teacher and her class. Findings from such a small sample should clearly be viewed with tentative interest at best. The significance of Russell and Lin's (1977) findings relates more to the fact that they appear to be the first to include non-verbal responses to the operational definition of teacher attention in the investigations of naturalistic rates of teacher approval and disapproval, than to the generalisability of their findings.

In similar vein, Fry (1983) observed teacher–student interactions in classrooms over a four-month period in order to examine similarities and differences between teacher–student interactions in the cases of 'problem' and 'non-problem' children. Due to the nature of the observation schedule used, teacher approvals and disapprovals were not recorded as such. Rather, 15 teacher and student process measure variables were used, covering eight teacher behaviours and seven student behaviours. Teacher variables pertinent to the present discussion included 'positive affect', operationally defined as teacher behaviours that show support or positive regard for students and their behaviour (including such behaviour as smiling, joking, reinforcement and praise), and 'negative affect', defined as verbal or non-verbal behaviours reflecting hostility or negative feelings of the teacher (including negative teacher evaluation of student behaviour, expressing anger or criticism) (Fry 1983).

Fry found that problem children received less positive affect from teachers, and received more negative affect from them, compared with their non-problem peers. Moreover, problem children obtained fewer 'social contacts' with their teachers, received less 'sustaining feedback' and were asked less frequently by their teachers 'to express their personal views and preferences on academic and class-related issues' (Fry 1983: 83).

In addition, the differences evident between the problem and non-problem groups increased over the period of a school term. Concomitant with the change in teacher behaviour, observations of problem children's behavioural interactions 'suggest an increase in serious misdemeanours and a corresponding decline in sustained attention' (ibid.: 79). It was reported that problem children's serious misbehaviours increased from one instance per hour to almost 2.8 instances per hour by the end of the four-month period (ibid.). Clearly, while causality between teacher behaviour and student behaviour cannot be established, this study provided an interesting perspective on the impact of teachers' social and affective orientation towards their students over time, particularly towards students who present as being behaviourally troublesome. Fry suggested that teachers needed to be more aware of their interactions with problem students, commenting that the results of the study:

> tentative as they are, suggest that problem children's disruptive behaviours and decline in sustained attention may not necessarily reflect true problem behaviour. It is quite likely that they are mediated more often than we suspect by the prevailing attitudes and orientations of the teacher.
>
> (Fry 1983: 87)

Strain *et al.* (1983), in the United States, investigated children's compliance to teachers' requests and the consequences for compliance. Nineteen teachers and 130 elementary school children from Kindergarten to Grade 3 were involved in this study of naturally occurring levels of teacher commands, and positive and negative teacher feedback. Students were selected on the basis of their social adjustment to school, being 'high-rated' (making a good adjustment to school) or 'low-rated' (not making a good social adjustment to school) (Strain *et al.* 1983: 243). In the low-rated group (*n* = 55), boys outnumbered girls 3 to 1. In the high-rated group (*n* = 75), girls outnumbered boys by a 1.5 to 1 margin. There was an approximately equal distribution of high- and low-rated students across the 19 classes in the study. As was the case in the Russell and Lin (1977) study, Strain *et al.* included gestures as teacher responses, as well as verbal behaviour. Teacher behaviour was classified as (a) teacher's commands, demands, requests; (b) teacher's positive social consequences; (c) teacher's negative feedback; or (d) teacher's *repeated* command, demand, request. Student behaviour was reported only as students' compliance (Strain *et al.* 1983: 246–7). For our purposes here, the findings for the classification 'teacher's positive social consequences' and 'teacher's negative feedback' are the most relevant.

Strain and colleagues reported that, given an episode of child compliance (by a member of either the low-rated or the high-rated group), the probability of positive social consequences was 0.10. Expressed differently, only 10 out of every 100 episodes of compliance were followed by positive feedback from the teacher. In addition to these low levels of approval, the differential treatment of the two groups was of particular interest. The vast majority (45/55 or 82 per cent) of low-rated children *never* received any positive social consequences for compliance, compared with only 27 per cent (or 20/75) of high-rated children. In terms of teachers' negative feedback, the probability that teachers would respond was 0.14 for the low-rated group, and 0.10 for the high-rated group. This difference was not statistically significant, however. Overall, the general level of feedback, including both positive and negative responses, was considered low (Strain *et al.* 1983).

In addition to corroborating and expanding on previous studies such as those of White (1975) and Thomas *et al.* (1978), all of whom found that teachers were generally inclined to provide more disapproval than approval, Strain *et al.* (1983) reported another significant finding. Teachers in their study demonstrated that a good proportion of positive feedback provided may have been contingent on *non-compliance*. In fact, misplaced positive contingencies occurred almost as often as appropriately delivered consequences. As Strain *et al.* concluded, it would appear that the group of children 'most in need of systematic feedback (low-rated group) were exposed regularly to contingency arrangements counterproductive to compliance' (ibid.: 248).

These findings, considered with the findings of Russell and Lin (1977) and those of Fry (1983) described above, suggest that teachers, at best, were not taking advantage of opportunities to reinforce appropriate behaviour in any overt, systematic way. At worst, they could have been reinforcing the inappropriate behaviours of their students. It would appear from these three studies that the students most affected by this style of behaviour management (or mismanagement) were those who most desperately needed classroom behaviour management to be effective.

The shift to more teacher approval than disapproval

With the exception of the studies reported by Brophy (1981), all other studies reported thus far found that teachers disapproved of student behaviour more than they approved of it. Findings from a study by Nafpaktitis *et al.* (1985) carried out in 84 classrooms in 29 intermediate schools in Los Angeles, however, changed this trend of results. The purpose of this study was to investigate the naturally occurring rates of verbal and non-verbal teacher approval of appropriate student behaviour, approval of inappropriate student behaviour, and teacher disapproval. The distinction between appropriate approval and inappropriate approval was as follows: appropriate approval was defined as approval following student on-task behaviour and inappropriate approval as following student off-task behaviour (Nafpaktitis *et al.* 1985).

As indicated above, and in contrast to most previous studies, Nafpaktitis *et al.* (1985) found that teachers provided students with *more appropriate approval* responses than disapproval responses. For most classes in the study, higher rates of student on-task behaviour were associated with higher rates of approval and lower rates of disapproval. Approval responses were observed as occurring at the mean rate of 1.3 per minute, although 0.40 of these were classified as 'inappropriate approval', leaving a mean rate of 0.90 appropriate approval responses per observed minute. (This finding confirmed the concern expressed by Strain *et al.* (1985) about inappropriately delivered consequences, described above.) Disapproving responses were occurring at the lower mean rate of 0.29 per minute observed (Nafpaktitis *et al.* 1985). Nafpaktitis *et al.* explored the relationship between teacher response and student on-task behaviour, to which we return later in this chapter.

In terms of the trend of findings reported so far (with the exception of those of Brophy 1981), it would seem prudent to heed the caution expressed by Nafpaktitis *et al.* (1985: 366) that it was perhaps 'premature' to conclude that the findings of the previous studies (such as those of White (1975); Heller and White 1975) reflect the norm in terms of teachers' use of approval and disapproval. In light of the work reported from the mid-1980s on, this advice would appear to be well founded.

A study in the United States designed largely as a follow-up to White (1975), and conducted by Wyatt and Hawkins (1987), confirmed that the caution issued by Nafpaktitis *et al.* (1985) was indeed warranted. In their study of 35 classrooms, which included classes from Kindergarten to Grade 4, as well as Grades 9 and 12, Wyatt and Hawkins utilised a modified version of the TAD observation schedule (the instrument used in White's study). The modification involved determining whether verbal responses to students' behaviour were descriptive or non-descriptive (Wyatt and Hawkins 1987). This study sought to determine the rates of teachers' *verbal* approval and disapproval in relation to grade level, classroom activity, student behaviour, and teacher characteristics. Teachers were observed for five 30 minute sessions over a two week period. The exclusion of non-verbal teacher responses made this study more similar to the early work in this area and dissimilar to the work of Nafpaktitis *et al.* (and later studies to be reported) who examined *both* verbal and non-verbal approval and disapproval. Wyatt and Hawkins (1987) stated that one of the reasons for their study was to clarify the discrepancy between the rates found by White and those found by Nafpaktitis *et al.*

Unlike White (1975), who found a preponderance of *disapproval* at every grade above Grade 2, Wyatt and Hawkins (1987) showed that approval was more frequent than disapproval *at every grade level* involved in their study. Approval was highest in Grade 1 where teachers provided 0.52 responses per minute, after which such responses generally declined (with the exception of Grade 9 where teachers were found to provide approval at the rate of 0.40 responses per minute, on average). By Grade 12, teachers were providing approval at the mean rate of 0.17 responses per minute.

In terms of disapproval, there was a similar pattern to the data with disapproval peaking in Grade 1 (0.52 responses per minute) and declining thereafter, except (again) for Grade 9 where teachers responded disapprovingly at the mean rate of 0.23 responses per minute. Again, by Grade 12, teachers were providing disapproval responses at the lowest rate across all grades (0.11 responses per minute, on average). While the pattern of disapproval responses was similar to that of approval responses across grades, such responses were significantly lower than approval responses in all grades except in Grade 1 and Grade 3 (Wyatt and Hawkins 1987).

Notwithstanding the difference in findings that showed approval predominating in teacher responses, Wyatt and Hawkins (1987) claimed that the *absolute* levels of responses found in their study were often similar to those found by White (1975). Extrapolating mean total approval and disapproval rates from information presented in the report of their study, Wyatt and Hawkins found a mean total approval rate of 0.38 responses per minute and a mean total disapproval of 0.28 per minute in the 1987 study. (*Note:* No mean total rates were reported by White (1975). Rather, results were presented discretely by grade.) Moreover, both studies found a (generally) declining trend across grades for teacher approval. (Disapproval tended to decline more consistently after Grade 9 in both studies.) Another area of agreement between the two studies related to the finding that approvals were primarily for academic behaviour (*instructional* was the term used in White's study), whereas disapprovals were primarily for conduct, (or *managerial* in the case of White's study) (Wyatt and Hawkins, 1987), a situation that pertained at every grade level, in *both* studies. For instance, when the data for all teachers were combined in the Wyatt and Hawkins' study, the average teacher praised *academic* behaviours at a rate of 0.33 per minute, whereas conduct behaviours were approved of infrequently at only 0.05 per minute (ibid.). Similarly, academic behaviours were disapproved of 0.09 times per minute, on average, whereas conduct behaviours were disapproved of at a rate of 0.19 times per minute.

The finding that there were no statistically significant relationships between teachers' ages, years of full-time teaching experience, recency of teachers' latest degree, and approval and disapproval rates led Wyatt and Hawkins (1987) to conclude that no assumptions should be made about the 'type' of teacher who is likely to deliver appropriate levels of approval and disapproval in the classroom. Rather, they claimed, any need for 'retraining' should be made on the basis of direct classroom observation and the outcomes teachers produce. Moreover, the researchers argued that such assessment and retraining should be carried out by behaviour analysts in schools; a likely outcome of such intervention being improved 'academic performance, conduct, and enjoyment of school for both students and teachers' (Wyatt and Hawkins 1987: 48).

The changing measurement of teacher approval and disapproval

In Brophy's (1981) functional analysis of teacher praise, referred to earlier, he made the distinction, both for 'praise' and 'criticism', between simple feedback statements and teacher reactions that go beyond 'mere affirmation of correctness of response' (Brophy 1981: 6). As Schwieso and Hastings (1987) pointed out, this distinction was particularly important for Brophy since he argued that feedback was virtually never harmful whereas praise might be. Moreover, they believed this distinction may, in part, be responsible for the depressed rates of both praise and criticism found in the studies Brophy reported compared with those found in, for example, White (1975) and Heller and White (1975) (Schwieso and Hastings 1987). Brophy considered that praise may be defined as having the same meaning and connotations as it does in everyday language: 'to commend the worth of or to express approval or admiration' (Brophy 1981: 5). Brophy also distinguished praise and criticism from more global approaches such as 'warmth' or 'hostility' (ibid.: 6).

While Schwieso and Hastings (1987) acknowledged that Brophy's (1981) distinction between feedback and praise made conceptual sense, they also conceded that, in practice, it 'may be difficult to decide when, for instance, a teacher says "Correct!", whether it includes an evaluative component or is pure feedback' (Schwieso and Hastings 1987: 116). Accordingly, they argued that observation systems that employed categories such as *approval, positive approval,* or *positive feedback* minimised the practical difficulties of classifying a response as an evaluative comment (for example, communicating approval) or purely as a feedback statement. Such observation schedules included within them all those teacher actions, 'which, on the face of it, seem to include some degree of evaluation' (ibid.: 116). Merrett and Wheldall (1986) developed such an observation system known as OPTIC (Observing Pupils and Teachers In Classrooms). Teacher approvals, which Merrett and Wheldall termed *positive events*, and teacher disapprovals, correspondingly called *negative events*, included both verbal and non-verbal manifestations of approval and disapproval.

Given that many of the remaining studies to be reported have utilised the OPTIC schedule, some details of the schedule's characteristics are included. OPTIC allows the observer to look systematically at two main aspects of classroom behaviour (namely teacher behaviour and student behaviour, specifically on-task behaviour) (Merrett and Wheldall, 1987b). In section A of the schedule, the observer is concerned with positive (approval or praise) and negative (disapproval or reprimand) teacher responses to students' academic and social behaviours. For the purposes of this schedule, instructional language is ignored. Section B is concerned with estimating students' on-task behaviour. Observers alternate between section A and section B at three-minute intervals, fives times for each section. Each observation session lasts a total of 30 minutes. Typically, a class is observed on at least three separate occasions (Merrett and Wheldall 1986). The instrument has been shown to be both reliable and valid, with inter-observer agreement figures for both sections of the schedule averaging over 90 per cent (Merrett and Wheldall 1986; Merrett and Wheldall 1987b).

Employing the OPTIC schedule, Merrett and Wheldall (1987b) reported the natural rates of teacher approval and disapproval in British primary and middle school classrooms. The sample consisted of 128 primary and middle school teachers and their classes. Merrett and Wheldall (1987b) found that teachers typically responded with more approval than disapproval to their students. This finding confirmed the earlier finding of Nafpaktitis *et al.* (1985), as well as the contemporaneous work of Wyatt and Hawkins (1987), whose studies were both conducted on the other side of the Atlantic in the United States of America, thereby providing evidence of generalisability of this phenomenon across countries and education systems. Expressed as a percentage of the total responses to student behaviour, Merrett and Wheldall (1987b) found total approval to academic and social behaviours (56 per cent) was slightly higher than total disapproval to these behaviours (44 per cent). Expressed as a mean rate per minute, total approval to student behaviour occurred at the rate of 1.15 (similar to the rate reported by Nafpaktitis *et al.* of 1.3 per minute, discussed earlier. Note, however, that 0.40 of this approval was deemed inappropriate approval, resulting in a rate of *appropriate approval* of 0.90 per minute). Total disapproval occurred at a rate of 0.93, a somewhat higher figure than that found by Nafpaktitis *et al.* (0.29), and that found by Thomas *et al.* (1978) for Grade 7 students in New Zealand (0.58), and reported earlier.

Although overall rates of approval were found to be higher than rates of disapproval in the study by Merrett and Wheldall (1987b), a high proportion of this teacher approval was in response to students' *academic* behaviour. For academic behaviour *alone*, positive responses were three times as frequent as negative responses. On the other hand, negative responses to *social* behavior were five times as frequent as positive responses. The findings from this study demonstrated that while teachers were very adept at recognising and rewarding appropriate *academic* behaviour, the same could not be said about their ability to recognise and reward appropriate *social* behaviour. Consequently, while approval for academic behaviour was much higher than disapproval, for social behaviour the reverse was the case. Merrett and Wheldall (1987b: 100) argued that teachers were:

> very quick to notice social behaviour of which they disapprove and continually nag children about it … But they hardly ever approve of desirable social behaviour … In other words, children are expected to behave well and are continually reprimanded if they do not.

Merrett and Wheldall's (1987b) findings in relation to teacher responses to social behaviour confirmed both earlier (see Brophy (1981); Heller and White (1975); Nafpaktitis *et al.* (1985); White 1975) and contemporaneous (see Wyatt and Hawkins 1987) findings.

Having investigated natural rates of teacher approval and disapproval in primary and middle schools, Wheldall *et al.* (1989) extended their work to British secondary school classrooms. A sample of 130 secondary school teachers and their classes were observed, the OPTIC schedule being employed once again. Students in the classes ranged in age from 11 to 16 years. In line with the findings from the earlier primary/middle school study, Wheldall *et al.* found that teachers used more approval (55 per cent of the total responses) than disapproval overall, a figure almost exactly the same as for the earlier study (56 per cent) reported above. Once again, 'most of the approval was directed at academic pupil behaviours, whereas most of the disapproval was for inappropriate social behaviour' (Wheldall *et al.* 1989: 38). For academic behaviour alone, positive responses were three times as frequent as negative responses, the exact opposite being the case for responses to social behaviour (i.e. there were three times as many negative responses as there were positive ones). The total approval rate expressed as a mean per observed minute was 0.65, substantially lower than the rate in the primary/middle school study (1.15). The total disapproval rate of 0.53 was, again, considerably lower than in the primary sample (Wheldall *et al.* 1989).

The rates of both approval and disapproval found by Wheldall *et al.* (1989) were higher than those found by Wyatt and Hawkins (1987), where approval occurred at rates of 0.40 and 0.17 per minute for Grades 9 and 12 respectively, while disapproval occurred at rates of 0.23 and 0.11 per minute for Grades 9 and 12 respectively. It should be remembered, however, that in the Wyatt and Hawkins (1987) study *verbal* responses only were recorded. This difference of approach could account for the higher levels of both approval and disapproval in the UK study (Wheldall *et al.* 1989).

When the data were analysed according to age of class taught, Wheldall *et al.* (1989) confirmed White's (1975) (general) finding that as students increased in age, teacher *approval* decreased accordingly (although Wheldall *et al.* concluded that, in general, differences between year groups were small). A similar finding was evident in the Wyatt and Hawkins (1987) study. While in agreement with White (1975) over the general trend of decreasing absolute rates of approval as age of students increased, the predominance of approval over disapproval is a major point of difference between Wheldall *et al.* (1989) and White (1975), as well as with other earlier high school studies such as those of Heller and White (1975) and Thomas *et al.* (1978) 'who found teachers in grades 7 and 9 more disapproving than approving' (Wheldall *et al.* 1989: 45). (As already indicated, White had found more disapproval than approval in *all* secondary classes included in her study (1975).) The data from Wheldall *et al.* (1989) is in line, however, with the findings of Nafpaktitis *et al.* (1985) and those of Wyatt and Hawkins (1987) in respect of teachers being, overall, more approving than disapproving of their students.

Further investigations into the natural rates of teacher approval and disapproval using OPTIC were carried out by Winter (1990) in secondary school classes in Hong Kong. Eighty-six teachers and their classes were observed (on one occasion only), providing data that confirmed many of the findings of Wheldall *et al.* (1989) (the secondary school study). Winter also found that teacher approval overall (63 per cent) exceeded teacher disapproval, with approval of academic behaviour (50 per cent of all responses) accounting for the vast majority of approval responses. While not provided in the article, absolute rates per minute can be extrapolated from the data Winter provided. Teacher approval occurred at the mean rate of 1.0 per minute, while teacher disapproval was a little more than half the rate of approval at 0.58 responses per minute. Positive responses to academic behaviour were the most prevalent (0.79 responses per minute), the approval of appropriate social behaviour being approximately one quarter of this figure at 0.21 responses per minute. When it came to disapproval, teachers provided more negative responses to the social behaviour of their students (0.33 responses per minute) than to their academic behaviour (0.25 responses per minute), and this was in line with the findings of previous studies (see Merrett and Wheldall (1987b); Wheldall *et al.* (1989); Wyatt and Hawkins 1987).

Further work in this area was reported by Charlton *et al.* (1995). Observations using the OPTIC schedule were undertaken in 15 classes on the isolated Atlantic island of St Helena. Students in the study ranged in age from 7 years to 10 years, being drawn from three 'first' and three 'middle' schools. Five classroom observations were obtained for each teacher and class. Findings from St Helena classrooms showed that teachers distributed more approval than disapproval responses to their students' behaviour (Charlton *et al.* 1995). Clearly, this finding replicated those found by Nafpaktitis *et al.* (1985), Merrett and Wheldall (1987b), Wyatt and Hawkins (1987), Wheldall *et al.* (1989), and Winter (1990). The mean rate per minute for total approval was 1.61 and 1.41 in first and middle schools respectively, with the mean rate for total disapproval being 0.50 and 0.89 for first and middle schools respectively. The approval rates reported here are higher than for any other study reported in this chapter.

A major difference in the findings of Charlton *et al.* (1995) was evident, however. In the case of first schools, more teacher responses were made to social (57 per cent) behaviours than to academic behaviours (43 per cent). In no other study has this been the case. In fact, three times as many approval as disapproval responses were made by first school teachers to *both* academic and social behaviours. In the middle schools group, marginally more responses were made to academic (52 per cent) than to social behaviours (48 per cent), being more in line with trends in other studies. The rate of approval to social behaviour was still high relative to other findings, however. Moreover, in this study, first and middle school student academic and social behaviour *both* attracted more approval responses from teachers than disapproval responses.

Charlton *et al.* posit a number of possible explanations as to why teachers in St Helena were so approving, ranging from reasons of geographical isolation, cultural differences in interactions, the absence of television, to the teachers on the island 'getting it right' (Charlton *et al.* 1995: 824) in terms of classroom behaviour management. High levels of on–task behaviour reported in this study (96 per cent for first and 92 per cent for middle schools), together with mode of teacher responses suggest that the classrooms of St Helena are an exemplar of effective classroom behaviour management.

Following the earlier work in this area (and specifically that of Merrett and Wheldall (1987b), Wheldall *et al.* (1989), and Wyatt and Hawkins 1987), Harrop and Swinson (2000) sought to examine teacher approval and disapproval 'a further ten years later' (Harrop and Swinson, 2000: 473) in the context of British classrooms. Harrop and Swinson used radio microphones (a technique not used in previous studies) to record teacher responses in 10 classes at each level of infants, junior, and secondary schooling. They reported that their results were generally in line with the investigations of the 1980s, specifically those of Merrett and Wheldall (1987b), Wheldall *et al.* (1989), and Wyatt and Hawkins (1987), where approval rates were higher than disapproval rates at each school level (Harrop and Swinson 2000). Similarly, they found (like many other researchers, such as Merrett and Wheldall (1987b); Wheldall *et al.* (1989); White (1975); Winter (1990); Wyatt and Hawkins 1987) that, overall, teachers gave higher rates of approval for academic behaviours than for social behaviours and higher rates of disapproval for social behaviours than for academic behaviours. Combining the data from all levels of schooling (there were very few differences in each level, see below), teachers in this study provided, on average, 1.30 approval responses per minute and 0.58 disapproval responses per minute. Of particular relevance to this chapter is the finding that secondary teachers in this study provided, on average, 1.27 approval responses and 0.42 disapproval responses per minute (Harrop and Swinson 2000). This is comparable with the findings of Wheldall *et al.* and Winter who, while finding lower rates of approval at the secondary level (0.65 and 1.0 responses per minute respectively), found very *similar* rates of disapproval (0.53 and 0.58 responses per minute) to those found in the study by Harrop and Swinson (0.58 negatives responses per minute).

The summary of reported rates of teacher approval and disapproval to academic and social behaviour detailed by Harrop and Swinson (2000) provides a clear picture of what was occurring in the classrooms in this study. While disapproval to *academic* behaviour occurred about 14 times every hour, disapproval to *social* behaviour occurred at the higher rate of about 21 responses per hour. In sharper contrast, approval to *academic* behaviour occurred at the high rate of about 72 times per hour, whereas approval to *social* behaviour occurred only about three times in an hour. It was clear that while students were receiving considerable positive feedback about their academic behaviour, being recognised for behaving *appropriately* was a rare occurrence. Furthermore, the finding that the ratio of approval to disapproval for *social* behaviour (0.04 to 0.61 or 1:15) was the same as reported in White (1975) for the parallel response category *managerial behaviour* (Harrop and Swinson 2000), is compelling evidence that not much had changed in terms of how teachers respond to the inappropriate social behaviour of their students in the quarter of a century since White first investigated natural rates of approval and disapproval.

Unlike earlier studies (such as those of White (1975); Wyatt and Hawkins (1987); Wheldall *et al.* 1989), the work completed by Harrop and Swinson (2000) did not find that teacher approval decreased with the increasing age of students and reported that there were no statistically significant differences in approval rates between infants, primary, and secondary classes involved in their study. As noted above, another point of difference between Wheldall *et al.* (1987) (the most relevant earlier study in terms of secondary classes) and Harrop and Swinson (2000), was that the level of *approval* in the latter study was twice that found in Wheldall *et al.* (1989) for British *secondary* classes. Moreover, a deviation from the pattern of typical responses was evident in the secondary classes (only) in this study, where teachers gave more disapproval to academic behaviours than to social behaviours (notwithstanding the general statements above). This anomaly was commented on by the authors who stated, 'That the results for the secondary study did not fit the overall pattern may or may not be a chance aberration' (Harrop and Swinson 2000: 481).

Table 12.1 provides a summary of the natural rates of teacher approval and disapproval reported in relevant studies. Comparative rates of approval and disapproval per minute are presented. Some of these data have been extrapolated from information in the studies where they were not reported directly. In addition, a summary is provided of teacher approval in the various studies, expressed as a percentage of all responses, to provide a means of comparing teacher approval behaviour over time.

As can be seen from Table 12.1, and as already mentioned, a shift from a preponderance of disapproval to approval was reported from the mid-1980s with the shift being sustained to the most recent study by Harrop and Swinson (2000).

Table 12.1 Natural rates (per minute) of teacher approval and disapproval and percentage of all responses being approvals – empirical studies

Study/Place	Approval	Disapproval	Percentage approval
White (1975) USA	0.41	0.46	47
Heller and White (1975) USA	0.29	0.52	36
Thomas, Presland, Grant and Glynn (1978) NZ	0.20	0.58	26
Nafpaktitis, Mayer and Butterworth (1985) US	0.90	0.29	76
Wyatt and Hawkins (1987) USA	0.38	0.28	58
Merrett and Wheldall (1987) UK	1.15	0.93	55
Wheldall, Houghton and Merrett (1989) UK	0.65	0.53	55
Winter (1990) Hong Kong	1.0	0.58	63
Charlton, Lovemore, Essex and Crowie (1995) (first schools) St Helena	1.61	0.50	76
Charlton, Lovemore, Essex and Crowie (1995) (middle schools) St Helena	1.41	0.89	61
Harrop and Swinson (2000) UK	1.30	0.58	69

But not all agree that this shift has represented much of a change in teacher responses. Others argue for the fact that there has been little change in classroom interactions since the mid-1970s. Galton *et al.* (1999), who conducted a repeat of the ORACLE (Observational Research and Classroom Learning Evaluation) study (the first of which commenced in 1975 and involved 58 British junior classrooms in the UK in a five-year project) found, among other things, results that suggested that the *balance* between teachers' use of praise and criticism had remained constant over the 20 years between 1976 and 1996 (Galton *et al.* 1999: 33). While changes such as increases in the amount of whole-class teaching were evident, there was no evidence of any radical shift in the pattern of the 'moment by moment exchanges taking place between teachers and pupils' (ibid.: 33). In spite of considerable evidence that teacher-manipulated rates of approval and disapproval can change the behavioural characteristics of the classroom, it would appear that many teachers still fail to take full advantage of this potentially powerful behaviour management tool. Or, as Wyatt and Hawkins (1987: 28) observed some time ago:

> [We] believe that teacher approval is a profoundly important and primarily positive tool in education. This opinion seems widespread because it is commonplace now to teach education students about the importance of contingent approval, although training them to *use* it appears to be unusual.

Relationships among teacher responses and between teacher response and student on-task behaviour

Relationships among teacher responses

Some researchers who have investigated discrete types of teacher attention have explored possible relationships among the various forms of teacher attention. For instance, at the primary school level, Merrett and Wheldall (1987b) found that *teacher approval* to academic behaviour was significantly, but weakly, related to *disapproval* of academic behaviour, but was also inversely related to *disapproval of social* behaviour. In addition, *disapproval* of *social* behaviour was significantly related to disapproval of *academic* behaviour. No other teacher responses were related in that study.

Wheldall *et al.* (1989), in their secondary school study, reported that teacher *approval* to *academic* behaviour was significantly related to *disapproval* of *academic* behaviour, a relationship that had only been weak in the parallel primary study (reported above). Teacher approval to academic behaviour was also strongly related to approval of *social* behaviour. Another relationship was evident between teacher disapproval of academic behaviour and approval of social behaviour. Except in respect of the similarities regarding approval and disapproval of academic behaviour (which were weak in the primary study), there were no similarities in terms of the relationships among teacher response variables in the Wheldall and Merrett (1987) and the Wheldall *et al.* (1989) studies.

Nafpaktitis *et al.* (1985) presented information regarding the intercorrelations among teacher behaviour and student behaviour (to be reported below). Among the teacher response variables alone, while there were no relationships evident between teacher disapproval and either appropriate approval or inappropriate approval, there was some relationship evident between teacher disapproval and inappropriate approval.

Winter (1990) provided a slightly different form of relationships analysis among teacher response variables and reported a significant relationship between total teacher approval and approval to academic behaviour. Conversely, there was a relationship between teacher disapproval and disapproval to social behaviour in his Hong Kong study. These relationships merely support the findings reported earlier that most teacher approval is directed at academic behaviour and most teacher disapproval is directed at the social behaviour of students.

Swinson and Harrop (2001) found that, while teacher approval and teacher disapproval were significantly and inversely correlated at the junior school level, this was not the case at the infants' school level. They interpreted this to mean that 'junior school teachers who give high levels of approval tend to give relatively low levels of disapproval and vice versa, as might be expected' (Swinson and Harrop 2001: 163–4). They attributed the absence of this relationship as possibly being the result of a different behaviour-management approach at the infants' level, where 'a certain amount of disapproval may constitute guidance for infant school pupils' (ibid.: 165). But these findings at the junior school level (in Swinson and Harrop 2001) are at odds with those of Merrett and Wheldall (1987b) in their junior school study. It would appear that there is little evidence for consensus or trends across studies regarding the nature of any relationships *among* the types of teacher response.

Relationship between teacher response and student on-task behaviour

Of more obvious educational relevance is the work done by several researchers who have explored the relationship between various teacher responses and students' on-task (or off-task) behaviour. Nafpaktitis *et al.* (1985) argued that the amount of disruptive and off-task behaviour was clearly related to the teacher's use of approval and disapproval. In their intermediate school study, they found that teacher disapproval scores were positively correlated with off-task behaviour (0.54). Nafpaktitis *et al.* also noted the relationships between their data and that of Thomas *et al.* (1978) who had similarly found a negative correlation (–0.48) for teacher *disapproval* and student on-task behaviour. In Nafpaktitis *et al.* (1985), the correlation between off-task behaviour and appropriate approval was weaker, at –0.21. (Thomas *et al.* (1978) found a correlation of 0.40 for teacher approval and student on-task behaviour.) These figures confirm, in effect, those of Thomas *et al.* (1978), where 'the disapproval correlation with student on- or off-task behavior was higher than the approval correlation' (Nafpaktitis *et al.* 1985: 365).

The effect of inappropriate approval, a phenomenon that Nafpaktitis and colleagues considered may occur frequently in the 'typical classroom' by way of teachers unintentionally reacting to 'inappropriate student behaviors with their attention and even approval' (ibid.: 362), was also considered in their study. The correlation between off-task behaviour and inappropriate approval from the teacher was found to be 0.40. But one of the largest positive correlations found in the study was that between inappropriate approval and disruptive student behaviour (0.52), higher rates of approval of off-task behaviour being associated with higher rates of disruptive behaviour. Moreover, in general, the higher the inappropriate approval, the lower the student on-task behaviour (Nafpaktitis *et al.* 1985).

While being cautious about the conclusions that can be drawn about cause and effect from a correlational, non-experimental study, Nafpaktitis *et al.* (1985) suggested that the attention provided by disapproval reinforces the inappropriate behaviour that it follows, given that a positive significant correlation existed between the rate of disapproval and the rate of off-task behaviour in their study. The researchers argued that inappropriate approvals:

> may also have a devastating effect on classroom management if respond-ing to disruptive behaviours such as talking out or being out of one's seat reinforces these behaviours ... [some students] may find it reinforcing to irritate teachers (resulting in disapproval) and may respond to inappropriate approval in the same way as they do to appropriate approval (i.e. with an increase in approved behavior).
>
> (Nafpaktitis *et al.* 1985: 365–6)

As was the case in the study by Nafpaktitis and colleagues, Wheldall *et al.* (1989) reported interesting correlational data in their secondary school study. Highly significant positive correlations were found between on-task behaviour and both approval to academic behaviour (0.44) and approval to social behaviour (0.37). The study found that a similarly significant negative correlation existed between teacher disapproval to social behaviour and on-task behaviour (–0.32) (Wheldall *et al.* 1989). The researchers concluded that, 'Teachers who used more praise and fewer instances of disapproval to social behaviour experienced higher levels of on-task behaviour in their classroom' (ibid.: 46). Earlier, however, Merrett and Wheldall (1987b) had found that the strongest predictor of on-task behaviour in their primary and middle school study was a negative correlation with disap-proval for social behaviour (–0.31).

Winter (1990) also found a strong positive correlation between total teacher approval and on-task behaviour (0.40) in secondary classes in Hong Kong (a very similar finding to that of the Wheldall *et al.* (1989) secondary school study). In addition, a strong negative correlation (–0.40) existed between disapproval and on-task behaviour (again similar to the findings of the British study reported above) (Winter, 1990). Although these findings confirmed the findings of Wheldall *et al.* (1989), a degree of caution should be exercised given that the data were based on one observation only per teacher, not the minimum of three as recommended when using OPTIC (Merrett and Wheldall 1986).

In a subsequent and related article to Harrop and Swinson (2000), the same researchers looked at the relationships between teacher approval and disapproval in the junior and infant classrooms and student on-task behaviour (Swinson and Harrop 2001). In line with the findings of other researchers (Wheldall *et al.*

(1989); Winter 1990), Swinson and Harrop (2001) found some evidence that student on-task behaviour increased with higher levels of teacher approval. At both school levels there was a positive *trend* in the relationship between teacher approval and on-task behaviour, but only in the infant school data was the trend statistically significant (Swinson and Harrop 2001). For both types of school there was an almost zero correlation between teacher disapproval and on-task behaviour.

The data relating to *optimal* rates of disapproval found in Swinson and Harrop (2001) provide food for thought. Tending towards a curvilinear relationship, higher levels of on-task behaviour were associated with mid-range levels of disapproval, while lower rates of on-task behaviour were associated with both low and high levels of disapproval. The authors drew the conclusion (while advisedly cautioning against drawing too firm a conclusion from correlational data) that it would seem reasonable to assume that both too little *and* too much disapproval in the classroom can be counterproductive (Swinson and Harrop 2001). According to the data available from their study of 10 classes at each school level, Swinson and Harrop argued that optimum levels of teacher disapproval were around 1.1 per minute in the infants' school and, almost half, at 0.6 per minute, in the junior school. They argued that it may be counterproductive to drop the rate of disapproval too low. As the authors pointed out, much is made of teachers increasing their use of approvals and decreasing disapprovals in courses dealing with effective classroom behaviour management. While reiterating that the evidence for the relationship between higher on-task levels and increased use of approvals was confirmed by the findings of their study, they also raised a caution about how teachers should be advised regarding their use of disapprovals. The researchers argued that the judicious use of disapprovals may have an important part to play in the management of the classroom, particularly in the infants' school where students are new to the mores of the classroom and the expectations of teachers in relation to appropriate classroom behaviour (Swinson and Harrop 2001).

By way of summary, the studies reviewed in this chapter are presented in Table 12.2. Presented in chronological order, this summary provides basic information regarding the location, participants, and main findings from each study. It is not intended to be a comprehensive critique of each study, but rather a guide to the relevant findings in respect of the present research focus.

Conclusion

Over the past 30 years, researchers have attempted to establish the rates of naturally occurring teacher responses to student behaviour. Reports of teacher behaviour indicate variable findings, although certain trends are evident. In the early work in the investigation of the naturally occurring rates of teacher responses, White (1975) and colleagues (Heller and White 1975) found that teachers used more disapproval than approval in the classroom. If the studies included in Brophy's

Table 12.2 Summary of studies and critiques on teachers' use of approval and disapproval

Author(s)	Year/Place	Subjects	Main findings
White	1975 USA	104 teachers Students in Grades 1–12	More verbal disapproval than verbal approval overall, after Grade 2.
Heller and White	1975 USA	10 teachers (5 mathematics) (5 social studies) Students in Grades 7–9	Teachers use more disapproval than approval overall. Teachers use more verbal disapproval in lower-ability classes than in higher-ability classes. Teachers use more approval than disapproval for instructional (academic) behaviour. Teachers use more disapproval for managerial (social) behaviour than for instructional behaviour.
Thomas, Presland, Grant and Glynn	1978 New Zealand	10 teachers 10 Grade 7 classes	Majority of teachers had higher individual verbal disapproval rates than individual verbal approval rates.
Russell and Lin	1977 South Australia	1 Grade 7 teacher 20 target students: 10 WB (Worst Behaved) 10 BB (Best Behaved)	Teacher responded at a higher rate to the inappropriate behaviour of the WB group than to that of the BB group.
Brophy	1981 USA	Reports the results of 6 studies between 1973 and 1980 from Grades 1–8.	Teachers overall showed more approval than disapproval; were more likely to approve of academic behaviour than to disapprove of it; were more likely to disapprove of academic behaviour than to approve of social behaviour.
Fry	1983 Canada	28 teachers and 400 students at elementary school level Subjects selected on the basis of being a problem/non-problem student.	'Problem' children received less positive affect and more negative affect from their teachers than their non-problem peers. A deterioration in interactions with the teacher over time was evident, as were increased serious misdemeanours with a corresponding decline in attention.

(continued)

Table 12.2 (continued)

Author(s)	Year/Place	Subjects	Main findings
Strain, Lambert, Kerr, Stagg and Lenkner	1983 USA	19 teachers and 130 children in kindergarten to Grade 3 Subjects classed according to making good (poor) social adjustment to school	Found low levels of feedback, both positive and negative. Found teachers used more disapproval than approval overall. Found a good proportion of positive feedback was contingent on non-compliance.
Nafpaktitis, Mayer and Butterworth	1985 USA	84 teachers in their classes in intermediate school	Mean rates of teacher approval were found to exceed rates of disapproval, in contrast to previous studies. Teacher disapproval scores were positively correlated with off-task behaviour.
Wyatt and Hawkins	1987 USA	35 classes in Grades K-4, 9 and 12. Designed as a replication of White (1975)	Mean rates of teacher approval found to be more frequent than disapproval at every grade level (unlike White 1975), confirming results of studies such as Nafpaktitis et al. (1985) (above). Approval and disapproval generally declined over grade level (peaking at Grade 1 for both approval and disapproval). Similar finding to White (1975). Absolute levels of approval and disapproval in several grades were similar to those found in White (1975).
Merrett and Wheldall	1987 UK	128 British primary and middle school teachers and their classes	Teachers used more approval (56%) than disapproval (44%) overall. For academic behaviour positive responses were three times as frequent as negative responses. For social behaviour, negative responses were five times as frequent as positive responses.

Table 12.2 (continued)

Author(s)	Year/Place	Subjects	Main findings
Wheldall, Houghton and Merrett	1989 UK	130 British secondary school teachers and their classes	Teachers used more approval (55%) than disapproval overall. For academic behaviour, positive responses were three times as frequent as negative responses. For social behaviour, the opposite was the case.
Winter	1990 Hong Kong	86 teachers and their classes	Teachers approved (63%) more than they disapproved overall. More approval to academic behaviour than to social behaviour.
Charlton, Lovemore, Essex and Crowie	1995 St Helena	15 teachers and their classes	Teachers distributed more approval than disapproval. Academic and social behaviours *both* received more approval than disapproval.
Harrop and Swinson	2000 UK	10 classes each at infants', junior and secondary school	Teachers distributed more approval than disapproval, although no decrease was found in approval rates with increasing age of students. More approval to academic behaviour than to social behaviour. For social behaviour, opposite was the case with the exception of secondary classes in this study.
Swinson and Harrop	2001 UK	10 classes each at infants' and junior school	Relationship between teacher responses and on-task behaviour was examined. Higher levels of approval were associated with higher levels of on-task behaviour. A curvilinear relationship existed between rate of disapproval and on-task behaviour suggesting reducing disapprovals too low may be counterproductive.

(1981) functional analysis are taken into account, however, the picture is more equivocal. Generally, however, it can be said that the earlier studies in this area typically found that teachers were more disapproving than approving of their students' behaviour. The seminal work of White (1975) has continued, but in a rather piecemeal way. Differences in the way data were collected and changes in operational definitions in terms of what constitutes a teacher response to student behaviour make it difficult to make direct comparisons between studies.

By the mid-1980s the trend towards teachers providing more disapproval than approval had been reversed (and this has continued to date) with teachers consistently using more approval than disapproval *overall* with broad agreement across the studies reviewed, which were carried out in the USA, Canada, the UK, Australia, New Zealand, Hong Kong, and in the tiny Atlantic island of St Helena (and also in New South Wales, Australia – see Addendum to this chapter). The findings of Wyatt and Hawkins (1987) in the USA lent support to the view that teacher behaviour did actually change in the 1980s (or the equivocation ceased, at least) from being more disapproving than approving. Given that Wyatt and Hawkins used the same instrument as White (recording only verbal responses) but had findings more *similar* to those of the later researchers in the 1980s such as Merrett and Wheldall (1987b), Wheldall *et al.* (1990), and Winter (1990), there would appear to be evidence of a genuine and sustained shift in teacher behaviour. More recent work by Harrop and Swinson confirms that approval rates are higher than disapproval rates at all school levels and that this is 'a robust finding' (Harrop and Swinson, 2000: 481). This latter finding confirms that the shift in trend that occurred in the mid- to late 1980s has been maintained into the late 1990s, at least.

While this sustained change in teacher behaviour is to be celebrated, there was little evidence to suggest that teachers, universally and systematically, deployed contingent approval or praise as positive reinforcement in spite of the considerable literature testifying to its effectiveness. One feature of teacher behaviour that was found to be constant over time (with one exception being the St Helena study of Charlton *et al.* 1995) was that the *academic* behaviour of students was much more likely to attract teacher praise or approval than students' conduct or *social* behaviour. Approval for appropriate classroom *social* (as opposed to *academic*) behaviour was only rarely observed and there was no evidence that appropriate social behaviour on the part of students attracted teacher approval or positive attention at any appreciable rate (other than in St Helena). Rather, it was the *inappropriate* behaviour of students that captured teachers' attention. Teachers responded far more frequently to the inappropriate social behaviour of their students than to the appropriate behaviours they may have wished to see increased. More recent work by Harrop and Swinson (2000) has confirmed that approval is given primarily to academic rather than to social behaviours, with the reverse being the case for disapproval. Given this, they claimed such a finding 'can be quoted as an established feature of observed teacher behaviour' (Harrop and Swinson 2000: 481).

Positive correlations between teacher approval and on-task behaviour, and negative correlations between teacher disapproval and on-task behaviour, suggests that teachers' less than optimal use of approval and disapproval may have been responsible for discouraging appropriate behaviour, and even increasing inappropriate social behaviour in classrooms. It has been suggested by some that students' inappropriate behaviour may actually be maintained or even increased by inappropriate or non-contingent teacher attention.

In summary, there is evidence that teachers today approve of students' *academic* behaviour much more frequently than they approve of students' appropriate classroom conduct, or *social* behaviour. Conversely, teachers typically provide large amounts of disapproval to students in relation to their social behaviour, while they rarely disapprove of their academic behaviour. This phenomenon has been observed in the United Kingdom, the United States of America, New Zealand, and Hong Kong (and also NSW, Australia – see Addendum to this chapter). Notwithstanding the fact that the power of contingent approval in increasing appropriate classroom behaviour has been consistently well documented, there appears to be a persistent resistance on the part of teachers to use approval to improve classroom behaviour.

References

Becker, W. C., Madsen, C., Arnold, C. and Thomas, D. (1967). Contingent use of teacher attention and praise in reducing classroom problems. *Journal of Special Education, 1*: 287–307.

Brophy, J. (1981). Teacher praise: A functional analysis. *Review of Educational Research, 51*: 5–32.

Charlton, T., Lovemore, T., Essex C. and Crowie, B. (1995). Naturalistic rates of teacher approval and disapproval and on-task behaviour in first and middle school classrooms in St. Helena. *Journal of Social Behaviour and Personality, 10*: 817–26.

Fry, P. S. (1983). Process measures of problem and non-problem children's classroom behaviour: The influence of teacher behaviour variables. *British Journal of Educational Psychology, 53*: 79–88.

Galton, M., Galton, M., Hargreaves, L., Comber, C., Wall, D. and Pell, A. (1999). Changes in patterns of teacher interaction in primary classrooms: 1976–96. *British Educational Research Journal, 25*(1): 23–37.

Harrop, A. and Swinson, J. (2000). Natural rates of approval and disapproval in British infant, junior and secondary classrooms. *British Journal of Educational Psychology 70*: 473–83.

Hattie, J. (1992). Measuring the effects of schooling. *Australian Journal of Education, 36*(1): 5–13.

Heller, M. and White, M. (1975). Rates of teacher approval and disapproval to higher and lower ability classes. *Journal of Educational Psychology, 67*: 796–800.

Madsen C. H., Becker, W. C. and Thomas, D. R. (1968). Rules, praise, and ignoring elements of elementary classroom control. *Journal of Applied Behavior Analysis, 1*: 139–50.

Merrett, F. (1981). Studies in behaviour modification in British educational settings. *Educational Psychology, 2*: 147–57.

Merrett, F. and Wheldall, K. (1986). Observing Pupils and Teachers In Classrooms (OPTIC): A behavioural observation schedule for use in schools. *Educational Psychology*, 6: 57–70.

Merrett, F. and Wheldall, K. (1987a). British teachers and the behavioural approach to teaching. In K. Wheldall (ed.), *The Behaviourist in the Classroom*, revised, 2nd ed. London: Allen and Unwin.

Merrett, F. and Wheldall, K. (1987b). Natural rates of teachers' approval and disapproval in British primary and middle school classrooms. *British Journal of Educational Psychology*, 57: 95–103.

Merrett, F. and Wheldall, K. (1990). *Positive Teaching in the Primary School*. London: Paul Chapman.

Nafpaktitis, M., Mayer, G. R. and Butterworth, T. (1985). Natural rates of teacher approval and disapproval and their relation to student behaviour in intermediate school classrooms. *Journal of Educational Psychology*, 77: 363–67.

Russell, A. and Lin, L. G. (1977). Teacher attention and classroom behaviour. *The Exceptional Child*, 24: 148–55.

Rutter, M., Maughan, B., Mortimore, P. and Ouston, J. (1979). *Fifteen Thousand Hours: Secondary schools and their effects on children*. London: Open Books.

Schwieso, J. and Hastings, N. (1987). Teachers' use of approval. In N. Hastings and J. Schwieso (eds.), *New Directions in Educational Psychology, Vol. 2 (behaviour and motivation in the classroom)*. London: Falmer, 115–36.

Strain, P. S., Lambert, D. L., Kerr, M. M., Stagg, V. and Lenkner, D. A. (1983). Naturalistic assessment of children's compliance to teachers' requests and consequences for compliance. *Journal of Applied Behaviour Analysis*, 16: 243–49.

Swinson, J. and Harrop, A. (2001). The differential effects of teacher approval and disapproval in junior and infant classrooms. *Educational Psychology in Practice*, 17(2): 157–66.

Thomas, D., Becker, W. and Armstrong, M. (1968). Production and elimination of disruptive classroom behavior by systemically varying teacher's behaviour. *Journal of Applied Behavior Analysis*, 1: 35–45.

Thomas, J. D., Presland, I. E., Grant, M. D. and Glynn, T. (1978). Natural rates of teacher approval and disapproval in grade 7 classrooms. *Journal of Applied Behavior Analysis*, 11(1): 91–4.

Wheldall, K. and Merrett, F. (1984). *Positive Teaching: the behavioural approach*. London: Allen and Unwin.

Wheldall, K. and Glynn, T. (1989). *Effective Classroom Learning: a behavioural interactionist approach to teaching*. London: Basil Blackwell.

Wheldall, K. and Merrett, F. (1989). *Positive Teaching in the Secondary School*. London: Paul Chapman.

Wheldall, K., Houghton, S. and Merrett, F. (1989). Natural rates of teacher approval and disapproval in British secondary school classrooms. *British Journal of Educational Psychology*, 59: 38–48.

White, M. A. (1975). Natural rates of teacher approval and disapproval in the classroom, *Journal of Applied Behavior Analysis*, 8: 367–72.

Winter, S. (1990). Teacher approval and disapproval in Hong Kong secondary school classrooms, *British Journal of Educational Psychology*, 60: 88–92.

Wyatt, W. and Hawkins, R. (1987). Rates of teachers' verbal approval and disapproval: Relationship to grade level, classroom activity, student behavior, and teacher characteristics. *Behavior Modification*, 11(1): 27–51.

Addendum

Note: The present authors have also completed research in this area in both primary and high school classrooms in New South Wales, Australia. Given that the work has yet to be formally published (and hence subjected to critical scrutiny), we have decided to report the findings in this addendum separate from the main body of the chapter that reviews the published research.

Wheldall and Beaman collected OPTIC data on samples of Australian teachers and their classes in the Sydney metropolitan area. The primary sample comprised 36 teachers and classes from seven different schools. More than 80 per cent of this group were female teachers, and most of the teachers (51.5 per cent) were aged between 30 and 39. The main findings from this observational study can be summarised as follows. Overall, teachers used an equal number of (total) positive and negative responses to student behaviour (50 per cent). Similarly, the total number of responses to academic (48 per cent) and to social behaviour (52 per cent) was almost the same. Positive teacher responses to academic behaviour (38 per cent) occurred at a rate nearly four times higher than that of negative responses (10 per cent). For teacher responses to social behaviour, however, the rate of negative responses (40 per cent) was more than three times greater than that for positive responses (12 per cent). The findings from this observational study in terms of ratios of responding concur with the results from the British sample of 128 primary teachers and their classes of Merrett and Wheldall (1987b). Differences are apparent, however, in the rates of responding. This group of Australian primary teachers had a total approval rate of 0.61 responses per minute, only half that of their British peers (1.15) whereas their total disapproval rate, 0.62 responses per minute, was only two-thirds that of the UK teachers (0.93). In essence, then, the Australian primary teachers simply responded less overall, but the resulting positive to negative ratio is very similar.

A sample of 79 secondary teachers and their classes from four metropolitan high schools in Sydney were also observed in Wheldall and Beaman's research. Of those indicating their age, 54 per cent were in the 30–9 year age group. Overall secondary teachers used slightly more positive (53 per cent) than negative responses (47 per cent) to student behaviour. Similarly, slightly more responses to academic behaviour (52 per cent) were used than to social behaviour (48 per cent). For responses to academic behaviour, the rate of positive responses (46 per cent) was nearly eight times greater than that for negative responses (6 per cent). Conversely, for social behaviour, the rate of negative responses (42 per cent) was nearly six times greater than the rate of positive responses (7 per cent). The findings from this study are again consonant with the results obtained from the sample of British secondary teachers as reported by Wheldall *et al.* (1989). But again, while the ratios are similar, there are differences in the rates of responding. Australian high school teachers approved overall at a rate of 0.45 responses per minute compared with 0.65 for their British high school peers, while their overall negative responses averaged a rate of 0.40 responses per minute compared with 0.53 for the British sample, both rates being appreciably lower.

Chapter 13

Classroom seating arrangements and classroom behaviour

Kevin Wheldall and Laraine Bradd

While there has been recent renewed interest in classroom seating arrangements (Kern and Clemens (2008); Wannarka and Ruhl 2008), seating arrangements and their effects on student behaviour have been studied for more than 80 years (see Dawe (1934); Griffith (1921); Schwebel (1969); Shores and Haubrich (1969); Wheldall *et al.* 1981). More recent studies of classroom seating arrangements completed since the late 1970s have provided important new insights into their effects on classroom behaviour involving a variety of different populations and settings. Populations studied have included regular students, children with mild, moderate and severe disabilities, and children with emotional and behavioural disorders, as well as their teachers. Studies have been conducted in regular and special schools at the primary and secondary level in the United Kingdom, the United States, Australia and Germany.

As anyone educated in school prior to the 1960s will recall, the norm for classroom seating was for students to be seated in rows facing the teacher, whose desk and blackboard were traditionally situated at the front of the classroom. This all changed with the publication of the Plowden Report on primary education in 1967 (Department of Education and Science 1967). The Plowden Report, reflecting the progressive mood of the times, argued that traditional classroom seating in rows should be eschewed in favour of small groups or table clusters (table groups) (Wheldall and Glynn 1989). Supposed benefits of small-group settings included strengthening the possibility of individual education programmes through increased individual teacher attention, albeit within a small group of students of similar academic achievement (Bennett and Blundell 1983). Groups also provide the opportunity and encouragement for students to socialise, for only with continued peer interaction, it was believed, could effective learning take place (Wheldall and Glynn 1989).

Table groups were also believed to provide a more effective means for students to participate in group work. The benefits of group work were thought to include an opportunity, as Bennett and Blundell (1983: 93–4) put it:

> to learn to get along together, to help one another and realize their own strengths and weaknesses, as well as those of others. They make meanings

clearer to themselves by having to explain them to others and gain from opportunities to teach as well as to learn. Apathetic children may be infected by the enthusiasm of a group or could sit back as idle passengers, a danger the teacher must watch for. Able children, on the other hand, benefit from being caught up in the thrust and counterthrust of conversation in a small group of children similar to themselves.

The majority of primary teachers readily adopted the recommendations made by the Plowden Report (Department of Education and Science 1967) with respect to classroom seating arrangements, and classroom seating in table groups became the norm in spite of the lack of any empirical research evidence supporting these recommendations (Bennett and Blundell 1983; Hastings and Schwieso 1995; Wheldall et al. 1981).

The ORACLE observational study of primary school classes carried out in the UK in the 1970s, however, highlighted some of the inconsistencies between seating arrangements and teachers' intentions (Galton et al. 1999). Children are required to sit in groups around tables, but are seldom asked to collaborate. Hastings (1995) concluded that cooperative learning tasks are, in fact, quite rare, while Bennett et al. (1984) found that a large part of the social interaction observed in table groups was, quite simply, non-work related.

The aim of this chapter is to review the extant *experimental* research literature on classroom seating arrangements and their effects on student classroom behaviour, with particular reference to comparisons of rows and table groups seating arrangements.

Spatial density

In one of the earliest experimental studies of classroom seating, Krantz and Risley (1977) evaluated the effects of spatial density on the behaviour of kindergarten children. Crowded and less crowded seating arrangements were systematically manipulated and observed during story sessions and teacher demonstrations. Masking tape was used to map out spaces two feet apart for the less crowded condition and a small blanket defined the area for the crowded condition. On-task behaviour was operationally defined as 'sitting cross-legged, with visual attendance to the teacher and/or book during a story, and not engaging in disruptive behaviour'. Observations revealed that the level of on-task behaviour was significantly lower in the crowded condition. Not only did the less crowded condition enhance on-task behaviour, but the frequency of disruptive behaviour was also reduced to levels achieved only by the systematic use of contingent reinforcement (praise and classroom privileges) during the crowded condition.

Same-sex versus mixed-sex seating

Wheldall and Olds (1987) carried out an experimental study with third- and fourth-grade students to determine whether a mixed-sex seating arrangement would produce clear effects on the on-task behaviour of two primary school classes. An ABA design was used where the participants of both classes were observed for two weeks in their usual seating positions. This was followed by a two-week intervention phase, and then a reversal phase with participants seated in their usual seating arrangement. During baseline, the Year 3 participants sat in their usual arrangement of three table groups for boys and three table groups for girls. During intervention, the boys and girls were mixed so that boys and girls were now sitting next to each other in table groups. In the fourth-grade class, the children were initially seated in their usual arrangement of three rows of double desks and next to a member of the opposite sex. During intervention all participants sat next to a member of the same sex.

On-task behaviour in the fourth-grade class (where participants were normally seated in rows next to a member of the opposite sex), decreased by 14 per cent from 90 per cent to 76 per cent when seating arrangements were changed to same-sex seating. During the reversal phase, on-task behaviour increased by 13 per cent to 89 per cent. Also, the mean levels of participant disruptions increased from 10 during baseline, to 19 during intervention, and then fell to 8 following the return to baseline. In the third-grade class (where participants normally sat in table groups next to a member of the same sex), on-task behaviour increased by 17 per cent (from 75 per cent to 92 per cent) when participants changed their seating arrangement to sit next to someone of the opposite sex. On-task behaviour fell by 25 per cent (from 92 per cent to 67 per cent) when same-sex seating was reintroduced in the reversal phase. Also, the level of participant disruptions fell from 22 during baseline to 11 during intervention and increased to 41 during the return to baseline. Thus, mixed-sex seating produced the highest levels of student on-task behaviour and the lowest levels of participant disruptions. Moreover, what emerged clearly from the results was that children with the lowest on-task study levels were most positively affected by the change from same-sex to mixed-sex seating.

Rows versus table groups during independent work

Most studies of classroom seating arrangements, however, have compared the effects of rows versus table groups on classroom behaviour when students were required to complete individual work. All studies consistently revealed appreciably higher levels of on-task, work-related behaviour when seating was arranged in rows. These studies are described below.

The seminal study by Axelrod et al. (1979) examined the effects of classroom seating arrangements in two United States elementary schools. They compared the impact of a table groups arrangement and a rows arrangement on the on-task behaviour and the total number of 'talk-outs' of second- and seventh-grade American students. The subjects in the first study were 17 second-grade academically below-average students. Study behaviour was operationally defined as orientation toward the appropriate material, attention to the teacher when the teacher was speaking, complying with teacher requests, raising a hand for teacher assistance, and being out of one's seat with teacher permission. An ABAB design was employed in which seating in table groups (A) alternated with seating in rows (B) at fortnightly intervals. Mean percentage on-task behaviour was 62 per cent during table groups 1 and rose to 82 per cent during rows 1, decreased to 63 per cent during table groups 2, and then rose again to 83 per cent during the final rows 2 phase. Rows promoted higher levels of on-task behaviour in 16 of the 17 students included in the study. The results clearly demonstrated that the participants achieved higher levels of on-task behaviour when participants were seated in rows compared with when they were sitting around tables during independent seat work.

In the second study, which employed an ABA design, Axelrod *et al.* (1979) compared the impact of table groups and rows seating arrangements on the disruptive behaviour (number of talk-outs) exhibited by 32 seventh-grade school students of average ability. The dependent variable, 'talk-outs', was defined as any audible, verbal sound made by a student without the teacher's permission. Talk-outs were counted as separate responses if there was at least a three-second lapse between successive talk-outs. Talk-outs averaged 58 per cent in table groups 1, 30 per cent during rows 1, and 50 per cent during table groups 2, demonstrating that disruptive behaviour was lower when students sat in rows compared with such behaviour when they were seated in table groups, during independent academic work.

Wheldall *et al.* (1981) subsequently replicated and extended the findings of Axelrod *et al.* (1979) in two ABA studies in British primary school classrooms. The participants comprised two classes of 10- to 11-year-old children of academically mixed ability. A time sampling technique at five-second intervals was used to collect data on student on-task behaviour. Students initially sat in their usual table groups formation and were observed daily for two weeks, followed by two weeks seated in rows, and finally, two weeks back around tables. In the first study involving 28 children, the mean on-task behaviour was 72 per cent in the table groups 1 phase, increasing to 88 per cent under the rows condition and decreasing again to 69 per cent after reversal to the table groups 2 condition. In the second study, involving 25 participants, Wheldall *et al.* (1981) found that the mean on-task behaviour of students was 67 per cent in the table groups 1 phase, increasing to 84 per cent under the rows condition, and decreasing to 72 per cent when seating was reversed to the table groups 2 condition. The results of both studies showed that the average amount of time students spent on-task in their mainstream classes, while carrying out independent tasks, was greater when students sat in rows.

The data were reanalysed, and the students grouped according to sex and according to high, average or low initial on-task behaviour. The change in seating conditions affected boys and girls equally in both classes (Wheldall *et al.* 1981), but differences were noted among participants when the participants' level of on-task behaviour during baseline table groups was considered. A negligible effect was found for students with high initial on-task behaviour, a moderate effect for students with average on-task behaviour and a substantial effect for students who had low on-task behaviour during baseline (Wheldall *et al.* 1981). Wheldall *et al.* (1981) concluded that manipulating seating in this way with children whose on-task behaviour is already high does not yield an appreciable effect. Students whose on-task behaviour is average when seated around tables may benefit from seating in rows, but students whose on-task behaviour is initially very low will benefit most, and appreciably, from sitting in rows in terms of increased on-task behaviour.

Both of these studies were partially compromised by ascending baselines in both studies, but the return to table groups in the third phase clearly showed lower on-task behaviour after reversal. These results support the findings of Axelrod *et al.* (1979) that on-task behaviour is higher when students sit in rows compared with table groups, for independent tasks.

In another British study, Bennett and Blundell (1983) followed up the work of Wheldall *et al.* (1981) by examining both the quantity and quality of work produced. They observed the effects of table groups and row seating arrangements in reading, language and mathematics classes. The participants were two classes (80 students) of 10- to 11-year-old children. Their results indicated that the quantity of work completed generally increased significantly when the children were seated in rows, but the quality of work was merely maintained or slightly improved.

Wheldall and Lam (1987) subsequently studied the effects of classroom seating arrangements (rows versus table groups) with three classes of 12- to 15-year-old students in a British school which catered for children with learning difficulties and behaviour problems. An ABAB design compared classroom behaviour in table groups and rows during mathematics classes at fortnightly intervals. A modified version of the OPTIC schedule (Merrett and Wheldall 1986) was used to measure student on-task behaviour and incidents of disruptive behaviour, as well as teacher positive and negative comments.

In all three mathematics classes, average on-task behaviour for the group more than doubled from 34 per cent in table groups 1 to 72 per cent during rows 1. In the return-to-baseline condition (table groups 2), average group on-task behaviour decreased to 35 per cent, and then nearly doubled again to an average of 69 per cent during the second intervention (rows 2). Eighty-eight per cent of the children were found to exhibit greater individual on-task behaviour when sitting in rows (Wheldall and Lam 1987). Also, disruptive behaviours reduced from an average of 31 disruptions during table groups 1 to 8 in rows 1. Disruptions increased to 24 during table groups 2 and fell again to 8 during the second intervention (rows 2) (Wheldall and Lam 1987). Consequently, classroom teachers significantly increased their positive comments and substantially decreased their negative comments about both student academic behaviour and conduct (Wheldall and Lam 1987). Wheldall and Lam (1987) concluded that students with learning and behaviour difficulties spend more time on-task and are better behaved when seated in rows during individual academic work (Wheldall and Lam 1987).

Yeomans (1989), using an ABA reversal design, observed a mainstream, second-year junior class consisting of 21 students, aged 7 to 8 years. The aim of her research was to increase the on-task behaviour of the class by manipulating seating conditions. The position of the desks was moved from their usual 'tables' to 'rows' but the children and their partners remained constant. The OPTIC Schedule was used for observations. The results showed that the mean on-task behaviour of the class was about 49 per cent during baseline. In the intervention phase, the desks were then arranged in single-desk formation, each table seating two students. The mean on-task behaviour increased to 79 per cent and dropped to 38 per cent on reversal to the original 'table' formation. The data collected clearly showed a 30 per cent increase in the average time on-task for single desks over group tables. Teacher behaviour was also observed and showed that positive responses to academic behaviour increased while negative responses decreased. Positive responses to social behaviour remained virtually unchanged while negative responses decreased substantially during intervention.

Hastings and Schwieso (1995) subsequently conducted two similar studies. Their first study evaluated the effects of seating arrangements on the on-task behaviour of two parallel classes of 9- to 11-year-old children in a British school. They attempted to examine whether any improvements made following a change in seating arrangements could be explained by novelty. The students were observed daily carrying out individual tasks. In both classes, an ABA design was used to record data over three, two-week phases. Class A was initially seated in a rows formation, then moved to table groups and then moved back to rows. In contrast, the students in Class B were initially seated in groups, moved to rows and then back to groups. The findings in both classes showed that the class average time on-task was greater in the rows condition. In Class A, the mean on-task behaviour during baseline (rows 1) was 75% per cent. This fell to 56% per cent when seating was changed to table groups and rose to 79% per cent when classroom seating resumed to a rows configuration. In class B, mean on-task behaviour was 66% per cent during baseline table groups. It rose to 76% per cent when seating arrangements were changed to rows and then decreased to 65% per cent when classroom seating reverted back to table groups. Consequently, Hastings and Schwieso (1995: 289) concluded that the improvements in the participants' on-task behaviour during rows arrangements could not be explained by novelty.

In the second study, Hastings and Schwieso (1995) examined the on-task behaviour and out-of-seat behaviour of three individual children (Kevin, Luke, and Mark) as well as the on-task behaviour of the whole class (eleven boys and nine girls, aged 8 to 9 years) using an AB design (table groups/rows). Observations took place for three weeks in each of the baseline and intervention phases. At baseline, the mean time on-task for the class as a whole was 48 per cent, while for Kevin, Luke and Mark on-task behaviour averaged 16 per cent, 26 per cent, and 6 per cent respectively. After intervention (rows) the average time-on-task rose to 78.5 per cent for the whole class, and 90 per cent, 94 per cent, and 89 per cent for Kevin, Luke and Mark respectively. The class as a whole was thus 30 per cent more on-task while Kevin, Luke and Mark were 74 per cent, 68 per cent and 83 per cent, respectively, more on-task when seated in rows compared with being seated in table groups. Out-of-seat behaviour during baseline was 86 per cent, 69 per cent and 91 per cent for Kevin, Luke and Mark, respectively, but fell to 11 per cent, 4 per cent, and 6 per cent, respectively, during intervention. These findings demonstrated that the change in seating arrangement from table groups to rows improved the on-task behaviour of the whole class, but was most effective for the three individual children who had the lowest on-task behaviour when seated in table groups (Hastings and Schwieso 1995: 289). These results replicated the findings of Wheldall *et al.* (1981) who also found that children with the lowest initial on-task behaviour when seated in table groups made the greatest gains in on-task behaviour when seated in rows during individual academic work.

Group collaborative work

In the United States, Rosenfield *et al.* (1985) evaluated the effects of classroom seating arrangements on three primary classrooms of regular fifth- to six-grade students. The participants comprised two high-ability, two low-ability, two high-interacting, and two low-interacting students. The researchers' aim was to test hypotheses about the relative effectiveness of different desk arrangements (rows, table groups and circles) for promoting student interactions identified as conducive to learning. All observation sessions took place while the participants were brainstorming ideas for written work. Participant on-task and off-task behaviours were observed. On-task behaviour was operationally defined to include 'actions directed toward solving the academic problem and verbal or physical actions contributing constructively to class academic activity' (Rosenfield *et al.* 1985: 107). Specifically, on-task behaviour included hand raising, discussion comment, questioning/pupil request, listening, out-of-order comment, and speaking. Off-task behaviour was operationally defined to include 'actions not directed toward solving the academic problem and verbal or physical action not joining constructively in class academic activity'. Specifically, off-task behaviour included disruptive conduct, withdrawal/ disassociation, and aggression (insulting/teasing, yelling, fighting) (ibid.: 107–8).

Rosenfield *et al.* (1985) found that circles produced a greater number of on-task oral responses and other on-task behaviours than did rows. The table groups arrangement also elicited more on-task behaviours and more hand-raising than did rows, while the rows arrangement produced a higher number of withdrawal responses than did the table groups or circle arrangements and more off-task responses than did the circle arrangement.

Marx et al. (2000) subsequently studied the impact of classroom seating arrangements (rows versus semi-circle) on the question–asking rate of 27 (15 female, 12 male) German fourth-grade students. In an ABAB within–subject design, the participants sat in their usual seating arrangement of rows for four weeks prior to data being collected. Commencing with a semi-circle arrangement, data was collected over eight weeks during mathematics and German classes. The participants alternated between two weeks in a semi-circle arrangement and two weeks in rows, and were randomly assigned to different seats during each phase of the study. The average rate of question asking per hour for the class as a whole over the eight-week observation period was three questions. The researchers' analysis revealed that a semi-circle seating arrangement resulted in a higher rate of question asking when compared with a rows configuration. Marx et al. (2000) reasoned that the closer distance of seats between the teacher and students, and the orientation of the students' seats in respect of the teacher and other students led to increased question asking. These findings are similar to those of Rosenfield et al. (1985) described above and further emphasise the importance of matching the type of activity (independent or collaborate work) and outcome desired with classroom seating arrangement.

Given the relative paucity of published studies, a number of (as yet) unpublished studies on classroom arrangements conducted in the United Kingdom, Australia and the United States may also be briefly considered, to the extent that they corroborate or extend the findings from the published studies reported so far. Given that these studies have not yet been subject to peer review, however, caution should be exercised in the degree to which they may be accepted as providing confirmatory (or contrary) findings. The experiments carried out in the United Kingdom and Australia, and reported below, were all conducted under the supervision of the first author of this chapter.

Unpublished British studies

Rendall (1983) examined whether the quantity and quality of academic work produced would increase concomitantly with increases in on-task behaviour when children's seating was changed from table groups to rows (Rendall 1983: 22). The participants were 108 top junior boys and girls aged 10 to 11 years in four classes. Rendall used an ABA design, with each phase being of two weeks' duration. On-task behaviour was observed in only one of the classes while academic product was measured in all four classes. Off-task behaviour during seating in rows was observed to be more passive, taking the form of daydreaming, looking out of the window, or looking around the room, while off-task behaviour when students were seated around tables involved communication with other children. On-task behaviour was again found to be higher under the rows condition, but there were no significant changes in the quantity or quality of work produced.

Croft (1986) assessed the effects of seating arrangements (table groups versus rows) on 27 (11 girls and 16 boys) mixed-ability 6- to 7-year-old children during the morning English session, and the afternoon mathematics session. The study examined the effect of seating arrangements on the participants' level of on-task behaviour and on the quality and quantity of work produced. The impact of the different seating arrangements on the teacher's behaviour (use of praise and reprimand) was also examined. A modified version of the OPTIC (Observing Pupils and Teachers in Classrooms) schedule (Merrett and Wheldall 1986) was employed which records both student on-task behaviour and teacher feedback responses.

The mean on-task percentage for the whole English class was approximately 74 per cent during baseline (table groups 1), which increased to 92 per cent during intervention (rows) (a mean increase of 18 per cent), and decreased to 73 per cent after reversal (table groups 2). During number work, the mean on-task behaviour increased from 74 per cent during baseline (table groups 1), to 91 per cent during intervention (rows) (an increase of 17 per cent), and fell to 73 per cent during the reversal phase (table groups 2). These results clearly showed that these infant-class children spent more time on-task when seated in rows for individual work. The teacher's use of praise for academic behaviour increased and reprimands for both academic and social behaviour decreased during the row formation (Croft 1986). These results concurred with the findings of Axelrod et al. (1979), Wheldall et al. (1981) and Wheldall and Lam (1987). The percentage of work completed increased when the children sat in rows and the quality of both language and number work also improved.

Fielder (1987) studied the impact of rows seating arrangements on both student on-task behaviour and teacher responses. A modified form of the OPTIC schedule was again employed to collect data. Each child in the study was assigned a code letter, which was printed on the modified OPTIC schedule. This provided for individual, group, whole-class, and gender data to be analysed (Fielder 1987). A multiple baseline across classes design was used with a gap in observations to allow for an assessment of maintenance. Data was collected in Class A as follows: table groups (one week); rows (two weeks); table groups (two weeks); table groups but with no observations (three weeks); table groups (one week), and rows (one week). In Class B, data were collected as follows: table group seating (two weeks); rows (three weeks); rows with no observations (three weeks); rows (one week), and table groups (one week) (Fielder 1987). On-task behaviour increased when the participants were seated in rows and decreased during the reversal to table groups. For Class A, participants increased their mean on-task behaviour from 58 per cent during table groups 1 to 78 per cent during rows 1 (20 per cent increase). On-task behaviour then fell to 61 per cent in table groups 2 (17 per cent decrease), fell further to 54 per cent during the table groups continuation, and then rose to 79 per cent in rows 2 (25 per cent increase). Similarly in Class B, participants increased their mean on-task behaviour from 66 per cent during table groups 1 to 83 per cent in rows 1 (17 per cent increase), increased further to 86 per cent during the rows continuation. On-task behaviour then fell to 66 per cent during table groups 2 (20 per cent decrease).

The data were also analysed to evaluate the performance of students with respect to sex, and with respect to high, medium and low initial on-task behaviour. Both girls and boys benefited from the intervention. The participants with the lowest initial on-task behaviour made the most significant gains during intervention, followed by slightly less significant gains by participants with medium initial on-task behaviour, and only slight improvements for participants with high initial on-task behaviour. These results concurred with the findings of Wheldall *et al.* (1981).

Unpublished Australian studies

Clifton (1992) examined the effects of classroom seating arrangements on the on-task behaviour of a class of five 13-year-old children with severe to moderate disabilities, in a language communication lesson. An ABAB reversal design was used to take data over four phases of equal length (horseshoe, rows, horseshoe, rows) over 20 days. In all phases, the children were encouraged to choose their own seats. The horseshoe table group formation was found to encourage more student social interactions and off-task behaviour, and this was associated with more negative teacher responses. In contrast, seating in rows increased student on-task behaviour and this was associated with increased teacher positive responses (1992). These results concurred with the findings of Axelrod *et al.* (1979), Wheldall and Lam (1987), and Wheldall *et al.* (1981).

Puckeridge (1992) investigated the effect of different seating arrangements (table groups versus rows) on the independent journal writing of three 15-year-old female secondary school students with mild intellectual disabilities during independent journal writing. An ABAB reversal design was used (table groups 1, rows, table groups 2). Average on-task behaviour was 72 per cent in table groups 1, and increased to 95 per cent in rows 1, decreased to 82 per cent during table groups 2, (but remained higher than baseline), and increased again to 96 per cent following the change to rows 2. The average percentage increase for time on task for rows over groups was 24 per cent during phases one and two, and 14 per cent during phases three and four. Mean time-on-task for each participant was highest when the students were seated in rows.

In a second study, Puckeridge (1993) observed the on-task behaviour of a small class of seven male students in a Year 9 secondary school during remedial English lessons. An ABAB design (table groups 1, rows 1, table groups 2, rows 2) was employed. The average level of on-task behaviour increased from 73 per cent in phases one and three to 92 per cent during intervention in phases two and four. Looking at the average number of words written across phases, the results showed 74 words in phase one (table groups 1), 105 words in phase two (rows 1),

87 words in phase three (table groups 2), and 109 words in phase four (rows 2). The results of this study clearly showed that when students were allocated seating in the two front rows, with at least a desk space between students, both on-task behaviour and productivity increased compared with when students were able to choose their own seating.

The subjects in a study completed by Pooley (1993) all had a mild intellectual disability. Pooley evaluated the effects of classroom seating arrangements on the behaviour of two classes of primary students and their teachers. Class A was observed during spelling and Class B during journal (diary) writing. An ABA reversal design was employed (table groups 1, rows, table groups 2) with data being taken for two weeks during each phase. The OPTIC schedule for collecting data on both teacher and student interaction was again employed.

In Class A (spelling), mean on-task behaviour was 41 per cent during baseline. This increased to a mean of 72 per cent during intervention and fell to a mean of 52 per cent during the return to baseline. Teacher positive comments increased from a mean of 6.5 during baseline to 13.3 during intervention and fell to 10.5 during the return to baseline. These findings were similar to those of Wheldall and Lam (1987).

In Class B (journal writing), mean on-task behaviour during baseline was 63 per cent. This increased to 80 per cent during intervention and fell to 71 per cent during the return to baseline. Contrary to what occurred in Class A, teacher positive comments were reduced during intervention from 3.7 during table groups 1, to 2 during intervention, and increased to 3.6 during table groups 2.

Baseline data showed that one-third of the participants had low on-task behaviour (less than 60 per cent) when seated around table groups while the remaining two-thirds had average on-task behaviour (60–80 per cent). Participants with low on-task behaviour increased their on-task behaviour by 20 per cent when seated in rows. However, the on-task behaviour for those with average levels during baseline did not increase significantly. When seating arrangements were reversed to table groups in the third observational phase, there was a significant decrease in the on-task behaviour of the students who had shown positive gains. The on-task behaviour of the other two-thirds of the class decreased only marginally. These results again concurred with those of Wheldall *et al.* (1981 – see p. 179), namely that students with the lowest on-task behaviour in table group settings benefit the most from classroom seating arranged in rows during academic work.

Sharma (1992) examined the on-task behaviour of a class of 11- and 12-year-old (Year 7) secondary students during mathematics. A modified version of the OPTIC schedule was again used, where each student's on/off task behaviour was rated every five seconds, using an interval recording system. On-task behaviour increased during intervention (rows) with the most significant gains being made by those with the lowest on-task behaviour during table groups seating arrangements. On-task behaviour was found to be 65 per cent in table groups 1, increasing to 79 per cent in rows and then decreasing to 71 per cent in table groups 2. These results concurred with those of Pooley (1993), Wheldall and Lam (1987), and Wheldall *et al.* (1981) that on-task behaviour is higher when seating is in rows than when students are seated in table groups for academic work.

Unpublished American studies

Wengel (1992) conducted a non-experimental study of four primary school classrooms in Virginia, USA. She observed each classroom for 25–40 minutes to determine any impact of classroom seating arrangements on student learning. Her sample comprised a combined first- and second-grade class which used a horseshoe arrangement, a second-grade class which used both rows and table groups, a third-grade class which used table groups, and a fourth-grade class which used a random design. She found no overall optimal classroom seating arrangement, but rather suggested that seating arrangement should be adjusted according to instructional method, classroom logistics, student personality, and task in hand (Wengel 1992: 43). Wengel (1992) stated that when given a choice, the participants usually chose rows or individual seats to do independent work, which concurred with the findings of Wheldall *et al.* (1981) where students also expressed a preference for rows seating.

In another study completed in the United States, Bonus and Riordan (1998) looked at the effects of different seating arrangements (table groups, U-shaped groups, and rows) on the on-task behaviour of 6- to 7-year-old children and on their teachers' behaviour. Their results were consistent with those of the Wheldall *et al.* (1981) study which found that on-task behaviour was higher when students were seated in rows. However, the US study was flawed in several respects and will not be detailed further here.

Conclusion

A review of the (limited) published literature over four decades has demonstrated, with remarkable consistency, that the manipulation of classroom seating arrangements can exert a powerful influence on student (and also teacher) classroom behaviour. Moreover, these findings were confirmed when a series of as yet unpublished studies were also considered.

When students were required to complete independent 'seat' work, there was little doubt that rows-style seating arrangements led to higher levels of on-task behaviour, usually accompanied by greater academic productivity. Students with the lowest on-task behaviour during (what is now typical) table groups seating arrangements made the most significant improvements in on-task behaviour and rates of disruption during academic work. Moreover, teacher praise statements were more frequent when students were seated in rows compared with when they were seated in table groups. On-task behaviour was also found to be higher when students were seated next to a student of the opposite sex. However, when students were required to verbally interact in whole–class discussions, on–task behaviour was higher and disruptions were lower when participants were seated in circles or semi-circles.

The clear implication to be drawn from these studies of classroom arrangements, particularly when attempting to meet the needs of students with learning and/or behavioural/attentional difficulties, is that teachers should consider the task in hand when determining the appropriate seating arrangement. There is no one seating arrangement that is appropriate for all classroom activities. If interaction among students is required for the successful completion of the classroom activity, or if group discussion is required for other purposes, then it makes little sense to seat students in rows; table groups seating is clearly and logically the preferred option.

It appears, however, that independent, individual seat work is more often required and that this is equally and clearly best accomplished when students are seated in non-social seating arrangements such as rows. Few adults would choose a social context in which to compose an important letter, for example, and it amounts to little short of (albeit unwitting) cruelty to require individual work to be completed in seating contexts specifically geared towards interaction and conversation. If we are seeking to meet the needs of students with learning and behavioural difficulties in the classroom, then teachers should carefully consider the most appropriate seating arrangement for the specific task in hand.

References

Axelrod, S., Hall, R. V. and Tams, A. (1979). Comparison of two common classroom seating arrangements. *Academic Therapy*, *15*: 29–36.

Bennett, N. and Blundell, D. (1983). Quantity and quality of work in rows and classroom groups. *Educational Psychology*, *3*: 93–105.

Bennett, S. N., Desforges, C. W., Cockburn, A. and Wilkinson, B. (1984). *The quality of pupil learning experiences.* London: Lawrence Erlbaum.

Bonus, M. and Riordan, L. (1998). Increasing student on-task behaviour through the use of specific seating arrangements. Unpublished Masters thesis. St Xavier University and IRI/Skylight Field-based Masters Program, Chicago.

Clifton, R. (1992). The effect of classroom seating arrangements on the on-task behaviour of children with severe to moderate disabilities. Unpublished report. Sydney: Macquarie University Special Education Centre.

Croft, A. M. (1986). Rows versus tables in the infant school: The effects of seating arrangements on quality and quantity of work produced. Unpublished dissertation. Birmingham, UK: University of Birmingham.

Dawe, H. C. (1934). The influence of size of kindergarten group upon performance. *Child Development*, *5*: 295–303.

Department of Education and Science. (1967). *Children and their primary schools.* Report of the Central Advisory Council for Education in England. London: HMSO. (Known as the 'Plowden Report'.).

Fielder, J. (1987). The influence of classroom seating arrangements upon children's behaviour levels and the rates of teacher approval and disapproval. Unpublished dissertation. Birmingham, UK: University of Birmingham.

Galton, M., Hargreaves, L., Comber, C., Wall, D. and Pell, A. (1999). *Inside the Primary Classroom: 20 years on*. London: Routledge.

Griffith, C. R. (1921). A comment upon the psychology of the audience. *Psychology Monographs, 30*: 36–47.

Hastings, N. (1995). Seats of learning? *Support for Learning, 10*(1): 8–11.

Hastings, N. and Schwieso, J. (1995). Tasks and tables: The effects of seating arrangements on task engagement in primary classrooms. *Educational Research, 37*(3): 279–91.

Kern, L. and Clemens, N. H. (2008). Antecedent strategies to promote appropriate classroom behavior. *Psychology in the Schools, 44*: 65–75.

Krantz, P. M. and Risley, T. R. (1977). Behavioral ecology in the classroom. In K. O'Leary and S. O'Leary (eds), *Classroom management: The successful use of behavior modification*, 2nd ed. New York: Pergamon, 349–67.

Marx, A., Fuhrer, U. and Hartig, T. (2000). Effects of classroom seating arrangements on children's question-asking. *Learning Environments Research, 2*: 249–63.

Merrett, F. and Wheldall, K. (1986). Observing pupils and teachers in classrooms (OPTIC): A behavioural observation schedule for use in schools. *Educational Psychology, 6*: 57–70.

Pooley, A. (1993). A study of the effects of two classroom seating arrangements on the behaviour of two primary classes of students with mild intellectual disability. Unpublished report. Sydney: Macquarie University Special Education Centre.

Puckeridge, J. (1992). Rows versus tables: The effects of two classroom seating arrangements on levels of on-task behaviour on three teenagers with special needs. Unpublished report. Sydney: Macquarie University Special Education Centre.

Puckeridge, J. (1993). Seating choice versus allocation: The effect upon student's on-task behaviour when seating in rows. Unpublished masters dissertation. Sydney: Macquarie University.

Rendall, S. E. (1983). The influence of classroom seating arrangements upon on-task behaviour and the accuracy and production of children's academic work. Unpublished dissertation. Birmingham, UK: University of Birmingham.

Rosenfield, P., Lambert, N. M. and Black, A. (1985). Desk arrangement effects on pupil classroom behaviour. *Journal of Educational Psychology, 77*: 101–8.

Schwebel, A. I. (1969). Physical and social distancing in teacher-pupil relationship. *Dissertation Abstract International, 31*: 973B–2378B. (University Microfilm No. 2370–16250.).

Sharma, V. K. (1992). Do students work better when sitting in rows or in tables settings in the classroom? Unpublished report. Sydney: Macquarie University Special Education Centre.

Shores, R. E. and Haubrich, P. A. (1969). Effects of cubicles in educating emotionally disturbed children. *Exceptional Children, 34*: 21–4.

Wannarka, R. and Ruhl, K. (2008). Seating arrangements that promote positive academic and behavioural outcomes: A review of empirical research. *Support for Learning, 23*: 89–93.

Wengel, M. (1992). *Seating arrangements: Changing with the times*. Eric Document Reproduction Service No. ED348 153.

Wheldall, K. and Lam, Y. (1987). Rows versus tables II. The effects of two classroom seating arrangements on classroom disruption rate, on-task behaviour and teacher behaviour in three special school classes. *Educational Psychology, 7*: 303–12.

Wheldall, K. and Olds, P. (1987). Of sex and seating: The effects of mixed and same-sex seating arrangements in junior school classrooms. *New Zealand Journal of Educational Studies*, *22*: 71–85.

Wheldall, K. and Glynn, T. (1989). *Effective classroom learning: A behavioural interactionist approach to teaching.* Oxford: Basil Blackwell.

Wheldall, K., Morris, M., Vaughan, P. and Ng, Y.Y. (1981). Rows versus tables: An example of the use of behavioural ecology in two classes of eleven-year-old children. *Educational Psychology*, *1*: 171–84.

Yeomans, J. (1989). Changing seating arrangements: The use of antecedent control to increase on-task behaviour. *Behavioural Approaches with Children*, *13*: 151–60.

Chapter 14

Teacher judgment of reading performance

Alison Madelaine and Kevin Wheldall

Teacher Judgment (TJ) is one of the most common ways of estimating academic achievement (Eaves *et al.* 1994). It can assist both in instructional decision making (Coladarci 1992; Hoge 1983; Hoge and Coladarci 1989) and in the identification of students at risk of academic failure (Gresham *et al.* 1987; Kenny and Chekaluk 1993; Patton 1976; Sharpley and Edgar 1986; Shinn *et al.* 1987). Other researchers view TJ with considerably more scepticism, however (Coladarci 1992; Shinn *et al.* 1987).

Teacher judgment of academic ability involves teachers estimating student proficiency based on their observations in the classroom. Gerber and Semmel (1984) have summarised the rationale for using TJ as follows:

> Teachers observe tens of thousands of discrete behavioral events during each school day. Formal tests of ability and achievement are based on analysis of only small samples of student behavior. Clearly, teachers have available to them, if they choose to use it, a far richer and varied sample of student behavior than the typical 'test'.
>
> (Gerber and Semmel 1984: 141)

Studies investigating the accuracy of TJ of student academic performance in general, or in specific areas such as maths (Helmke and Schrader 1987), have yielded varying results. Eaves *et al.* (1994) found that TJ provided better estimates for reading than for maths. Hoge and Coladarci (1989) summarised 16 studies examining the relationship of TJ with academic performance, with correlations ranging from 0.28 to 0.92 (median = 0.66). These correlations were classified as medium to strong. In terms of agreement, the figure was about 70 per cent.

This chapter will review the relevant literature over the last 30 years or so relating to teacher judgment. The review will look initially at the methodological issues in TJ research and the research on TJ for the purpose of screening or referral. The focus of this chapter, however, will be TJ of reading skills, with particular reference to the ability of teachers to identify low-progress readers in their classrooms.

Methodological issues in research

Method of data collection

The method of data collection used in TJ research varies. Hoge and Coladarci (1989) provided a good summary of the main methodological issues related to data collection and how much these have affected the results of TJ research.

Direct or indirect evaluation of TJ

Direct evaluation refers to the case where teachers are asked to estimate scores on a particular standardised test. Indirect evaluation, on the other hand, refers to teachers being asked to rate the performance of students on some sort of scale. Hoge and Coladarci (1989) found little difference between the results of studies using direct evaluation and those using indirect evaluation.

Specificity

Ratings are identified as lowest in specificity, with rankings, grade equivalence, number correct, and item response increasing in specificity. Hoge and Coladarci (1989) found rankings to have the greatest agreement.

Norm-referenced or peer-independent TJ evaluation

This refers to whether or not students are compared with each other. According to Hoge and Coladarci (1989), the results of TJ research were not affected by whether the evaluation was norm-referenced or peer-independent.

Accuracy data

Although many TJ studies report correlation coefficients as a measure of teacher accuracy, several authors have discussed the problems with using correlation coefficients for this purpose (Coladarci 1986; Flynn and Rahbar 1998; Kenny and Chekaluk 1993; Salvesen and Undheim 1994). Coladarci (1986) points out the fact that correlation coefficients indicate the degree of association between two variables. They do not indicate the degree of similarity between the individual values themselves. Flynn and Rahbar (1998) argue that studies reporting correlation coefficients have limited predictive validity. Kenny and Chekaluk (1993) express concern at studies reporting correlation coefficients as the only measure of accuracy of TJ, with particular reference to the identification of high-risk children. Salvesen and Undheim (1994) make a similar point in relation to the use of correlation coefficients: 'although a highly significant relationship may be revealed, this is less important than correctly classifying individual children' (Salvesen and Undheim 1994: 60). It is more important for the teachers to accurately identify the lowest-performing students in their classes, than it is to be able to rank all students in relation to each other.

Unit of analysis

This refers to whether pooled data (where class membership is ignored), or within-class data are used. Hoge and Coladarci (1989) warn that results can be over- or underestimated when pooled data are used. In Hoge and Coladarci's (1989) analysis, pooled data produced lower correlations than within-class data.

Validity

There seems to be some disagreement amongst researchers as to whether the validity of TJ should be established using standardised or other tests as the criterion, or vice versa (Gerber and Semmel 1984; Gresham et al. 1997; Gresham et al. 1987; Shinn et al. 1987). If TJ and reading tests are going to be used to evaluate reading achievement and identify students experiencing reading problems, they need to be valid; that is, they need to be measuring the same thing – reading. Most of the research in this area has used standardised (or other) tests to evaluate the accuracy of TJ. This has been done both in concurrent and in predictive contexts.

Concurrent validity is established when the test scores of a group of participants are related to a criterion measure administered at the same time or within a short period of time (Borg and Gall 1989). Most studies addressing the concurrent validity of TJ have used regular classes; that is, they have looked at the relationship between TJ and performance on standardised tests (Hoge and Coladarci 1989) using regular classes. For example, Bates and Nettleback (2001) used the Neale Analysis of Reading Ability – Revised (Neale 1988) and Eaves et al. (1994) used the Woodcock Reading Mastery Test – Revised (Woodcock 1987).

Predictive validity is the degree to which predictions made are confirmed by the later behaviour of the subjects (Borg and Gall 1989). Most studies addressing the predictive validity of TJ collected TJ data in Kindergarten and then administered standardised tests a few years later. The results of the tests are then used to confirm or deny the initial TJ. Studies addressing both the concurrent (for example, Bates and Nettlebeck (2001); Eaves et al. (1994); Fletcher et al. 2001) and predictive validity (for example Coleman and Dover (1993); Flynn and Rahbar 1998) of TJ will be discussed in detail below.

Moderator variables

The available research on TJ of reading has identified several possible moderator variables. These include the following.

- Differences among teachers. These differences can be controlled for by using within-class data (Hoge and Coladarci 1989).
- Student gender. No significant student gender effect has been found in the literature (Gaines and Davis 1990; Hoge and Butcher 1984; Hoge and Coladarci 1989).
- Student ability. There is some evidence that teachers are less able to accurately judge lower-performing students. There are in fact few studies looking at lower-performing students. From their review of the literature, Hoge and Coladarci (1989) conclude that there is a strong suggestion that students' academic ability influences the accuracy with which teachers judge students' achievement. This is discussed in more detail below.
- The relationship of the student and teacher. Doherty and Connelly (1985) suggest this as a factor in response to the 'expectancy effect' research. Nash (1973) found that the teacher's relationship with students affected their academic judgment.
- Tidiness of the child. This refers to tidiness of written work (Doherty and Conolly 1985).
- Race (Gaines and Davis 1990).
- Social class (Gaines and Davis 1990; Hoge 1983).

Teacher issues

Several studies have investigated the effects of teacher experience on TJ with varying results. Bates and Nettlebeck (2001) found no evidence that judgments were affected by teacher experience. Freeman (1993), on the other hand, found that teacher experience was a contributing factor in the number of overestimated scores of TJ of reading, with inexperienced teachers more likely to overestimate reading scores. Hoge and Coladarci (1989) suggest that the number of years of teaching experience is a possible explanation for the accuracy of the judgments in their study.

There is also some suggestion that teacher gender can affect TJ. Freeman (1993), for example, found that female teachers tended to overestimate predictions for girls and underestimate predictions for boys (when asked to predict scores on a standardised test). Male teachers tended to overestimate more in general.

Teacher familiarity with students was identified as a limitation by Eaves *et al.* (1994). In their study, in which low correlations were found between TJ and standardised tests, students attended a five-week summer remedial reading clinic and had contact with teachers just four mornings per week. The rationale here is that teachers would be more accurate in their judgments if they had spent longer time in contact with their students.

Teacher familiarity with tests is also an issue in this type of research. The idea here is that teachers who are more familiar with a certain test will be better able to predict the scores of students on that test. Gaines and Davis (1990) asked teachers to identify students who would score in the top and bottom quartiles on the Iowa Test of Basic Skills (ITBS) (see Gaines and Davis 1990) and the Degrees of Reading Power Test (DRP) (Degrees of Reading Power Services 1988). Similarly, Bates and Nettlebeck (2001) asked teachers to estimate percentile scores on the Neale Analysis of Reading Ability – Revised (NARA-R) (Neale 1988).

Salvesen and Undheim (1994) describe halo effects as teachers' tendencies to allow their rating of one aspect of a child's behaviour to be influenced by their overall evaluation of the child. They found a halo effect in their study, but argued that ratings of reading would be accurate despite this halo effect because, as reading is such a dominant activity at the primary school level, reading evaluations were more likely to influence other areas rather than be influenced by them. Cadwell and Jenkins (1986) also reported that teachers in their study had difficulty rating students on one characteristic independently of other information they had about the students.

Teacher judgment for screening, referral and classification

The main purpose of looking at teacher judgment of low-progress readers is that teachers should be able both to identify students having reading problems and to programme appropriately for them. TJ seems to be a major part of the screening/referral decision-making process (Bates and Nettlebeck 2001; Hoge 1983; Kastner and Gottlieb 1991).

There appears to be some disagreement among researchers as to how best to identify children at risk of reading failure. According to Flynn and Rahbar (1998), the two possibilities are teacher rating scales and screening tests. Issues specific to teacher rating scales will be discussed later in this chapter. Flynn and Rahbar (1998) note some concerns regarding screening tests, such as limited educational relevance and inadequate psychometric qualities. In their study on improving prediction of children at risk of reading failure, they hypothesised that asking teachers to rate current skills would be more valid than asking them to predict future ability. The findings indicated that teacher prediction of children at risk of having reading problems may be improved by the use of 'rating instruments where research validated precursors to reading are involved' (Flynn and Rahbar 1998: 170).

Screening for reading problems needs to be fast and accurate (Morrison *et al.* 1988). Another consideration is the cost involved. Gaines and Davis (1990) make the point that TJ is important in identifying students at risk of academic failure due to limited resources and that, if TJ is relied upon, over-identification would reduce the effectiveness of remedial programmes by increasing the strain on resources.

According to Patton (1976), the identification of students with special needs is often left to the discretion of teachers, administrators and school psychologists, with teachers having a key role in the initial identification. For this reason, Patton sees the classroom teacher as one of the key decision makers. Similarly, Kastner and Gottlieb (1991) found that information provided by the classroom teacher was influential in decision making regarding the classification of students in special education. Despite this, they found only a 64 per cent accuracy rate in classification of students to programmes for students with a learning disability (LD) or emotional disturbance.

Studies looking at teacher identification of students with academic problems show that a certain proportion of students are misclassified. This can occur in two ways. False positives occur when a child is identified as being at risk of having a learning problem but does not have one. In this case, a child may receive intervention when none was needed and therefore resources would be wasted. False negatives occur when a child is not identified as being at risk of having learning problems but later experiences them. False negatives can clearly be disastrous for the student.

Gottlieb and Weinberg (1999) looked at the differences between students with LD who had been referred for special education, and low-achieving students (LA) who had not been referred. In 1982, Ysseldyke, Algozzine, Shinn and McGue had found that these two groups were virtually indistinguishable in terms of their performance on standardised achievement tests (cited in Gottlieb and Weinberg 1999). Behaviour has been suggested as a possible difference. The authors state that the methodology used to determine differences between these two groups would usually be to compare performance on standardised tests. This, however, may not be an accurate indicator of any difference after LD students had received special education services since they may score higher. This methodological problem was Gottlieb and Weinberg's (1999) rationale for collecting data for their study at the time of referral. The aim, then, was to look at whether referred and non-referred students differed in behaviour and academic achievement.

The participants were 57 students in kindergarten to Year 3 from nine schools (32 referred, 25 non-referred). In addition to a number of behaviour rating scales, teachers completed an academic rating scale developed by special educators, though it is not clear whether this scale specifically measured reading. Scores on the Degrees of Reading Power Test (Degrees of Reading Power Services 1988) were obtained from the schools. Analysis of variance was used to compare the two groups with the initial teacher ratings. No significant main interaction effect was found, so the two groups were initially perceived by teachers as being the same. In addition, no significant correlations between referral status and any of the teachers' variables were found. Referred students scored significantly lower on the standardised reading test, however.

The aim of the study by Gresham et al. (1987) was to look at the accuracy of TJ in identifying students classified as LD or non-handicapped as compared with standardised test results. The authors hypothesised that teachers would be as accurate as standardised tests in identifying students classified as LD or non-handicapped. One hundred students who had previously been classified as having LD and 100 students who had not been thus classified participated in the study. These participants were all selected randomly from 25 classes in 14 schools. The LD group were mainstreamed but had been receiving special education services. The non-LD group had never been referred or considered for referral.

The predictor variables were scores on an intelligence test (WISC-R) (Wechsler 1974), the Peabody Individual Achievement Test (Dunn and Markwardt 1970), and the teacher rating of academic performance (TRAP) (see Gresham *et al.* 1987). The TRAP requires teachers to rate reading, maths and overall academic performance. The dependent variable was group membership. The correlation between the predictor variables and group membership was 0.73, which accounted for 53 per cent of the variance. TJ correlated with the standardised tests at between 0.39 and 0.72 with a median value of 0.56. The teacher ratings accurately classified 91 per cent of students. The intelligence and achievement tests accurately classified 89 per cent and 84.5 per cent respectively. The authors concluded that TJ is highly accurate in classifying students as LD or not.

The main methodological problem with this study is that it used a re-evaluation sample; that is, the students had previously been identified as LD according to state guidelines. Gresham *et al.* (1987) state that 95–8 per cent of students classified as LD retain their classification three years later. This obvious bias is acknowledged, but, given that the students' previous classification would influence TJ, these results, if useful at all, may only be generalised to other re-evaluations and therefore are not necessarily an indication of the accuracy of TJ of referral of students with LD per se. It would be interesting to see how accurate TJ would be for identifying LD students at the point of referral.

Teacher decision making

According to Borko *et al.* (1981), teachers use 'best guesses' to make decisions. Coladarci (1992) cites a study by McNair (1978–9) which indicated that many instructional decisions were based on what teachers 'surmised' was going on. Teachers make instructional decisions based, at least in part, on TJ, and therefore accuracy is important. Errors in TJ can be costly for school systems and, most importantly, for students themselves. Shinn *et al.* (1987) identified two main types of error in decision making. These are biases based on factors such as ethnic background and gender, and teacher accuracy. Accuracy of teacher judgment, with particular reference to the identification of low-progress readers, is of most interest in this chapter.

Coladarci (1992) has identified several factors that seem to be influencing the accuracy of TJ. Firstly, TJ has been shown to vary across teachers within studies. In other words (and unsurprisingly) some teachers display better academic judgment than others. Secondly, TJ depends on the task being judged. In the area of reading comprehension, for example, teachers made more accurate judgments of students' performance on literal rather than on figurative tasks (Coladarci and Spector (1985), cited in Coladarci 1992). Thirdly, it depends on the student being judged. Teachers have been found to be less accurate in judging students of lower ability (Bates and Nettlebeck 2001; Hoge and Butcher 1984). As Coladarci states, 'These results point to the disturbing conclusion that low-performing students, while doubtless the most in need of accurate teacher judgments, are the least likely to get them' (Coladarci 1992: 36).

Variation in teacher tolerance may also result in significant variability in the decisions teachers make (Gerber and Semmel 1984; Shinn *et al.* 1987). According to both Shinn *et al.* (1987) and Gerber and Semmel (1984), it is still unclear as to whether variations in teacher tolerance create systematic bias, due to methodological problems with research.

Teacher judgment of reading ability

The available research on the relationship between TJ and reading performance can be divided into two types: studies looking at predictive validity and studies looking at concurrent validity. Although the research on predictive validity will be included in this review, the main focus will be on those studies establishing concurrent validity.

Coladarci (1992) identified three different types of TJ study on reading: (i) Those using ratings and reporting correlations between ratings on a scale and the results of standardised tests; (ii) studies in which teachers predicted how students would score on a particular test – for example, grade equivalence, percentiles and raw scores; and (iii) studies in which, for individual students, teachers went through the test and predicted on which items a student would make errors. From a group of studies examining the relationship between TJ and academic achievement, there was a moderate to strong relationship, with a mean correlation of 0.67. The author concluded that 0.67 was sufficient to suggest the validity of TJ and likened it to the validity coefficients between two standardised tests. Coladarci's (1992) overall conclusion was that TJ of reading is valid overall, but that this is really only true for some teachers on some tasks regarding some students. He then raises the question: What makes some teachers better judges? In answer to this question, Coladarci suggests that it is the teachers' empirical orientation, or the extent to which the teacher frequently and systematically collects information on student learning. There appears to be little or no research linking teachers' empirical orientation and the accuracy of their judgments.

Eaves *et al.* (1994) used the Woodcock Reading Mastery Test (Woodcock 1987) to investigate the accuracy of TJ using a group of 45 learning disabled and at-risk students attending a five-week summer remedial reading clinic. A median correlation of 0.38 with a range of 0.22 to 0.46 was found. The authors concluded that this represented a low to moderate relationship between TJ and reading test performance and is considerably lower than that found by other studies (for example, Bates and Nettlebeck 2001). Several possible reasons are offered for this low correlation: the remedial reading clinic only lasted five weeks; the teachers were unfamiliar with the students at the beginning of the clinic and only had contact with the students for four mornings per week; and, as the teachers were special educators, the authors argue that they may not have had a good idea of what is considered to be 'average' for a particular grade. A potential limitation that was not acknowledged by the authors was the timing of the data collection. The tests were administered before the clinic began and the TJ data was collected at the end of the clinic. There was no mention made of the effect of any possible progress made over the duration of the clinic.

There have been a few Australian studies in this area. One such study by Bates and Nettlebeck (2001) looked at the accuracy of TJ of reading accuracy and reading comprehension in respect of students with and students without behaviour problems. In this study, the NARA-R (Neale 1988) was used as the criterion measure. One hundred and eight 6- to 8-year-old students participated in this study. After being provided with some information on the NARA-R, the teachers were asked to estimate a percentile rank for each student. Overall, the correlation between TJ and reading accuracy was 0.77, and it was 0.62 between TJ and reading comprehension.

Looking at individual estimations revealed some interesting findings. Bates and Nettlebeck (2001) scored estimations that were within one standard deviation of the student's actual score as correct. Even based on this generous criterion, 75 per cent of estimations were incorrect. Using a criterion of two standard deviations, 50 per cent were correct for reading accuracy and 40 per cent were correct for reading comprehension. These results lend support to the concerns of several authors (Coladarci 1986; Flynn and Rahbar 1998; Kenny and Chekaluk 1993; Salvesen and Undheim 1994) regarding using correlation coefficients as the sole indicator of accuracy of TJ, as discussed below. Estimations were also translated to errors in reading ages in months. For reading accuracy, 32 per cent of teacher estimations were more than 12 months in error. This figure was 40 per cent for reading comprehension. Bates and Nettlebeck (2001) found that errors as large as these were made at least once by approximately two-thirds of teachers in the study.

Bates and Nettlebeck (2001) also looked at over- and underestimation. They found that teachers tended to overestimate the reading accuracy and reading comprehension of students more in lower-ability groups and to underestimate students in higher-ability groups. Overestimation occurred more than underestimation in general (60 per cent and 40 per cent respectively). When overestimations were analysed separately, 39 per cent of estimations were in error by 12 months or more for reading accuracy and 45 per cent of estimations were in error by 12 months or more for reading comprehension. The authors conclude that, as TJ is a major source of information used in the identification of students with special needs and in making educational decisions, such over-estimation is problematic.

Another Australian study by Fletcher et al. (2001) investigated the accuracy of teachers' identification of children with language and literacy difficulties. The participants were Year 2 students evaluated by 12 teachers from five schools in Western Australia. The rating scales used were the Strength and Difficulties Questionnaire (SDQ) (Goodman 1997), the Child Development Clinic Language Questionnaire (LQ) (Humphries et al. 1994), and the Literacy Rating Scale (LRS) (see Fletcher et al. 2001). Developed for this study, the LRS is a rating scale measuring performance in written expression, spelling and reading comprehension on a five-point scale. The standardised measures used were the NARA-R (Neale 1988); the Woodcock Reading Mastery Tests – Revised (WRMT-R) (Woodcock 1987) (word identification and word attack subtests); the South Australian Spelling Tests (SAS) (Westwood 1999); the Peabody Picture Vocabulary Test (PPVT) (Dunn and Dunn 1981), and the Clinical Evaluation of Language Fundamentals – Revised Screening Test (CELF-RS) (Semel et al. 1989).

Complete test data was available for 50 children (including a comparison group). Standardised tests were administered by testers (blind to the teacher's ratings) over two individual and one group sessions. After the standardised tests had been scored, children were classified as either having language/literacy problems, or not. Correlations between teacher ratings (LRS) and the NARA-R were 0.73 for accuracy and 0.69 for comprehension.

Doherty and Conolly (1985) asked seven teachers to predict the scores of 145 Grade 3 and Grade 4 students on three standardised tests, including The Reading Test (Doherty and Conolly 1985). In contrast to the Bates and Nettlebeck (2001) study, all teachers underestimated more than they overestimated reading ability. The correlation between TJ and scores on the reading measure was 0.68, which is comparable to that found by Coladarci (1992).

Gaines and Davis (1990) conducted two studies looking at the accuracy of TJ of academic achievement. In Study One, 22 teachers and 530 students participated. The teachers were asked to identify students in the top and bottom quartiles on the ITBS (see Gaines and Davis 1990) and the DRP (Degrees of Reading Power Services 1988). Results for bottom-quartile students indicated TJ accuracy of 64 per cent for the ITBS and 61 per cent for the DRP. Accuracy was slightly higher for top-quartile students (63 per cent for the DRP and 68 per cent for the ITBS). A significant correlation was found between total years of teaching experience for the DRP. Where correlations were significant, more experienced teachers were more accurate.

In Study Two, teachers were required to code student test papers as one, two or three (first to fifteenth, sixteenth to thirty-fifth, and thirty-sixth to fiftieth percentiles respectively). Accuracy was calculated based on strict (right category) and more liberal (first to thirty-fifth percentile) criteria. The more liberal criteria allowed the first two categories to be combined. The findings indicated that teachers were more accurate in identifying low-performing students, a finding that seems to be in contrast to that of Coladarci (1992), who concluded that teachers are less accurate at judging the reading performance of lower-performing students. In addition, a significant difference between the grade levels included in the study was found, with Year 6 teachers proving to be more accurate judges of reading performance than either Year 4 or Year 2 teachers.

Hopkins et al. (1985) investigated the concurrent validity of the Comprehensive Test of Basic Skills (CTBS) (Hopkins et al. 1985) against TJ in reading and four other areas. The concurrent validity coefficient between TJ and reading perform-ance on the CTBS was very high at 0.93. Similarly, a 1988 study by Wright and Wiese compared a teacher rating grading system with performance on the SRA Achievement Test (SRA) (Science Research Associates Inc. 1978) for 145 students. Ratings were made on a five-point Likert scale for achievement and effort in several areas, including reading. Predictions of percentile scores on the SRA were also made. In the area of reading ability, the correlation between TJ and the SRA was 0.82 and between the TJ rating and the SRA, the correlation was 0.71. These high correlations provide support not only for the concurrent validity of the CTBS, but also for TJ of reading performance.

Freeman (1993) used the vocabulary and comprehension subtests of the Gates-MacGinitie Reading Test Level D (MacGinitie et al. 1980) to investigate the accuracy of TJ in respect of 214 students from grades four to six. Teachers in this study were required to estimate the number of correct responses on the test. Overall, the relationship between TJ and the test scores was 0.72 (p<0.001). The correlations by grade were 0.72, 0.74 and 0.71 for Grades 4, 5 and 6 respectively. Overestimation was made for 67 per cent of students. According to the authors, teacher experience and teacher gender accounted for this. No variable was found to account for underestimations.

An early study by Farr and Roelke (1971) aimed to investigate the validity of various assessment procedures for measuring the following subskills of read-ing: vocabulary, comprehension and word analysis. Standardised tests, teacher judgment and informal reading tests administered by reading specialists were compared. Convergent and discriminant validity were examined. The tests used were the McCullough Word Analysis (McCullough 1963), the Gates-MacGinitie Reading Test (Gates and MacGinitie 1965), and the California Reading Test (Tiegs and Clark 1963). Teacher judgments were measured using a rating scale based on the operational definition of each subskill. Validity coefficients ranged from 0.48 to 0.92, which is highly variable.

Hoge and Butcher (1984) aimed to investigate the accuracy of teacher judg-ment of the achievement levels of students. Participants were 322 students (in Years 3 to 8) and 12 teachers in a rural area. Teachers were required to estimate student performance on the Gates-MacGinitie Reading Test (MacGinitie et al. 1978) in terms of a grade equivalent score; provide an estimate of confidence in this rating (on a five-point scale); rate basic intellectual ability (on a five-point scale), and rate student motivation to do schoolwork (also on a five-point scale). The Gates-MacGinitie Reading Test (MacGinitie et al. 1978) and the verbal subscales of the Canadian Lorge-Thorndike Intelligence Test (Wright 1967) were administered approximately two weeks after TJ was completed.

The results indicated a close relationship between TJ and standardised tests ($\beta=0.71$) but that IQ may be a biasing factor. The correlation between TJ of reading ability and TJ of intellectual ability was 0.87. There was no evidence of a gender effect in this study. It was concluded that teachers are able to accurately judge student achievement.

The fact that only teachers who volunteered participated in this study may introduce some bias as it is likely that they would have greater confidence in their own judgments. The authors suggest number of years of teaching experience of the teachers in this study as a possible explanation of the accuracy of the judgments. Perhaps the most significant finding in this study is that, although teachers seem to be accurate judges of student ability overall, they may not be as accurate at all ability levels. Teachers in this study tended to overestimate the ability of higher-achieving students and underestimate the ability of lower-achieving students.

Coleman and Dover (1993) used the RISK Screening Test (Coleman and Dover 1989) to predict future placement in resource classrooms. The RISK Screening Test requires teachers to rate students on 43 school behaviour items. This study found that, overall, over 94 per cent of students were accurately selected to the relevant educational placement (Coleman and Dover 1993), but that this figure was only 79 per cent for at-risk students. The RISK Screening Test missed about one in every five students who were ultimately placed in a resource classroom (Coleman and Dover 1993).

In a study investigating the early prediction of reading achievement, Mantzicopoulos and Morrison (1994) asked teachers to rate each student's likelihood of developing a learning disability later in their schooling. Results indicated that TJ was an accurate indicator of future reading performance, particularly where test-based false positives and false negatives occurred.

The accuracy of TJ for predicting reading achievement by the end of first grade was compared with two screening tests in a study by Kapelis (1975). The criterion measure was the Metropolitan Achievement Test (MAT) (Durost 1959). Moderate correlations were found for all three predictors, with the two screening tests correlating with the MAT at 0.58–0.68. The correlation between TJ and the MAT was lower, at 0.46–0.49.

Flynn and Rahbar (1998) aimed to improve teacher prediction of students at risk for reading failure by developing a screening test. The Teacher Rating Scale (TRS) (Flynn 1977) is a ten-item rating scale. A sample of 210 students was used to investigate the predictive validity of the TRS. This was carried out by asking teachers to rate current skills rather than asking them to predict future ability. Flynn and Rahbar (1998) hypothesised that this would improve valid positive rates for teacher predictions. Teachers ratings on the TRS correctly predicted 64 per cent of poor readers. The authors concluded that the accuracy of teacher prediction of students at risk of reading failure can be improved by using a rating scale.

Similarly, teachers in the Feshbach et al. (1977) study were required to complete the Student Rating Scale (SRS) (see Adelman and Feshbach 1971). The Cooperative Primary Reading Test (Feshbach *et al.* 1977) was then administered in Years 1 to 3 and correlations of 0.43 to 0.49, 0.48 to 0.52, and 0.39 to 0.44 were found for the two cohorts in each of the three grades, respectively. The authors concluded that the SRS was at least as effective as psychometric measures while being more descriptive and economical.

The research reviewed above is inconsistent regarding the relationship between TJ and reading performance. Although Coladarci (1992) regarded TJ as valid overall, if the relationship between TJ and performance on standardised tests is to be likened to the relationship between two tests, a validity coefficient of 0.67 seems quite low. In addition, despite favourable results in some studies, large variations in accuracy scores and validity coefficients have been found (for example, Farr and Roelke 1971) with some disturbing findings (for example, Bates and Nettlebeck 2001). For these reasons, perhaps a more objective method of evaluating reading performance, and, in particular, of identifying low-progress readers is needed.

Other related studies

The following studies do not directly address TJ of reading ability, but further illustrate the relationship between TJ and academic ability, including reading. Studies such as that by Airasian *et al.* (1977) reinforce the lack of objectivity in TJ, whereas the study by Jorgensen (1975) highlights the difficulty of the task that can be faced by teachers in making judgments about reading.

A study by Airasian *et al.* (1977) investigated the effect of information gained from standardised tests on TJ. The researchers aimed to determine the proportion of students for whom TJ was affected by test information, and to identify the directionality of any changes. A pre/post-test design with 1,566 students was used in Irish schools. Schools were randomly allocated to one of three conditions. In one condition, no standardised tests were administered. In the second condition, standardised tests were administered but the school did not receive the results. In the third condition, standardised tests (Educational Research Centre 1973) were administered and the schools received the results.

Teachers rated the students on a five-point scale for English and maths ability. Standardised test were administered and teachers rated the students a second time about six months later. The authors found that test information is not powerful in influencing TJ, except in the case of a very small proportion of students. Where there were changes, standardised test information tended to raise TJ.

Jorgensen (1975) investigated teachers' accuracy in judging the difficulty level of reading passages. Six paragraphs from an informal reading inventory were presented to teachers in random order. The teachers had to indicate the grade level for which they thought each paragraph was suited. Results indicated that the teachers could estimate the difficulty of the easiest passages, but that, as the difficulty level increased, the accuracy of their judgments decreased, and the variability in teacher responses increased. Overall, Jorgensen (1975) concluded that teachers vary widely in their ability to judge the level of difficulty of reading material.

In a similar study, Oliver and Arnold (1978) compared standardised test scores, informal reading inventory (IRI) placement levels, and TJ. A group of Year 3 students was given the Iowa Test of Basic Skills (ITBS) and an informal reading inventory, and teachers were asked to estimate their reading levels. Oliver and Arnold (1978) found correlations of 0.82 between TJ and the IRI, and 0.74 between TJ and the ITBS. The IRI placed students on easier material than either the standardised tests or TJ.

Another related study is that by Leinhardt (1983), which looked at novice and expert teachers' knowledge of student achievement. In this study, teachers had to go through a standardised achievement test and indicate whether individual students were given sufficient instruction to get each item correct or not. They were not asked to indicate whether or not the students would get each item correct or not. The novice teachers were slightly less accurate, but the difference between the two groups was not large. A major weakness of this study, however, was the fact that, although the test scores were not made available to teachers until after the judgments were made, the tests were administered by the teachers themselves.

The use of curriculum-based measures

As stated above, most studies of TJ of reading ability have used standardised or norm-referenced tests. Few studies have compared TJ with curriculum-based assessment and, in particular, curriculum-based measurement.

Curriculum-based measurement (CBM) of reading is a quick, reliable and valid means of tracking progress in basic skills, such as reading, towards a long term goal. One way in which this can be done is by using a passage reading test (PRT) (Deno *et al.* 1982; Hasbrouk and Tindal 1992). A PRT requires students to read aloud from a passage of text for one minute. The index of student proficiency is the number of words read correctly per minute, or oral reading fluency (ORF). Research has consistently and repeatedly demonstrated the reliability and validity of CBM using PRTs (Deno *et al.* 1982; Fuchs *et al.* 1988; Jenkins and Jewell 1993; Madelaine and Wheldall 1999).

In addition to being used for monitoring, a PRT can also be used for screening purposes (Deno 1987; Fuchs and Deno 1992; Mehrens and Clarizio 1993; Rodden-Nord and Shinn 1991) and would be a suitable alternative for initial identification of students experiencing reading problems, as PRTs have established technical characteristics and can quickly and easily be administered, taking as little as one minute per student. Marston *et al.* (1984) suggest CBM as an alternative to other diagnostic/placement approaches. In their study, they found that students identified via CBM were likely candidates for referral. One of the most important findings of this study was that only about one-third of the students referred by TJ met the district criterion for placement in LD programmes, whereas about 80 per cent of students referred on the basis of continuous evaluation were eligible for an LD placement (Marston *et al.* 1984). Rodden-Nord and Shinn (1991) used PRTs in a study designed to investigate the academic performance ranges in reading, with identification of students likely to be referred to special education services in mind.

In their study of 300 Year 2 to Year 7 students, Fewster and Macmillan (2002) carried out a discriminant analysis to examine the ability of CBM scores to predict group placement. Their results indicated that CBM scores could reliably predict placement in each of four groups: special education, remedial, general education, and honours class (p<0.0005 for the oral reading fluency measure) (Fewster and MacMillan 2002).

Wilson *et al.* (1992) examined the relationship between TJ, reading test scores and CBM of reading. They hypothesised that CBM would be the best predictor of instructional group placement. The correlation between CBM and instructional group placement was 0.43–0.44. The teacher rating scale used was the Teacher Rating of Academic Performance – Revised (TRAP-R) (see Wilson *et al.* 1992). This contained two items specifically related to reading. The reading comparison item asked teachers to rate individual students' reading in comparison with that of the other students in their classroom. The grade level expectations item required teachers to rate each student against what they considered typical for a particular grade level. The CBM measure correlated with the TRAP-R reading comparison item at 0.58 and with the TRAP-R grade level expectations item at 0.63. Interestingly, the Iowa Tests of Basic Skills (ITBS) (see Wilson *et al.* 1992) correlated higher with the two TRAP-R reading items (0.72 and 0.75 respectively). Wilson *et al.* (1992) carried out a discriminant function analysis to indicate the percentage of correct classifications (instructional group placement) for each assessment method. The TRAP-R was the most accurate overall, at 78 per cent. The CBM measure correctly classified 68 per cent of students, and 65 per cent of students were correctly classified by the ITBS (Wilson *et al.* 1992). The authors concluded that the three types of measures predicted reading equally well, and suggest that the combination of CBM, group achievement tests and teacher ratings be used to replace norm-referenced tests in the screening and referral process.

In a study aimed at establishing the validity of CBM of English reading with bilingual Hispanic students, Baker and Good (1995) administered CBM probes, the Stanford Diagnostic Reading Test (Karlsen and Gardner 1985) and a series of language measures to 76 students in Year 2. In addition, teachers were required to rate reading skills on a seven-point Likert scale. The teacher ratings of reading correlated with the Stanford Diagnostic Reading Test at 0.59 and with the CBM measure at 0.80 (Baker and Good 1995).

Other studies that have employed a measure of CBM and TJ include that of Hartman and Fuller (1997), who found correlations of 0.69 to 0.78 between TJ and CBM in their study on the development of CBM norms in literature-based classrooms, and that of Morgan and Bradley-Johnson (1995) who measured TJ in their study of the use of CBM with Braille readers. Morgan and Bradley-Johnson (1995) found overall correlations of 0.80–0.85, but correlations were lower for decoding and comprehension separately (0.51–0.54 and 0.39–0.40 respectively). These results should be viewed with a degree of caution, however, as analyses were conducted on samples of 14–15 students. Shinn *et al.* (1987) used curriculum-based measures as the main dependent measure in their study on teacher bias in the referral process. The CBM scores reflected differences in groups of teacher-referred and non-referred students at all grade levels. Overall, the teachers in this study were found to be both accurate and biased in referring low-achieving students for special education services.

A series of studies conducted by Madelaine and Wheldall (Madelaine and Wheldall 2003 2002a 2005) in Australia have used the Wheldall Assessment of Reading Passages (WARP) (Wheldall and Madelaine 2006) as the criterion against which the accuracy of teacher judgment is evaluated. The WARP has consistently been found to be both reliable and valid (Madelaine and Wheldall 1998 2002b 2002c; Wheldall and Madelaine 2000). This series of studies focused on the ability of teachers to identify low-progress (LP) readers in their classes using several different methodologies.

In the first study, teachers were asked to identify one LP and four average readers from their classes. Results indicated that more than one-quarter of the teachers in the study found this task difficult (Madelaine and Wheldall 2003). The second study required teachers to categorise their students into the top 25 per cent, middle 50 per cent and bottom 25 per cent for reading perform-ance. Compared with categorisation based on the more objective CBM measure, the mean accuracy of TJ was 67 per cent, varying between 29 per cent and 100 per cent (Madelaine and Wheldall 2002a). The third study used a similar methodology, with 24 teachers required to categorise ten randomly selected students from their classes into the top three, middle four and bottom three for reading performance. Results similar to those of the second study were obtained with mean accuracy of TJ at 65 per cent, varying between 20 per cent and 100 per cent (Madelaine and Wheldall 2002b). The final study involved 33 teachers and their Year 3 to Year 5 classes. Twelve students were randomly se-lected from each class and their teachers were asked to rank them based on their judgments of student reading performance. All students were also assessed on the WARP. The obtained oral reading fluency measures for the students were ranked for each class and compared with TJ rankings. The results indicated that only half of the teachers identified the same poorest reader as did the curriculum-based PRT. Moreover, only 15 per cent of the teachers identified the same three lowest-performing readers as the PRT (Madelaine and Wheldall 2005).

Conclusion

When considering the actual purpose of TJ, it is important to think about what it is we want teachers to judge, and why. Do we need them to be able to state the reading ages of individual children? Perhaps the ability to classify children into a set of groups is more important. Several authors discuss the need for a means of identifying children at risk of learning difficulties that is accurate (Sharpley and Edgar 1986), cost effective and time efficient (Shinn *et al.* 1987), and suggest that teachers need an effective screening tool that they can use with little disruption to their classes (Fletcher *et al.* 2001). As classroom teachers need to be able to accurately identify students experiencing difficulty with reading so that they may make instructional changes or referrals, a method other than judgment may be needed.

In this review, we have examined studies investigating TJ of overall academic ability, and in greater detail those investigating TJ of reading ability. While it seems that TJ of reading ability is relatively accurate overall, there is enormous variability in the accuracy of TJ. We have considered the methodological issues relevant to research in this area, with an emphasis on validity. As TJ is said to have an important role in the screening and referral process (Bates and Nettlebeck 2001; Hoge 1983; Kastner and Gottlieb 1991), we have reviewed studies in this area, with a focus on the ability of teachers to identify LP readers. The research in this area indicates that TJ might not be the most accurate means of identifying low-progress readers. Finally, we have examined the body of literature on TJ of reading using CBM as the criterion measure. By virtue of its established reliability, validity, simplicity and cost-effectiveness, CBM is a promising alternative to TJ for the purpose of identifying low-progress readers.

The literature indicates that overreliance on TJ for instructional decision making, or for selecting low-progress readers for appropriate instruction, may be misplaced and that a more objective, quick alternative based on CBM may be preferable. Such a method would expand the range of assessment options available to educators for the purpose of identifying low-progress readers, thus enhancing the professional lives of teachers. The identification of low-progress readers allows remedial instruction to be targeted more precisely. Teachers' professional lives would, thereby, be made easier because they would have access to a quick and objective measure, rather than just 'feel'.

References

Adelman, H. and Feshbach, S. (1971). Predicting reading failure: Beyond the readiness model. *Exceptional Children*, *37*, 349–54.

Airasian, P. W., Kellaghan, T., Madaus, G. F. and Pedulla, J. J. (1977). Proportion and direction of teacher rating changes of pupils' progress attributable to standardized test information. *Journal of Educational Psychology*, *69*, 702–9.

Baker, S. K. and Good, R. (1995). Curriculum-based measurement of English reading with bilingual Hispanic students: A validation study with second-grade students. *School*

Psychology Review, 24: 561–78.

Bates, C. and Nettlebeck, T. (2001). Primary school teachers' judgements of reading achievement. *Educational Psychology, 21*: 179–89.

Borg, W. R. and Gall, M. D. (1989). *Educational research: An introduction*, 5th ed. New York: Longman.

Borko, H., Shavelsen, R. J. and Stern, P. (1981). Teachers' decisions in the planning of reading instruction. *Reading Research Quarterly, 16*: 449–66.

Cadwell, J. and Jenkins, J. (1986). Teachers' judgments about their students: The effect of cognitive simplification strategies on the rating process. *American Educational Research Journal, 23*: 460–75.

Coladarci, T. (1986). Accuracy of teacher judgments of student responses to standardized test items. *Journal of Educational Psychology, 78*: 141–6.

Coladarci, T. (1992). Teachers' knowledge of what students' know: The case of reading. *Reading Improvement, 29*: 34–9.

Coleman, J. M. and Dover, G. M. (1989). *Rating Inventory for Screening Kindergarteners.* Austin, TX: Pro-Ed.

Coleman, J. M. and Dover, G. M. (1993). The RISK screening test: Using kindergarten teachers' ratings to predict further placement in resource rooms. *Exceptional Children, 59*: 468–77.

Degrees of Reading Power Services. (1988). *Degrees of reading power norms: All forms.* Brewster, NY: Touchstone Applied Science Associates.

Deno, S. L. (1987). Curriculum-based measurement. *Teaching Exceptional Children, 20*: 41–2.

Deno, S. L., Mirkin, P. K. and Chiang, B. (1982). Identifying valid measures of reading. *Exceptional Children, 49*: 36–45.

Doherty, J. and Conolly, M. (1985). How accurately can primary school teachers predict the scores of their pupils in standardised tests of attainment? A study of some non-cognitive factors that influence specific judgements. *Educational Studies, 11*: 41–60.

Dunn, L. and Markwardt, F. (1970). *Peabody Individual Achievement Test.* Circle Pines, MN: American Guidance Service.

Dunn, L. M. and Dunn, L. M. (1981). *Peabody Picture Vocabulary Test – Revised.* Circle Pines, MN: American Guidance Service.

Durost, W. N. (ed.). (1959). *Directions for Administering the Metropolitan Achievement Tests.* New York: Harcourt, Brace and World.

Eaves, R. C., Williams, P., Winchester, K. and Darch, C. (1994). Using teacher judgment and IQ to estimate reading and mathematics achievement in a remedial-reading program. *Psychology in the Schools, 31*: 261–72.

Educational Research Centre. (1973). *Drumcondra Test Series.* Dublin: Educational Research Centre, St Patricks College.

Farr, R. and Roelke, P. (1971). Measuring subskills of reading: Intercorrelations between standardised reading tests, teachers' ratings, and reading specialists' ratings. *Journal of Educational Measurement, 8*: 27–32.

Feshbach, S., Adelman, H. and Fuller, W. (1977). Prediction of reading and related academic problems. *Journal of Educational Psychology, 69*: 299–308.

Fewster, S. and MacMillan, P. D. (2002). School-based evidence for the validity of curriculum-based measurement of reading and writing. *Remedial and Special Education, 23*: 149–56.

Fletcher, J., Tannock, R. and Bishop, D. V. M. (2001). Utility of brief teacher rating scales to identify children with educational problems. *Australian Journal of Psychology, 53*: 63–71.

Flynn, J. M. (1977). *Teacher Rating Scale.* LaCrosse, WI: Lacrosse Area Dyslexia Institute.

Flynn, J. M. and Rahbar, M. H. (1998). Improving teacher prediction of children at risk for reading failure. *Psychology in the Schools, 35*: 163–72.

Freeman, J. G. (1993). Two factors contributing to elementary school teachers' predictions of students' scores on the Gates-MacGinitie Reading Test, Level D. *Perceptual and Motor Skills, 76*: 536–8.

Fuchs, L. S. and Deno, S. L. (1992). Effects of curriculum within curriculum-based measurement. *Exceptional Children, 58*: 232–42.

Fuchs, L. S., Fuchs, D. and Maxwell, L. (1988). The validity of informal reading comprehension measures. *Remedial and Special Education, 9*: 20–8.

Gaines, M. L. and Davis, M. (1990). 'Accuracy of teacher prediction of elementary school achievement'. Paper presented at the Annual Meeting of the American Educational Research Association, Boston, April.

Gates, A. I. and MacGinitie, W. H. (1965). *Gates-MacGinitie reading tests.* New York: Teachers College Press, Columbia University.

Gerber, M. M. and Semmel, M. I. (1984). Teacher as imperfect test: Reconceptualizing the referral process. *Educational Psychologist, 19*: 137–48.

Goodman, R. (1997). The strengths and difficulties questionnaire: A research note. *Journal of Child Psychology and Psychiatry, 34*: 581–6.

Gottlieb, J. and Weinberg, S. (1999). Comparison of students referred and not referred for special education. *The Elementary School Journal, 99*: 187–99.

Gresham, F. M., Reschly, D. J. and Carey, M. P. (1987). Teachers as 'tests': Classification accuracy and concurrent validation in the identification of learning disabled children. *School Psychology Review, 16*: 543–3.

Gresham, F. M., MacMillan, D. L. and Bocian, K. M. (1997). Teachers as 'tests': Differential validity of teacher judgments in identifying students at-risk for learning difficulties. *School Psychology Review, 26*: 47–60.

Hartman, J. M. and Fuller, M. L. (1997). The development of curriculum-based measurement norms in literature-based classrooms. *Journal of School Psychology, 35*: 377–89.

Hasbrouk, J. E. and Tindal, G. (1992). Curriculum-based oral reading fluency norms for students in grades 2 through 5. *Teaching Exceptional Children, 24*: 41–4.

Helmke, A. and Schrader, F.-W. (1987). Interactional effects of instructional quality and teacher judgement accuracy on achievement. *Teaching and Teacher Education, 3*: 91–8.

Hoge, R. D. (1983). Psychometric properties of teacher-judgment measures of pupil aptitudes, classroom behaviours, and achievement levels. *The Journal of Special Education, 17*: 401–29.

Hoge, R. D. and Butcher, R. (1984). Analysis of teacher judgments of pupil achievement levels. *Journal of Educational Psychology, 76*: 777–81.

Hoge, R. D. and Coladarci, T. (1989). Teacher-based judgments of academic achievement: A review of the literature. *Review of Educational Research, 59*: 297–313.

Hopkins, K. D., George, C. A. and Williams, D. D. (1985). The concurrent validity of standardized achievement tests by content area using teacher's ratings as criteria. *Journal of Educational Measurement, 22*: 177–82.

Humphries, T., Koltun, H., Malone, M. and Roberts, W. (1994). Teacher-identified oral language difficulties among boys with attention problems. *Developmental and Behavioral Pediatrics, 15*: 92–8.

Jenkins, J. R. and Jewell, M. (1993). Examining the validity of two measures for formative teaching: Reading aloud and maze. *Exceptional Children*, *59*: 421–32.

Jorgensen, G. W. (1975). An analysis of teacher judgments of reading level. *American Educational Research Journal*, *12*: 67–75.

Kapelis, L. (1975). Early identification of reading failure: A comparison of two screening tests and teacher forecasts. *Journal of Learning Disabilities*, *8*: 638–41.

Karlsen, B. and Gardner, E. (1985). *Stanford Diagnostic Reading Test*, 3rd ed. San Antonio, TX: The Psychological Corporation.

Kastner, J. and Gottlieb, J. (1991). Classification of children in special education: Importance of pre-assessment information. *Psychology in the Schools*, *28*: 19–27.

Kenny, D. T. and Chekaluk, E. (1993). Early reading performance: A comparison of teacher-based and test-based assessments. *Journal of Learning Disabilities*, *26*: 227–336.

Leinhardt, G. (1983). Novice and expert knowledge of individual student's achievement. *Educational Psychologist*, *18*: 165–79.

MacGinitie, W. H., Kamons, J., Kowalski, R. L., MacGinitie, R. K. and MacKay, T. (1978). *Gates-MacGinitie reading tests*. Don Mills, ON: Thomas Nelson.

MacGinitie, W. H., Kamons, J., Kowalski, R. L., MacGinitie, R. K. and MacKay, T. (1980). *Gates-MacGinitie reading test, Canadian edition – teacher's manual*. Toronto, ON: Nelson Canada.

Madelaine, A. and Wheldall, K. (1998). Towards a curriculum-based passage reading test for monitoring the performance of low-progress readers using standardised passages: A validity study. *Educational Psychology*, *18*: 471–8.

Madelaine, A. and Wheldall, K. (1999). Curriculum-based measurement of reading: A critical review. *International Journal of Disability, Development and Education*, *46*: 71–85.

Madelaine, A. and Wheldall, K. (2002a). A comparison of two quick methods for identifying low-progress readers: Teacher judgment versus curriculum-based measurement. *Australasian Journal of Special Education*, *1/2*: 32–47.

Madelaine, A. and Wheldall, K. (2002b). Establishing tentative norms and identifying gender differences in performance for a new passage reading test. *Australian Journal of Learning Disabilities*, *7*: 40–5.

Madelaine, A. and Wheldall, K. (2002c). Further progress towards a standardised curriculum-based measure of reading: Calibrating a new passage reading test against the New South Wales Basic Skills Test. *Educational Psychology*, *22*: 461–71.

Madelaine, A. and Wheldall, K. (2003). Can teachers discriminate low-progress readers from average readers in regular classes? *Australian Journal of Learning Disabilities*, *8*: 4–7.

Madelaine, A. and Wheldall, K. (2005). Identifying low-progress readers: Comparing teacher judgment with a curriculum-based measurement procedure. *International Journal of Disability, Development and Education*, *52*: 33–42.

Mantzicopoulos, P. Y. and Morrison, D. (1994). Early prediction of reading achievement: Exploring the relationship of cognitive and noncognitive measures to inaccurate classification of at-risk students. *Remedial and Special Education*, *15*: 244–51.

Marston, D., Mirkin, P. and Deno, S. L. (1984). Curriculum-based measurement: An alternative to traditional screening, referral and identification. *The Journal of Special Education*, *18*: 109–17.

McCullough, C. M. (1963). *McCullough word analysis tests*. Boston: Ginn.

Mehrens, W. A. and Clarizio, H. F. (1993). Curriculum-based measurement: Conceptual and psychometric considerations. *Psychology in the Schools*, *30*: 241–54.

Morgan, S. K. and Bradley-Johnson, S. (1995). Technical adequacy of curriculum-based measurement for braille readers. *School Psychology Review, 24*: 94–103.

Morrison, D., Mantzicopoulos, P.Y. and Stone, E. (1988). Screening for reading problems: The utility of SEARCH. *Annals of Dyslexia, 38*: 181–92.

Nash, R. (1973). *Classrooms observed.* London: Routledge and Kegan Paul.

Neale, M. D. (1988). *Neale Analysis of Reading Ability – Revised.* Melbourne: Australian Council of Educational Research.

Oliver, J. E. and Arnold, R. D. (1978). Comparing a standardized test, an informal reading inventory and teacher judgment on third grade reading. *Reading Improvement, 15*: 56–9.

Patton, C.V. (1976). Selecting special students: Who decides? *Teachers College Record, 78*: 101–24.

Rodden-Nord, K. and Shinn, M. R. (1991). The range of reading skills within and across general education classrooms: Contributions to understanding special education for students with mild handicaps. *The Journal of Special Education, 24*: 441–53.

Salvesen, K. A. and Undheim, J. O. (1994). Screening for learning disabilities with teacher rating scales. *Journal of Learning Disabilities, 27*: 60–6.

Science Research Associates Inc. (1978). *SRA Achievement Series.* Chicago: Science Research Associates.

Semel, E., Wiig, E. H. and Secord, W. (1989). *Clinical evaluation of language fundamentals – revised: Screening test.* USA: Psychological Corporation.

Sharpley, C. F. and Edgar, E. (1986). Teachers' ratings vs standardized tests: An empirical investigation of agreement between two indices of achievement. *Psychology in the Schools, 23*: 106–11.

Shinn, M. R., Tindal, G. A. and Spira, D. A. (1987). Special education referrals as an index of teacher tolerance: Are teachers imperfect tests? *Exceptional Children, 54*: 32–40.

Tiegs, E. W. and Clark, W. W. (1963). *California Reading Tests.* Monterey, CA: California Test Bureau.

Wechsler, D. (1974). *Wechsler Intelligence Scales for Children – Revised.* NY: Psychological Corporation.

Westwood, P. (1999). *Spelling: Approaches to teaching and assessment.* Camberwell, VIC: Australian Council for Educational Research.

Wheldall, K. and Madelaine, A. (2000). A curriculum-based passage reading test for monitoring the performance of low-progress readers: The development of the WARP. *International Journal of Disability, Development and Education, 47*: 371–82.

Wheldall, K. and Madelaine, A. (2006). The development of a passage reading test for the frequent monitoring of performance of low-progress readers. *Australasian Journal of Special Education, 30*: 72–85.

Wilson, M. S., Schendel, J. M. and Ulman, J. E. (1992). Curriculum-based measures, teachers' ratings, and group achievement scores: Alternative screening measures. *Journal of School Psychology, 30*: 59–76.

Woodcock, R. W. (1987). *Woodcock Reading Mastery Test – Revised.* Circle Pines, MN: American Guidance Service.

Wright, D. and Wiese, M. J. (1988). Teacher judgment in student evaluation: A comparison of grading methods. *Journal of Educational Research, 82*: 10–14.

Wright, E. N. (1967). *Canadian Lorge-Thorndike Intelligence Test.* Don Mills, ON: Thomas Nelson.

Index